Issues in
Clinical Psychology

Issues in Clinical Psychology

Subjective versus Objective Approaches

MICHAEL WIERZBICKI
Marquette University

ALLYN AND BACON
Boston   London   Toronto   Sydney   Tokyo   Singapore

Editor-in-Chief of Social Sciences: Susan Badger
Senior Editor: Laura Pearson
Senior Editorial Assistant: Dana Lamothe
Production Administrator: Annette Joseph
Production Coordinator: Holly Crawford
Editorial-Production Service: Carlyle Carter
Cover Administrator: Linda K. Dickinson
Cover Designer: Suzanne Harbison
Manufacturing Buyer: Mary Beth Lynch

Copyright © 1993 by Allyn and Bacon
A Division of Simon & Schuster, Inc.
160 Gould Street
Needham Heights, MA 02194

Library of Congress Cataloging-in-Publication Data

Wierzbicki, Michael.
    Issues in clinical psychology: subjective versus objective approaches/Michael Wierzbicki.
    p.   cm.
    Includes index.
    ISBN 0-205-13972-8
    1. Clinical psychology—Methodology—Evaluation.
    2. Psychodiagnostics—Validity. 3. Psychotherapy—Evaluation.
    I. Title.
    [DNLM: 1. Mental Disorders—diagnosis. 2. Outcome and Process Assessment (Health Care). 3. Personality. 4. Projective Techniques. 5. Psychology, Clinical—methods. 6. Psychotherapy.
    WM 105 W 648i]
    RC467.W54 1993
    616.89—dc20
    DNLM/DLC
    for Library of Congress   92-10689
                                                                          CIP

Printed in the United States of America

10 9 8 7 6 5 4 3 2 1   97 96 95 94 93 92

Contents

Preface

Clinical psychology experienced substantial changes in the second half of the twentieth century. Whereas psychoanalytic theory dominated the field during the first half of the century, other views, including the humanistic, behavioral, cognitive, and biological schools, gained followings in the latter half that now rival if not surpass that of psychoanalysis.

Many influences led to the rise of these alternatives to psychoanalysis. For example, economic and other pragmatic factors contributed to the field's moving away from expensive long-term psychoanalytic therapy toward less expensive and more readily accessible short-term therapies.

Scientific factors also contributed to this movement. In the 1950s, clinical psychologists began to examine empirically the traditional assumptions and methods that stemmed from Freudian psychology.

The purpose of this book is to review six issues which have been debated and empirically tested by clinical psychologists since the 1950s. These issues concern the assumptions and methods of traditional subjective approaches to clinical psychology. The issues discussed in this book are: (a) the effectiveness of psychotherapy, (b) the stability of personality, (c) the reliability and validity of projective tests, (d) the reliability of psychiatric diagnosis, (e) the relative accuracies of clinical and statistical prediction, and (f) the validity of clinical judgment.

This book will review these issues, highlighting the major arguments and empirical investigations concerning each. The thesis of this book is that, from the 1950s on, empirical examination failed to provide sufficient support for clinical psychology's traditional views concerning these issues and so led the field to consider and adopt alternative theoretical approaches.

Regardless of whether readers are of the subjective or objective persuasion, they should be aware of these issues, of the major findings and arguments concerning each, and that the empirical examination of these issues led many clinical psychologists to prefer objective over traditional subjective approaches to clinical psychology.

This book was written for three groups of readers. First, it is intended for undergraduate students in upper-division courses in clinical psychology (Introduction to Clinical Psychology, Principles of Psychological Assessment, Theories of Personality, and so on). For these students, this book will serve as a supplementary textbook, introducing the students to these issues and helping to explain why clinical psychology has increased its emphasis on empirically oriented approaches.

Second, this book is intended for graduate students in psychology. Graduate students in experimental areas may use this book to see how a scientific examination of major issues in clinical psychology influenced the field's movement in a more empirical direction. Graduate students in clinical and counseling psychology can use this book as an introduction to these issues and then pursue the primary readings on their own.

A third audience for the book is psychologists. Although psychologists should already be familiar with these issues and the corresponding arguments and empirical results, they may wish to have a single source to serve as a reference guide to the primary works and as a summary of the major works and arguments.

I began this work when on an academic sabbatical at Washburn University and completed it after joining the faculty of Marquette University. I would like to thank my colleagues at both institutions, especially Gene Pekarik, Laura Stephenson, Laura Hubbs-Tait, and Gary Forbach for their ideas and encouragement. I would also like to acknowledge my research assistants, including Johnette Clark, Christine Robison, and Stephen Frommelt, for their help in locating the sources cited in the book. I also appreciate the many helpful comments and suggestions from the psychologists who reviewed early drafts of the book: James Calhoun, University of Georgia; Peter Finn, Indiana University—Bloomington; Jeffrey Hecker, University of Maine; and Robert G. Meyer, University of Louisville. Most importantly, I wish to thank my family for their love and support. Alexis, Jane, and Kaye, you make it all worthwhile.

Biographical Statement

Michael Wierzbicki received his Ph.D. from Indiana University in 1980. He is an Assistant Professor of Psychology at Marquette University and previously was a member of the faculty of Washburn University. Since 1980, Dr. Wierzbicki has been involved with the training of graduate students in clinically oriented master's degree programs. Dr. Wierzbicki has published numerous research articles on depression and other clinical topics. He is a member of the APA Division of Clinical Psychology and is a licensed clinical psychologist.

CHAPTER ONE

Introduction

Clinical psychology has experienced substantial changes since the 1950s. Whereas psychoanalytic theory dominated the field during the first half of the century, other views (including the humanistic, behavioral, cognitive, and biological schools) have now emerged and gained followings that rival if not surpass that of psychoanalysis.

From the time of Freud until the 1950s, clinicians readily accepted both the assumptions and methods associated with the psychoanalytic movement. For example, clinicians assumed that psychological disorders were related to underlying disturbances in the psyche, and so it followed that the appropriate treatment for such disorders was to delve into the unconscious of the client through lengthy, insight-oriented therapy. Clinicians assumed that underlying personality characteristics were stable and therefore a primary influence on an individual's behavior across situations. From this, it followed that an appropriate method of assessing personality was the projective test, because underlying traits would be expressed in how one responded to the ambiguous projective test stimuli.

Since the 1950s, however, clinical psychologists have questioned and either replaced or provided alternatives for many of the traditional assumptions and practices associated with psychoanalysis. For example, Garfield (1981), when reviewing the recent history of psychotherapy, noted among several trends over the last forty years that psychotherapy has changed its emphasis away from psychoanalysis and toward alternatives, such as cognitive, behavioral, and community approaches.

Similar changes have occurred in other areas of clinical psychology. In the area of personality assessment, clinicians at one time relied almost exclusively on projective tests, which were subjective in both their scoring and interpretation. However, today's clinicians have alternatives, such as

1

empirically constructed personality inventories, which rival traditional projective tests in their frequency of administration.

Another example is in the area of diagnosis. Clinicians at one time made diagnostic decisions in a quite subjective manner. Diagnostic rules were imprecise and often based on symptoms, such as internal dynamics, that were unseen and could only be inferred. Today's diagnostician, however, makes diagnoses in a more objective way. The current diagnostic system was developed precisely to increase the reliability (by reducing the subjectivity) of diagnosis, basing diagnostic decisions on the observable symptoms of the client (American Psychiatric Association, 1987).

The changes in clinical psychology since the 1950s have been due to many influences. For example, economic and other pragmatic factors contributed to the move from long-term to short-term therapy. During the 1950s, the emphasis on long-term insight-oriented psychotherapy came under increasing fire because its expense limited it to only a small segment of the population. Several influential studies, including those of Hollingshead and Redlich (1958) and Srole, Langner, Michael, Opler, and Rennie (1962), demonstrated that members of lower socioeconomic groups had greater need for treatment services but actually received less (and less desirable forms of) treatment than members of higher income groups. World War II highlighted the need for short-term therapy. The discovery of drugs useful in treating schizophrenia led to the development of treatments, typically problem-focused rather than insight-oriented, which were useful in the aftercare of formerly hospitalized patients. Studies in the 1950s demonstrated that the need for mental health services could not be met by the current number of practitioners, especially if they continued to use long-term treatments (e.g., Albee, 1959).

In addition to these very practical influences, scientific factors also contributed to the changes in clinical psychology. Both theoretical and empirical factors played a significant role. The 1950s saw the rise of the theoretical school of humanism and the application of behavioral psychology to clinical problems. The 1960s and 1970s witnessed a revival of both the cognitive and biological approaches to the conceptualization of clinical disorders.

A complete discussion of the development of these schools and their influence on clinical psychology is beyond the scope of this book and is more suited to works on the recent history of the field. This book will help to explain the rise of these alternatives to the traditional psychoanalytic school by reviewing six issues which have been debated by clinical psychologists since the 1950s. Each issue concerns the relative merits of the assumptions and methods of subjective versus objective approaches to clinical psychology.

Freud and his followers typically employed subjective methods to develop and evaluate psychoanalytic principles and techniques. Such methods include: (a) the case study, wherein a subject is described in detail and hypotheses are generated concerning the influences on the subject's functioning; (b) the uncontrolled group study, wherein the outcome of a set of cases is described and judgments are formed as to the principles that operate across subjects to produce the observed outcome; and (c) the rational derivation of conclusions from an existing theory. These methods are subjective in that the criteria used to evaluate them are largely related to individual judgment.

For example, an investigator who conducts a case study may speculate about the causes of the observed outcome. However, no matter how experienced, well-trained, intelligent, and honest the investigator, these speculations have only uncertain scientific value. The investigator may have overlooked facts related to the true cause of the outcome, misinterpreted the events, or unknowingly biased the observations or interpretations.

Because of these problems, scientists regard the case study methodology as having very low internal validity (Campbell & Stanley, 1963), or ability to prove that what one believes to be the cause of an observed event is the actual cause. To accept as valid the conclusions drawn from a case study, then, is to rely on the interpretations of the investigator, a subjective practice.

Similar problems exist with the uncontrolled group study. An investigator can report as accurately as possible the outcome of a group of subjects and then argue that the intervention, such as a clinical treatment, was the cause of the outcome. The difficulty here is that the investigator may have overlooked some set of factors that actually caused the observed outcome. Perhaps some aspect of the intervention, other than that which the investigator believed to be the cause, was the true "active ingredient" which produced the outcome. The investigator may have indeliberately biased the observations or interpretations. Thus, the uncontrolled group study, like the case study, has very poor internal validity. To accept as valid claims based on such uncontrolled studies is to rely on the accuracy of the interpretations of the investigator, a subjective practice.

Finally, Freud and his followers also relied on the method of deriving rationally from a theory some conclusion, such as a practical application or a further theoretical statement. Although this certainly occurs in all science, Freud did not then engage in the next scientific step—the attempt to systematically test or refute his conclusions. Rather, he preferred to support them with the kind of case study or uncontrolled group study described above.

Scientists recognize that deriving hypotheses from a theory is only a prelude to their empirical evaluation. According to the scientific method, the scientist must establish conditions that permit the critical examination of a hypothesis—that determine whether the hypothesis in question or some alternative hypothesis is the more accurate. To accept as valid a rationally derived hypothesis without submitting it to controlled empirical examination relies on the accuracy of the judgment of the individual who derived the hypothesis, a subjective practice. After all, it is possible that another theorist could draw a different conclusion from the theory that is inconsistent with the first.

By the 1950s the weaknesses in these methods were recognized by clinical psychologists. At that time, clinical psychologists began to apply more objective methods to evaluate the traditional assumptions and methods, which stemmed from Freudian psychology.

The purpose of this book is to discuss six major issues, debated and tested by clinical psychologists since the 1950s, which concern the empirical adequacy of the methods and assumptions of traditional approaches to the field. The debate over each issue involved the fact that empirical evaluations of the traditional methods and assumptions questioned their validity and utility. Thus, the field was required either to gather empirical evidence to support the traditional positions or to develop alternative approaches supported by empirical evidence.

The issues that will be discussed in this book are the following:

1. The effectiveness of psychotherapy. Through the first half of the century, mental health professionals, along with their clients, assumed that psychotherapy worked. There was little objective evidence, however, to support this assumption. In 1952, Hans Eysenck published a classic paper in which he reviewed the uncontrolled group studies to date, which reported success rates of psychotherapy with neurotic patients. He used the estimates of two other studies to determine the spontaneous remission rate, or the rate at which neurotic patients improve without psychotherapy. Eysenck found that the recovery rate of treated patients did not exceed the spontaneous remission rate and so he concluded that the field did not have scientific evidence at that time to support the claim that psychotherapy worked. This paper sparked a heated controversy that contributed to the development of the scientific evaluation of psychotherapy.

2. The stability of personality. In 1968, Walter Mischel published a book entitled *Personality and Assessment*. In this book, Mischel reviewed the research on another traditional assumption of clinical psychology—that personality traits are stable and, therefore, useful predictors of behavior. Mischel reviewed the empirical literature concerning the stability of personality traits and concluded that, although there was good evidence for

the stability of some personal characteristics, there was little evidence for the stability of trait-related behavior across dissimilar situations. Thus, Mischel strongly questioned the validity of the traditional assumption that underlying personality traits were stable and, therefore, useful predictors of behavior across situations.

3. The reliability and validity of projective tests. For the first half of this century, clinical psychologists relied heavily on projective tests for personality and diagnostic assessment. However, there was little objective evidence to support the reliability and validity of such tests; rather, clinical psychologists relied on subjective judgments to support the continued use of projective tests. Since the 1950s, research on the psychometric properties of projective tests has seriously questioned both their reliability and validity. This led to the development of other assessment instruments, other ways of employing projective tests, and a decrease in the weight placed on information obtained from projective tests.

4. The reliability of psychiatric diagnosis. Traditional psychiatric diagnosis was a subjective process, often relying upon the clinician's judgment concerning the client's psychological functioning—internal processes that had to be inferred rather than observed. Numerous studies in the 1950s and 1960s demonstrated that the reliability of psychiatric diagnosis was not sufficient to be useful, particularly for specific diagnoses within broad categories. Research in the 1960s and 1970s aimed at the development of a diagnostic system that would be more reliable. The result of these efforts was the development of the third edition of the *Diagnostic and Statistical Manual of Mental Disorders* (DSM-III; American Psychiatric Association, 1980), which bases diagnoses on observable symptoms, hence reducing the subjectivity and increasing the reliability of psychiatric diagnosis.

5. Clinical versus statistical prediction. In 1954, Paul Meehl attempted to determine whether the clinical (subjective) or the statistical (objective, empirical) method was the more accurate in predicting behavior. Traditionally, clinical psychologists assumed that the clinical method was superior. Meehl reviewed all published studies to date that compared the two methods of making predictions and found that the statistical method almost always equalled or surpassed the clinical method. This review, like Eysenck's (1952) paper, sparked a controversy that led to further studies on the relative accuracies of the two methods and to a reconsideration of the validity of clinical prediction.

6. The validity of clinical judgment. Through the first half of the century, clinicians assumed that the clinical method was both appropriate and accurate for understanding individuals. The clinical method involves attempting to understand the underlying dynamics of an individual and then basing one's interaction with the individual on this understanding.

Numerous studies from the 1950s through the present have demonstrated that clinical judgment is not as accurate as was once believed. These studies have shown that clinicians are susceptible to the same kinds of errors and biases that affect the judgment of people in general.

The purpose of this book is to review these six issues, highlighting the major arguments and empirical findings concerning each. This book will not attempt to resolve these issues conclusively. Throughout the discussion of each issue, arguments in favor of both the objective and subjective approaches will be provided.

The review of each issue will include a presentation of the empirical work that questioned traditional assumptions and methods along with the counter-arguments of the traditional position. The thesis of this book is that clinical psychology's adoption of theoretical approaches other than psychoanalysis and increasing adoption of an objective orientation were stimulated by the empirical examination of these issues since the 1950s. Regardless of whether readers prefer the subjective or objective approach, they should be aware of these issues, the major findings and arguments concerning them, and that the discussion of these issues led many clinical psychologists to prefer a more empirical approach to examining clinical issues.

References

Albee, G. W. (1959). *Mental health manpower needs*. New York: Basic Books.

American Psychiatric Association. (1980). *Diagnostic and statistical manual of mental disorders* (3rd ed.). Washington, DC: American Psychiatric Association.

American Psychiatric Association. (1987). *Diagnostic and statistical manual of mental disorders* (3rd ed.—Revised). Washington, DC: American Psychiatric Association.

Campbell, D. T., & Stanley, J. C. (1963). *Experimental and quasi-experimental designs for research*. Chicago: Rand McNally.

Eysenck, H. J. (1952). The effects of psychotherapy: An evaluation. *Journal of Consulting Psychology, 16*, 319–324.

Garfield, S. L. (1981). Psychotherapy: A 40-year appraisal. *American Psychologist, 36*, 174–183.

Hollingshead, A. G., & Redlich, F. C. (1958). *Social class and mental illness: A community study*. New York: Wiley.

Meehl, P. E. (1954). *Clinical versus statistical prediction*. Minneapolis, MN: University of Minnesota Press.

Mischel, W. (1968). *Personality and assessment*. New York: Wiley.

Srole, L., Langner, T. S., Michael, S. T., Opler, M. K., & Rennie, T. A. C. (1962). *Mental health in the metropolis (Vol. 1). The midtown Manhattan study*. New York: McGraw-Hill.

CHAPTER TWO

The Effectiveness of Psychotherapy

Introduction

The practice of psychotherapy is booming. Goldberg (1986) estimated that there were over 100,000 mental health practitioners in the United States. Gross (1978) estimated that six million individuals receive psychotherapy annually in the United States from clinics, hospitals, and private therapists, while another one million receive psychotherapy from lay therapists.

Although the delivery of mental health services has become widespread, the scientific evaluation of the effectiveness of these services has lagged behind. Bergin and Garfield (1971) acknowledged this in the preface to their handbook on empirical studies of psychotherapy: "For most of its history, the field of psychotherapy has appeared to rely almost exclusively on clinical reports, case studies, and theoretical accounts . . ." (p. ix).

Although case studies are rich sources of information and so are useful in generating clinical hypotheses, they are relatively poor tests of hypotheses. For example, it has been shown that therapists' ratings of therapy outcome tend to overestimate client improvements (Feifel & Eells, 1963). Thus, therapists' subjective estimates of their clients' progress may be biased in the direction favorable to the evaluation of psychotherapy.

Similarly, judgments of the cause of improvement in a case study may be inaccurate. Although a therapist may attribute client improvement to the therapy that was provided, it is possible that other factors, either outside the therapy context altogether or within the therapy context but not recognized by the therapist, may be the actual causes of client change. Because the case study does not control for such alternative explanations for client improvement, they have poor internal validity (Campbell & Stanley, 1966) and do not provide much support for claims of the effectiveness of a particular treatment.

Perhaps one of the reasons for the field's delay in conducting controlled studies of psychotherapy is that Sigmund Freud, the founder of psychoanalysis and an early proponent of psychological treatments, repeatedly expressed resistance to such methods. For example, Freud (1917/1963) rejected a suggestion that analysts prepare statistics regarding their successes, because "statistics are worthless if the items assembled in them are too heterogeneous; and the cases of neurotic illness which we had taken into treatment were in fact incomparable in a great variety of respects" (p. 461). Later, when presented the results of ten years' cases of the Berlin Psychiatric Institute, Freud (1933/1964, p. 152) responded that "statistics of that kind are in general uninstructive; the material worked upon is so heterogeneous that only very large numbers would show anything. It is wiser to examine one's individual experiences."

This antipathy toward controlled studies of therapy continued within psychoanalysis, which dominated the field of psychotherapy in the first half of the 1900s. For example, Knight (1941) attempted to evaluate the effects of psychoanalytic therapy because, in his opinion, there was "not a single report in the literature on the therapeutic results of an analyst in private practice or of any such group of analysts" (p. 434). In 1947, in a discussion of clinical research, Kris noted that there was "still a tendency among psychoanalysts to look upon rigorous procedures of verification, upon what has come to be called 'experimental psychoanalysis' with a scornful or patronizing eye . . ." (p. 211).

Other schools of psychotherapy experienced a similar lag in and indifference toward conducting experimental studies of the effectiveness of their psychotherapies. For example, Wertheimer (1978) reported the response of his colleagues to his request for data addressing the effectiveness of humanistic psychotherapy. "In the first place, and perhaps most disturbing, these approaches are typically inimical to solid data: It is almost heretical, 'dehumanizing,' to raise a question about the effectiveness of these procedures. . . . But there is no documentation that any of these forms of treatment—'humanistic' or otherwise—produces results that cannot readily be explained as due to self-fulfilling prophecies" (p. 744).

Many of the critics of controlled studies of the effectiveness of psychotherapy raise the objection of individual differences: because all people are different, group averages are not representative of any real individual; because all people are different, group studies ignore the individual's unique aspects, which must be addressed in his or her treatment. This is interesting in that it repeats the very same criticisms that were raised in the early 1800s when Pierre Louis advocated the use of statistics and controlled outcome studies to evaluate medical treatments (Shryock, 1947).

It is only since the 1950s that psychologists have widely endorsed the practice of conducting controlled scientific evaluations of psychotherapies, and it is only since the 1960s that large numbers of such controlled studies have been conducted. The purpose of this chapter is to review the issue of the effectiveness of psychotherapy, addressing in particular the arguments raised since the 1950s concerning empirical investigations of therapy outcome.

Eysenck's Argument

In 1952, Hans Eysenck published a short article in which he attempted to evaluate the effectiveness of psychotherapy. Although this was neither the first attempt to assess the degree to which psychotherapy was effective (e.g., Landis, 1938; Miles, Barrabee, & Finesinger, 1951; Wilder, 1945) nor the first call for controlled studies to evaluate psychotherapy (e.g., Hunt, 1952; Thorne, 1952; Watson, 1952; Zubin, 1953), Eysenck's paper was by far the most critical and controversial.

Eysenck asked a simple question: Does psychotherapy work? In an attempt to answer the question, Eysenck reviewed all the studies published to date that reported success rates of various types of psychotherapy. Eysenck limited his review to psychotherapy with "neurotics," excluding schizophrenic, manic-depressive, and paranoid patients who are more difficult than neurotics to treat with psychotherapy. In this way, Eysenck identified 5 studies of psychoanalytic therapy and 19 studies of other "eclectic" psychotherapy.

In order to evaluate the effectiveness of any treatment, it is necessary to compare the outcome of patients who receive the treatment to that of other patients who do not receive the treatment. If one did not compare treated to untreated patients but merely relied on the rhetorical impact of a reported treatment recovery rate, then imagine the impact of reports of 100 percent success rates—such as would be obtained when treating patients suffering from the common cold or other time-limited conditions with any intervention.

Because the studies reviewed by Eysenck did not include control groups of untreated neurotics, he had to estimate the recovery rate of untreated neurotics. He did so by combining the results of two additional studies. Landis (1938) reported that the percentage of neurotics in state hospitals (and who presumably received little more than custodial care) who are discharged as recovered or improved was approximately 72 percent. Denker (1946) examined 500 cases of neurotics who received insurance disability due to their disorder and who saw general practitioners rather than mental health professionals. Denker found that, over a two-year period, 72 percent of the neurotics recovered. From these studies, Eysenck suggested that a reasonable estimate of the spontaneous recovery rate for neurotic disorders was 72 percent.

Eysenck then combined the therapy outcome results within the two classes of psychoanalytic and eclectic psychotherapy. Because studies did not report outcome in a uniform way, Eysenck "forced" the results from the 24 studies into a uniform classification system using four headings: (a) cured or much improved, (b) improved, (c) slightly improved, and (d) not improved, died, discontinued treatment, etc. Using this system, Eysenck reported that the overall improvement rate (which combines the first two headings listed above) was 44 percent for psychoanalytic therapy and 64 percent for eclectic psychotherapy.

When the overall improvement or recovery rate of psychotherapy with neurotics is compared to the spontaneous recovery rate, the result is not favorable to psychotherapy. Eysenck concluded that these data "fail to prove that psychotherapy, Freudian or otherwise, facilitates the recovery of neurotic patients" (1952, p. 322).

Eysenck correctly noted that these data do not disprove the possibility of the effectiveness of psychotherapy (remember that, in statistical tests, failure to reject the null hypothesis that there is no difference between groups does not mean that one accepts the null hypothesis as true) and also noted the weaknesses of his actuarial comparison. Finally, he encouraged the field to gather more facts concerning the effectiveness of psychotherapy and to conduct rigorous controlled studies that might support the claim that psychotherapy is effective.

Responses to Eysenck

The response to Eysenck's paper was quick and vigorous (Bergin, 1971; Cartwright, 1955; deCharms, Levy, & Wertheimer, 1954; Luborsky, 1954; Rosenzweig, 1954; Sanford, 1953; Strupp, 1963a, 1963b). Criticisms of Eysenck's argument generally fell into the following categories:

The "Apples and Oranges" Argument

The 24 studies reviewed by Eysenck covered a wide range of disorders, which were treated with a wide range of therapies by therapists who had different training and levels of experience and who used a variety of techniques to measure outcome. To combine such a heterogeneous group of studies is questionable because the average therapy outcome will not be a realistic summary of any of the studies. For example, Sanford's (1953) response to Eysenck's review was that "the only wise course with respect to such a challenge is to ignore it. From the point of view of science, the question 'Does psychotherapy do any good?' has little interest because it is virtually meaningless. . . . The question is, which people, in what circumstances, responding to what therapeutic stimuli?" (pp. 335–336).

The Control Group Argument

Eysenck's comparison was not a true experiment (which requires the random assignment of subjects to experimental and control groups), but was based on previously formed treatment and control groups. Thus, at best, Eysenck's review typifies what has been called quasi-experimental research (Campbell & Stanley, 1966). The problem with the quasi-experimental design is that the control and experimental groups may not have been equivalent at the beginning of the study, and so differences between groups at the end of the study may be due to their initial differences and not to the quasi-experimental procedure.

It is likely that the untreated subjects in the Landis (1938) and Denker (1946) studies were different from the neurotic subjects in the 24 treatment reports reviewed by Eysenck. For example, subjects in the Landis (1938) study were neurotics who were treated as inpatients in state hospitals. Because most neurotics do not require hospitalization, it is likely that these subjects had disorders of greater severity than those of the neurotics in the 24 treatment studies. Similarly, inpatient treatment in state hospitals suggests that these individuals were lower than average in income, education, and other indices of socioeconomic status. Although greater severity of disorder and lower socioeconomic status would suggest that these subjects would be less likely to experience spontaneous remission than the treated subjects in Eysenck's review (and so would act to increase the apparent effectiveness of psychotherapy), the likely initial difference in levels of severity between the two groups reduces the meaningfulness of any comparisons of their outcome.

Similarly, subjects in the Denker (1946) study very likely were less severely disturbed than those in the 24 treatment studies. Denker's subjects were individuals who received insurance payments due to a "disabling" neurosis of at least three months' duration. Although Denker considered these individuals severely disturbed because of the disabling nature of their disorder, these individuals were not sufficiently disturbed to seek help from a mental health professional. Instead, they received help from regular contacts with a general medical practitioner. Because Denker's data were gathered between 1934 and 1940, a time of severe economic depression in the United States, it is possible that there were reasons other than a disabling neurosis for these individuals to be unemployed. If Denker's subjects were less severely disturbed than subjects in the 24 treatment studies, then one would expect that they would show a higher spontaneous remission rate than the treated subjects. Again, possible differences in severity between the treated and untreated subjects raise doubts about the validity of Eysenck's comparison and conclusions.

The Spontaneous Remission Argument

Eysenck concluded that the data do not support the claim that treated neurotics have a better outcome than "untreated" neurotics. However, whether the subjects in the Landis and Denker studies were in fact "untreated" can be seriously questioned.

Subjects in the Landis study were neurotics treated as inpatients in state hospitals. Although such patients were regarded as receiving little more than custodial care, it is possible that they did receive some treatment. In addition, they were likely exposed to such nonspecific therapeutic elements as attention, caring, expectations of improvement, and so on. It might be more appropriate to regard these subjects as being in a minimal treatment or placebo treatment group rather than a no-treatment group.

Similarly, subjects in the Denker study saw their own physicians regularly. Although this is not the same as formal psychotherapy, Denker noted that these subjects received "suggestions" and "reassurance" along with medical interventions. Because suggestion and reassurance can be considered as nonspecific therapeutic elements in psychotherapy, it is not proper to regard Denker's subjects as a "no-treatment" comparison group. Rather, they can be more properly described, like subjects in the Landis study, as a minimal or placebo treatment group.

Another possible flaw with Eysenck's spontaneous remission argument is that many individuals who are not in formal psychotherapy (Gurin, Veroff, & Feld, 1960) or who are on psychotherapy waiting lists (Frank, 1961) seek help from resources other than mental health professionals. Thus, it becomes difficult to maintain that individuals in a no-treatment control group did not actually receive any treatment. They may well have received help from non–mental health professionals in either formal contacts (e.g., physicians, clergy) or informal contacts (e.g., friends, family).

If these criticisms are valid, then the subjects that Eysenck used to estimate the spontaneous remission rate may actually have received some form of therapy. Thus, they would have recovered more than would subjects who in fact received no therapy. This would lead to the overestimation of the "true" spontaneous remission rate.

Bergin (1971) summarized the results of 14 studies which led him to conclude that the spontaneous remission rate for neurotics was approximately 30 percent, much lower than Eysenck's estimate of 72 percent. If Bergin's estimate is correct (and it may well not be—see Rachman [1971] for a criticism of the studies used by Bergin to generate this figure), then Eysenck's estimates of 44 and 64 percent recovery rates for psychoanalytic and eclectic psychotherapies would actually support the claim that psychotherapy is effective.

The Outcome Criteria Argument

The studies reviewed by Eysenck employed a variety of methods to determine outcome. It is possible that the criteria for the determination of outcome in the studies by Landis (1938) and Denker (1946) differed substantially from the criteria employed in the 24 treatment studies. For example, Landis (1938) used the hospital discharge determination as his outcome criterion. Patients discharged as "recovered" or "improved" were judged by Landis as having recovered spontaneously. The problem here is that criteria that are appropriate to judge outcome in state hospital inpatients may well be different from and less stringent than the criteria that are appropriate to assess outcome in clinic outpatients. Whereas a hospitalized inpatient may be discharged as "improved" when his symptoms no longer present a danger to himself or to others (although he may still be experiencing significant disturbances), a psychoanalytic outpatient may not be judged as "improved" until he has undergone a substantial personality restructuring. Because the criteria in the Landis study are very likely less stringent than the criteria in the 24 treatment studies, it is difficult to maintain that outcome was comparable in the treated and untreated hospital groups. Thus, Eysenck's finding of similar outcomes in treated and untreated groups becomes suspect.

Similarly, outcome criteria in the Denker (1946) study may have differed from those employed in the 24 treatment studies. Denker's cases were neurotics whose disability prevented them from working for at least three months and who received insurance disability benefits. Denker's criteria for determining a successful outcome included: return to work for a five-year period, complaint of no further or only slight difficulties, and successful social adjustment.

Because Denker's data were obtained from insurance company files concerning the payment of disability benefits, the outcome data regarding return to work are likely of high quality. On the other hand, it is difficult to imagine that the assessments of social adjustment and personal difficulties could be accurate, especially after the subject returned to work and was no longer under the scrutiny of the insurance company. For this reason, the criteria used by Denker to determine outcome can essentially be reduced to the individual's successfully returning to work.

Because it is possible that a neurotic individual could return to work without experiencing much if any improvement in his disorder (especially in the late 1930s when the general state of the economy of the United States was improving), the criteria used by Denker to judge outcome were very likely less stringent than outcome criteria used in the treatment studies reviewed by Eysenck.

Since the outcome criteria in the Landis and Denker studies were very likely less stringent than the outcome criteria in the 24 treatment studies, it is difficult to maintain that outcome was comparable in the treated and untreated groups. Thus, Eysenck's finding of similar outcomes in treated and untreated groups becomes suspect.

The Alternative Interpretations Argument

In tabulating the results from the 24 treatment studies, Eysenck made numerous subjective judgments in order to fit all the results into a uniform classification scheme. Other reviewers might differ from Eysenck in their judgments of each study, and could derive conclusions much different from Eysenck's.

For example, Eysenck limited his attention to neurotic patients, excluding psychotics who would not be as likely as neurotics to respond favorably to psychotherapy. However, Eysenck included patients with "psychopathic states" and "character disorders," two disorders that are more difficult to treat than traditional neuroses. If one excluded these patients from the 24 treatment studies, the overall improvement rate of therapy should be higher than that estimated by Eysenck.

A second judgment by Eysenck concerned the interpretation of outcome results. Many of the initial investigators classified outcome using different categories from those in Eysenck's four-category scheme. Eysenck made subjective decisions in order to "force" these initial classifications of results into his four outcome categories. However, other reviewers might disagree with Eysenck's decisions. For example, Bergin (1971) discussed a study by Fenichel at the Berlin Psychoanalytic Institute and demonstrated how a different subjective interpretation of results could lead to a conclusion very different from that of Eysenck. Fenichel's study reported outcome using categories of Cured, Very Much Improved, Improved, Uncured, and Dropout. Eysenck's tabulation of this study listed 99 subjects in his Slightly Improved category, which he then combined with the Not Improved group to obtain the rate of clients who did not recover. The problem is that Fenichel did not classify any subjects as Slightly Improved. The only way, according to Bergin, that Eysenck could have obtained his figures would have been to assume that a portion of Fenichel's Improved cases were only Slightly Improved and then to estimate this figure.

Another judgment by Eysenck concerned the classification of dropouts and deaths as failures. Although it is true that some clients drop out of therapy precisely because it has not proved beneficial, it is also the case that other clients drop out of therapy for reasons other than the success or failure of therapy (e.g., lack of time, money, and so on). Eysenck's decision to classify all dropouts as failures leads to a conservative estimate of the effectiveness of therapy.

Similarly, his counting patient deaths as treatment failures can be questioned. Certainly, if the death was related to the patient's disorder (such as a suicide while depressed), then this practice is legitimate. However, if the death was due to causes unrelated to the patient's neurosis, then the practice of counting deaths as treatment failures leads to a conservative estimate of the effectiveness of therapy.

Other reviewers might differ from Eysenck in each of the ways described above and derive very different estimates of the effectiveness of therapy. For example, Bergin (1971) reexamined the 24 treatment studies reviewed by Eysenck. Bergin eliminated dropouts and psychopathic patients from the subject pool and judged cases that the original authors considered to be Improved as Improved (rather than splitting them into Improved and Slightly Improved, with the Slightly Improved cases counted as treatment failures). In this way, Bergin estimated that the improvement rates of psychoanalytic and eclectic psychotherapy were, respectively, 83 and 65 percent (compared with the 44 and 64 percent figures derived by Eysenck).

Because Eysenck interpreted the 24 treatment studies in such a rigorous fashion, he has sometimes been accused of having a theoretical bias that colors his interpretations. For example, critics of Eysenck have suggested that he has a theoretical bias favorable to behavioral therapy and opposed to traditional psychotherapy. Such a bias could affect the selection of studies to review (Eysenck has been accused of overlooking studies that yield outcomes favorable toward psychotherapy), the evaluation of the design quality to determine which low-quality studies to exclude (Eysenck has been accused of using inconsistent criteria for evaluating the quality of studies, using more stringent criteria to reject studies with outcomes favorable to psychotherapy), and the judgments that must be made to force a large class of studies into a uniform classification system (Eysenck has been accused of deciding to count dropouts as failures in order to reach a conclusion unfavorable to psychotherapy).

To criticize a reviewer on the basis of theoretical bias is to raise a sensitive and double-edged issue. It is a sensitive problem that must be addressed carefully, or else the criticism can deteriorate into an invalid ad hominem argument. (The exchanges between Eysenck and his critics have occasionally sunk to this level—somewhat entertaining for the reader but not very helpful to the field.) The issue is also double-edged, because the accusation of theoretical bias can be reversed and used against anyone who attacks Eysenck's theoretical stance.

It is not the purpose of the author to claim that Eysenck's theoretical leanings led him to review the research in a biased way, merely to note that others have raised this issue. Still, it is important to recognize that it is possible for a bias to affect the review process—in the selection, evaluation, and interpretation of studies—and that such a factor may affect any reviewer's conclusions regarding a body of research.

Eysenck's Response to His Critics

Although these criticisms of Eysenck's argument are powerful and have often been quoted in the literature on the effectiveness of psychotherapy, two additional points should be noted. First, Eysenck was aware of all of these issues. In his 1952 paper (and in his responses to his critics, e.g., Eysenck, 1955, 1964), he anticipated these criticisms and qualified his arguments appropriately. Although he did not detail these criticisms as extensively as did his critics and although he did not make the qualifiers as explicit as his critics would have liked, these criticisms were all familiar to Eysenck.

Second, even if these arguments completely invalidate Eysenck's argument, they still do not prove that patients treated with psychotherapy have a more favorable outcome than untreated patients. To demonstrate that Eysenck's argument is flawed does not substitute for empirical evidence from controlled experimental studies that demonstrate the effectiveness of therapy.

Eysenck's 1952 paper, then, issued a challenge that the field of clinical psychology was honor bound to accept. If psychotherapy works, then psychotherapists should be able to demonstrate this empirically in controlled studies. If traditional psychotherapies do not work (or if it is not possible to demonstrate their effectiveness empirically), then the field should consider the development of alternative therapies that can be supported empirically.

The 1950s and 1960s witnessed an increase in the number of controlled studies on the effectiveness of psychotherapy, in part as a response to Eysenck's challenge. In 1960, Eysenck updated his review. He added one study which supported his earlier estimate of the spontaneous remission rate for neurotics. He discussed four controlled psychotherapy studies, of which three produced results unfavorable to therapy (the fourth, which supported the effectiveness of therapy, was dismissed as having a weak methodology). He summarized the work of Levitt (1957), who repeated Eysenck's (1952) methodology in a review of the literature on the effectiveness of psychotherapy with children and who concluded that there was no empirical evidence that therapy with children produced outcomes superior to no therapy. Finally, Eysenck summarized the results of several studies which suggested that psychotherapy based on learning theory produced results superior to no therapy and to other forms of psychotherapy.

Eysenck's (1960) conclusions regarding psychotherapy echoed his 1952 conclusion: "When untreated neurotic control groups are compared with experimental groups of neurotic patients treated by means of psychotherapy, both groups recover to approximately the same extent" (p. 719). However, he now acknowledged that research evidence supported the claim that neurotics, "treated by means of psychotherapeutic procedures based on learning theory, improve significantly more quickly than do patients treated by means of psychoanalytic or eclectic psychotherapy, or not treated by psychotherapy at all" (p. 720).

In 1965, Eysenck once again updated his review of therapy outcome studies. Although seven additional controlled studies were included, Eysenck's (1960) conclusions regarding traditional psychotherapy and therapy based on learning theory were repeated. (Eysenck [1966] reprints the 1965 article along with 17 responses—both critical and supportive. Interested readers might begin their independent study with this book.)

Although critics of Eysenck and defenders of therapy did not appreciate Eysenck's conclusion regarding traditional psychotherapy, it is significant that Eysenck, such a severe critic of psychotherapy, evaluated any form of treatment favorably. This indicated that a rigorous empirical approach to evaluating psychotherapy could produce a favorable conclusion to at least some form of psychotherapy, and signalled a rise in the popularity of and attention to behavioral therapies, especially among empirically oriented clinical psychologists.

Other Reviews of Psychotherapy Outcome

Since Eysenck's 1952 challenge, psychotherapists have conducted an increasing number of controlled outcome studies. For example, Smith, Glass, and Miller (1980) identified 475 experimental studies in which one form of psychotherapy was compared either to no therapy or to another form of therapy. Because the empirical literature has become so extensive, it is difficult for the professional to read and critically evaluate all of the research. For this reason, many research reviews have appeared in the literature. Such reviews examine a portion of the literature with the goals of summarizing the results, interpreting the findings, and making recommendations concerning the practice of therapy and the conduct of future studies.

Because reviewers vary in the portions of the literature they examine, the criteria they use to evaluate studies, and their theoretical leanings, they may easily reach different conclusions. The purpose of this section of the chapter is to summarize the results of several well-known reviews of the research on the effectiveness of psychotherapy. This will serve to illustrate how subjective judgments made by reviewers may affect their evaluations of the research.

Bergin (1971)

Bergin (1971) published a very important work on the effectiveness of psychotherapy. In this paper, Bergin critiqued Eysenck's argument, offered alternative interpretations of the studies reviewed by Eysenck, and summarized the results of 14 studies which led him to conclude that the spontaneous remission rate for neurotics was approximately 30 percent. In this work, Bergin also examined a selected sample of 52 reports of the effectiveness of psychotherapy. Bergin presented a tabular summary (or what has been called a "box-score" analysis) of the outcomes of these studies, expressing therapy outcome as a function of the characteristics of the studies. On the basis of 22 positive, 15 doubtful, and 15 negative findings, Bergin concluded that research supported the claim that psychotherapy has at least a moderately positive average effect. In addition, Bergin reported that both design quality and therapist experience are positively related to therapy outcome, but that neither duration nor type of therapy is related to outcome.

Meltzoff and Kornreich (1970)

Another important review of the research literature on the effectiveness of psychotherapy was published by Meltzoff and Kornreich (1970). They attempted to identify and summarize all controlled studies on the effectiveness of psychotherapy. They described the results of 101 studies, 57 rated as having "adequate" and 44 rated as having "questionable" designs. They found that a large majority of the studies yielded results favorable to the effectiveness of psychotherapy (48 of 57 adequate studies, 33 of 44 questionable studies) and concluded that the research evidence supported the claim that psychotherapy is effective. In addition, they reported that therapy outcome was positively related to the quality of design of the study but was not related to most other facets of therapy (such as therapist style, group versus individual format, and so on). Although Meltzoff and Kornreich did not find support for claims of the superior effectiveness of one traditional school of psychotherapy over another, they did find that recent studies showed behavioral techniques, particularly systematic desensitization, to be consistently superior to verbal therapies aimed at insight and self-understanding.

Luborsky, Singer, and Luborsky (1975)

Luborsky, Singer, and Luborsky (1975) published a well-known review of therapy outcome studies. They excluded analogue studies, examining only controlled studies of actual patients. They also included only studies that treated either adults or young adults and that met minimum design standards. Luborsky et al. then tabulated the results, using a box-score analysis to determine the effectiveness of therapy in general and the relationship of several therapy characteristics to therapy effectiveness.

Luborsky et al. reported that the outcome of treated subjects equalled that of untreated subjects in 13 studies and surpassed that of untreated subjects in 20 studies. In addition, they found little relationship between therapy outcome and quality of the research design or aspects of therapy such as format (individual versus group) and duration. In several comparisons, they found little difference between therapy type and outcome, supporting the phrase in the title of the article that "everyone has won and all must have prizes."

The only differences Luborsky et al. found in effectiveness between types of therapy were that drug treatment was superior to psychotherapy (found primarily in studies of schizophrenics), and that multiple treatments were superior to treatments in isolation. In addition, the only "matches" they found between specific disorders and effective treatments were the following: behavior therapy was superior to other therapies for the treatment of phobias; and psychotherapy and medication in combination were superior to other approaches for the treatment of psychosomatic disorders.

Critiques of These Reviews

Although these are not the only reviews of therapy outcome from this period, they are among the most respected and well known and can be accepted as representative of the field's evaluation of psychotherapy research. Although these reviewers agreed that (at least) some forms of psychotherapy are effective, they disagreed about the extent to which psychotherapy is effective, the relative efficacies of different forms of therapy, the relationship between therapy duration and outcome, and the relationship between quality of the research design and therapy outcome.

None of these research reviews generated as large a written response as had Eysenck's 1952 paper. Perhaps this was due to the fact that these reviews were based on larger and more recent samples of investigations than Eysenck's review, and so the field perceived these reviews to be more accurate representations of the state of the literature. (Or perhaps this occurred because these reviews presented conclusions that were more acceptable than Eysenck's to mainstream psychotherapeutic thought and were written in a less "challenging" style than Eysenck's papers).

In any event, followers of the psychotherapy literature should be aware that these reviews are not without flaws and that their conclusions have not gone unchallenged. Just because the conclusions are more appealing to psychotherapists than Eysenck's original conclusion does not mean that the reviews should be received uncritically. The next section of the chapter presents a brief critique of the research reviews summarized above.

Critique of Bergin (1971)

Bergin's (1971) paper has been extremely influential, considered by some to be the definitive response to Eysenck. Still, Bergin's review of therapy outcome studies should be examined critically. Because the populations treated in the 52 studies reviewed by Bergin were quite heterogeneous (inpatients and outpatients; students, teachers, and psychologists; neurotics and psychotics; delinquents, homosexuals, and ulcerative colitis patients), the same "apples and oranges" argument directed at Eysenck can be applied here. Because over half of the studies did not employ control groups, the "control group" and "spontaneous remission" arguments can be applied, now questioning the finding of support for the effectiveness of psychotherapy. Because of the heterogeneity in the designs of the studies, the "outcome criteria" and the "alternative interpretations" arguments can be applied. Because Bergin did not specify the criteria used for selecting the studies (although he did note that all were published between 1952 and 1967 and were, in his opinion, representative of the literature), the criticism of selection bias can be raised. In other words, the very same arguments used to criticize Eysenck's position can be applied to other reviews, including those that reached conclusions opposite to that of Eysenck.

The most vigorous critic of Bergin (1971) has been Rachman (1971; Rachman & Wilson, 1980). Rachman (1971) examined the 14 studies Bergin used to estimate a spontaneous remission rate for neurotic disorders of 30 percent. Rachman systematically critiqued each of these studies, arguing either that their methodologies are so weak that they cannot provide support for Bergin's claim or that Bergin systematically misinterpreted the results in order to support his claim. Rachman concluded that the studies cited by Bergin do not refute Eysenck's estimate of about a two-thirds spontaneous remission rate.

Rachman then examined the studies Bergin interpreted as supporting the effectiveness of psychoanalysis. Rachman criticized Bergin's contention that dropouts should be excluded altogether from the subject pool. After all, if a psychoanalytic patient drops out of therapy after seven years of treatment, is it fair to exclude this patient from the sample? If the client has not progressed in such a long time, is it not more reasonable to consider the client a treatment failure? Eysenck's position that dropouts should be counted as treatment failures is particularly justified in the case of psychoanalytic therapy, according to Rachman, because psychoanalytic treatment is characterized both by lengthy durations and by high dropout rates. To exclude dropouts from the sample would systematically bias any review in favor of the effectiveness of long treatments with high dropout rates.

Rachman also critiqued the methodology of the studies, noting that most do not include appropriate no-treatment control groups. Rachman concluded that the studies which Bergin regarded as supporting the effectiveness of psychonalytic therapy do not provide "acceptable evidence to support the view that psychoanalytic treatment is effective" (1971, p. 63).

Similarly, Rachman critiqued the methodologies of several of the studies cited by Bergin to support the effectiveness of eclectic psychotherapy. Following the identification of such flaws as high dropout rates, use of measures of doubtful psychometric worth, and weak follow-up data, Rachman concluded that "the best studies of psychotherapy yield discouraging results while the inadequate studies are overoptimistic" (1971, p. 83).

Critique of Meltzoff and Kornreich (1970)

The review by Meltzoff and Kornreich (1970) examined 101 controlled studies and concluded that there is substantial evidence for the effectiveness of psychotherapy. However, this review has been criticized on several grounds. Both the range of disorders (including ulcerative colitis, warts, delinquency, alcoholism, retardation, and psychosis) and the range of treatments (including hypnosis, desensitization, televised confrontation, single-session psychotherapy, and street-corner counseling) included in the review were extremely wide. Thus, the conclusion of the effectiveness of psychotherapy could not be made specifically for traditional psychotherapy with neurotic outpatients. In addition, the "apples and oranges" argument limits the extent to which such a heterogeneous collection of studies can be meaningfully integrated.

Malan (1973) noted that Meltzoff and Kornreich, although attempting to evaluate quality of research design, were uncritical of the outcome criteria employed and of the use of follow-up evaluations, two design elements that other reviewers might weigh heavily. Thus, the subjective judgments made by Meltzoff and Kornreich in evaluating design quality may have affected their overall conclusions.

Meltzoff and Kornreich had identified 32 findings from studies with "adequate" design that supported the effectiveness of psychotherapy and that they considered to be "major" results. Malan (1973) attempted to reduce this list to those findings that were most pertinent to Eysenck's question concerning the effectiveness of psychotherapy with neurotics. Malan eliminated from consideration those studies that did not have at least a six-month follow-up and that treated psychotics, children or adolescents, and volunteers or analogues (rather than true patients). Malan concluded that the review of Meltzoff and Kornreich provided only four major findings supporting the effectiveness of psychotherapy with adult nonpsychotic patients. These four studies provided support for didactic lectures as treatment for peptic ulcer patients, psychodynamic treatment of ulcerative colitis patients, client-centered treatment of alcoholics, and desensitization treatment of phobics. As Malan (1973) concluded, "Studies of dynamic psychotherapy on adult psychoneurotic outpatients are entirely absent" (p. 724).

Critique of Luborsky et al. (1975)

The review by Luborsky et al. (1975) has also met with wide criticism. For example, Smith, Glass, and Miller (1980) noted that the only criterion Luborsky et al. used to evaluate outcome was whether a study produced significant results. Smith et al. (1980) argued that this biased the review in favor of studies with large samples, because larger studies can produce statistically significant results with smaller effect sizes than can smaller studies. This practice also ignores the fact that, when a statistical test is insignificant and the null hypothesis is not rejected, the null hypothesis may still be false. There may be a difference between experimental groups which the study failed to detect (perhaps on methodological grounds, such as a small sample size, use of an insufficiently reliable measure, and so on). It is possible for a true difference to exist between groups, which is not detected in any of a series of individual studies, but which is apparent when the data from all of the studies are combined.

In addition, Smith et al. (1980) noted that, because the review of Luborsky et al. excluded analogue studies and studies of habit disorders (such as bedwetting), it may have underestimated the effectiveness of behavior therapy. Luborsky et al. (1975) excluded analogue studies, including only those with "real" patients, in order to increase the external validity or generalizability of the results of their review. However, excluding analogue studies and studies of habit disorders introduces a bias against behavior therapy in two ways. First, it leads to the exclusion of many more studies of behavior therapy than traditional insight-oriented therapy. Because a box-score analysis rests on a simple tally of the number of results favorable to a form of therapy, the practice of excluding analogue studies and studies of habit disorders leads to the loss of many more opportunities for behavior therapy to be found effective than traditional psychotherapy.

Second, excluding analogue studies and studies of habit disorders ignores the fact that behaviorists consider analogue studies to be appropriate methods of conducting tests of the effectiveness of new treatments before they are applied to more severely disturbed clients. It also ignores that, for behaviorists, habit disorders are "real" disorders. Behavioral theory suggests that disorders are the result of conditioning and can be treated with conditioning, that the same kinds of conditioning occur in the development of analogue and "real" disorders, and that the same kinds of conditioning can be used to treat analogue and "real" patients. Thus, within behavioral theory, it is perfectly appropriate to conduct analogue studies as tests of the effectiveness of behavioral treatments. To exclude analogue studies and studies of habit disorders, then, is to introduce a theoretical bias against behavior therapy.

Rachman and Wilson (1980) also critiqued the Luborsky et al. (1975) review. They agreed with Smith et al. (1980) that the exclusion of analogue studies and studies of habit disorders eliminated a wealth of behavioral treatment studies. In addition, Rachman and Wilson noted that Luborsky et al. were inconsistent in their application of their exclusion criterion. For example, Luborsky et al. included a study in which two forms of psychotherapy were found to produce equivalent changes on a measure of ethnocentrism, certainly not a "real" disorder.

Rachman and Wilson (1980) also raised criticisms originally directed against Eysenck; for example, the familiar problems of combining "apples and oranges," of having alternative interpretations of the quality of research designs, and of lacking appropriate control groups (for example, if two treatments were found to produce equal improvements, this does not mean that either is more effective than a placebo or than no treatment whatsoever).

Kazdin and Wilson (1978) critiqued the review of Luborsky et al. (1975), noting numerous weaknesses of the box-score method of analysis. In addition to the "apples and oranges" problem and the fallacy of giving equal weight to studies that reject and fail to reject the null hypothesis (noted by Smith et al. [1980] and summarized above), Kazdin and Wilson identified the following problems.

First, they argued that box-score analyses fail to consider the methodological adequacy of individual studies. For example, in a box-score analysis, several low-quality studies are given more weight than a single well-designed investigation. In addition, Kazdin and Wilson noted that combining several weak studies, all of which include the same kind of methodological problem, yields no more information than a single inadequate study. They therefore argued that research reviews ought to evaluate the quality of the research and to give priority to those studies with the strongest methodological designs.

Second, Kazdin and Wilson identified several problems concerning the subjectivity of reviewers' judgments. For example, labels such as *behavior therapy* and *psychotherapy* are not well defined, and so reviewers may disagree as to whether a specific treatment technique should be included within one category or the other. Kazdin and Wilson (1978) cited a paper which listed cognitive therapy in a category other than "behavior modification" and argued that cognitive therapy is more typically and appropriately classified among behavioral therapies.

Similarly, the interpretation of the box-score tallies is subjective and open to alternative evaluations. For example, Luborsky et al. (1975) reported that 19 comparisons of behavior therapy and psychotherapy resulted in 13 tie scores and 6 comparisons that favored behavior therapy. From this, Luborsky et al. (1975) concluded that there was no difference in effectiveness between the two types of therapy. However, an alternative interpretation, equally supported by this comparison, is that behavior therapy always equalled or surpassed psychotherapy.

Finally, Kazdin and Wilson suggested that a box-score analysis is misleading. It suggests greater empirical support for its results than is actually the case and which would be apparent given a more critical analysis.

The Smith and Glass Meta-analyses of Therapy Outcome Studies

Although the reviews described in the previous section of this chapter generally agreed that (at least some form of) therapy is effective, they disagreed on issues such as the extent to which psychotherapy is effective, the relative efficacies of different forms of psychotherapy, and the relationship between therapy outcome and quality of research design, duration, and other aspects of treatment. In addition, all of the arguments which had been directed against Eysenck could now be cited in opposition to the conclusions of reviewers who reported that therapy is effective.

During this period of confusion and contention over the effectiveness of psychotherapy, Smith and Glass (1977) published a review of the research which, like Eysenck's 1952 paper, would become a classic. Smith and Glass (1977) employed a statistical technique called "meta-analysis" to examine the results of 375 therapy outcome studies. Meta-analysis refers to a set of statistical techniques which have been developed expressly for the purpose of combining the data from various studies of a single topic (Cook & Leviton, 1980). What meta-analysis does is to derive measures that are comparable across studies (such as a study's effect size), regardless of the differences in the studies' methodologies (such as differences in the assessment instruments used or the groups compared). Once comparable measures are obtained for all studies, the meta-analyst can then examine the measure as a function of any aspect of the study (such as the quality of the study's design or the nature of the subjects' disorder).

Smith and Glass (1977) examined 375 experimental studies (including analogue studies and dissertations) in which one form of psychotherapy was compared to at least one control condition or other form of therapy. Their definition of psychotherapy was that given by Meltzoff and Kornreich (1970, p. 6):

> *Psychotherapy is taken to mean the informed and planful application of techniques derived from established psychological principles, by persons qualified through training and experience to understand these principles and to apply these techniques with the intention of assisting individuals to modify such personal characteristics as feelings, values, attitudes, and behaviors which are judged by the therapist to be maladaptive or maladjustive.*

Using this definition, Smith and Glass excluded studies of drug therapy, hypnotherapy, bibliotherapy, occupational therapy, milieu therapy, peer counseling, sensitivity training, marathon encounter groups, consciousness-raising groups, and psychodrama.

The "dependent variable" in the Smith and Glass (1977) analysis was the magnitude of the treatment effect or "effect size." This was defined as the mean difference between the treatment and control groups, divided by the standard deviation of the control group. Effect sizes were calculated for every outcome measure reported by an investigator. In this way, the 375 studies generated 833 effect sizes.

Smith and Glass then examined effect size as a function of 16 characteristics of both the treatment employed and the design of the study.

These "independent variables" were: type of therapy (classified as one of ten types); duration of therapy; therapy format (group versus individual); therapist experience; client diagnosis (neurotic versus psychotic); client age; client IQ; source of clients (self-referred, committed, solicited); therapist training (education, psychology, psychiatry); social and ethnic similarity between clients and therapists; type of outcome measure; duration of follow-up; reactivity (or "fakability") of outcome measure; date of publication; form of publication; and internal validity of the study.

Smith and Glass (1977) found that, over 375 studies, the average effect size of treated patients was .68. According to Smith and Glass, this means that "the average client receiving therapy was better off than 75% of the untreated controls" (p. 754).

Consistent with conventional psychotherapeutic wisdom, effect size was found to be significantly related to client IQ and similarity between client and therapist. That is, therapy produced greater differences between treatment and control groups when clients were higher in intelligence and when clients and therapists were more similar in social and ethnic backgrounds. Effect sizes were also significantly related to the type of outcome measure employed: the largest effect sizes were found for measures of fear, anxiety, and self-esteem, whereas more moderate effect sizes occurred for measures of general adjustment and work/school achievement.

In addition, effect size was found to be significantly related to several characteristics of the design of the study, including duration of the follow-up, internal validity, date of publication, and reactivity of the outcome measure. That is, larger effect sizes were produced by shorter follow-up durations, better designed studies, more recent studies, and studies which used less reactive (or more objective) outcome measures. Interestingly, no significant relationship was observed between effect size and treatment format (individual versus group), therapy duration, therapist experience, client diagnosis (neurotic versus psychotic), or client age.

Perhaps the most well-known results of the Smith and Glass (1977) meta-analysis concern the relative efficacies of different types of therapy. They calculated the average effect size for ten types of therapy and found that the largest effect sizes occurred for the following: Systematic Desensitization (.91), Rational-Emotive Therapy (.77), Behavior Modification (.76), Adlerian (.71), and Implosion (.64).

They then created two "superclasses" of therapy, combining Systematic Desensitization, Behavior Modification, and Implosion into a "Behavioral" group, and six of the remaining seven therapies (excluded was Gestalt therapy, due to an "inadequate" number of studies) into a "Nonbehavioral" group. Smith and Glass then reported that the average effect size of the behavioral treatments was .8, while the average effect size of the nonbehavioral treatments was .6. Although some might regard this difference as significant (since it was some five to seven times as large as the standard errors of the two mean effect sizes), Smith and Glass regarded it as insignificant. They noted that studies of behavioral therapies had two advantages over studies of nonbehavioral therapies, namely shorter average follow-up (two versus five months) and more reactive (subjective) outcome measures. When they examined 50 studies in which a behavioral treatment was compared to both a nonbehavioral treatment and to an untreated control condition, they found that the superiority of the behavioral treatments had decreased to .07.

Smith and Glass (1977), then, reached two major and often-cited conclusions. First, their analyses "demonstrate the beneficial effects of counseling and psychotherapy" (p. 760). Second, "the results of research demonstrate negligible differences in the effects produced by different therapy types" (p. 760).

Smith and Glass later extended their meta-analysis, examining 475 studies with a total of 1,766 effect sizes (Smith, Glass, & Miller, 1980). The average effect size in this analysis was .85 and, when placebo treatments were excluded, the average effect size increased to .89. As in the previous meta-analysis, no relationship was found between effect size and treatment format (group versus individual), therapy duration, or therapist experience. Also, as in the earlier meta-analysis, differences between types of therapy were interesting.

Smith et al. (1980) calculated the average effect size of 18 different types of therapy, the largest of which were observed for Cognitive Therapies (2.38), Hypnotherapy (1.82), Cognitive-Behavioral Therapy (1.13), Systematic Desensitization (1.05), Eclectic-Dynamic Therapies (.89), Eclectic Behavioral Therapies (.89), and Behavior Modification (.73).

They then grouped these therapies into six classes, with the following average effect sizes: Cognitive (1.31), Cognitive-Behavioral (1.24), Behavioral (.91), Dynamic (.78), Humanistic (.63), and Developmental (.42).

Finally, they classified these into three major headings: Behavioral (including Behavioral and Cognitive-Behavioral Therapy), Verbal (Dynamic, Humanistic, and Cognitive Therapy), and Developmental. The average effect sizes for these three major classes were, respectively, .98, .85, and .42.

As in the earlier meta-analysis, Smith et al. (1980) found that studies of behavioral treatments tended to use more reactive measures than studies of verbal treatments and, after correcting for this difference, they found little difference between the average effect size of Behavioral and Verbal therapies. However, when they examined only those studies which compared directly a therapy from the Behavioral and Verbal classes, they found that "behavioral therapies produced reliably larger effects" (p. 107).

One result from this second meta-analysis differed from their earlier results. Smith et al. (1980) found that the relationship between effect size and the internal validity of the study (or design quality) was insignificant (remember that their previous meta-analysis suggested that better designed studies produced larger effect sizes). That is, effect size was comparable in studies with high (.88), medium (.78), and low (.78) design quality. This led Smith et al. (1980) to question the practice in traditional research reviews of excluding studies of poor quality.

In summarizing their meta-analysis, Smith et al. (1980) concluded that "the results show unequivocally that psychotherapy is effective" (p. 124). The average effect size calculated from 1,766 measures in 475 studies was .85; this means that the average treated client was superior to 80 percent of untreated clients. In addition, they suggested that, whereas the issue of the comparative effectiveness of different types of psychotherapy "does not yield a single answer," some therapies such as cognitive, cognitive-behavioral, hypnosis, and systematic desensitization appear to be the most effective. When therapies were divided into major classes, the "behavioral therapies were more effective than the verbal therapies, which were in turn more effective than the developmental therapies" (p. 124).

Criticisms of the Smith and Glass Meta-analyses

The meta-analyses of Smith and Glass stimulated an immediate and large response, perhaps larger than that of any other review of therapy outcome since the original Eysenck (1952) paper. Although the technique of meta-analysis has become accepted as a standard method of evaluating therapy outcome studies (e.g., Kazdin, 1986), and although the conclusions of Smith and Glass (1977; 1980) are often cited as evidence supporting the effectiveness of psychotherapy (e.g., Lambert, Shapiro, & Bergin, 1986), a large number of criticisms have been directed against the techniques and conclusions of Smith and Glass (e.g., Eysenck, 1978, 1983; Gallo, 1978; Kazdin & Wilson, 1978; Mansfield & Busse, 1977; Presby, 1978; Rachman & Wilson, 1980; Rimland, 1979; Searles, 1985; Strahan, 1978). The purpose of the next part of the chapter is to summarize the arguments for and against the techniques and conclusions of the Smith and Glass meta-analyses of the psychotherapy outcome literature.

The Strengths of Meta-analysis

Precision
Smith et al. (1980) described meta-analysis as a more precise method of reviewing large bodies of research than the traditional, qualitative

method employed by Eysenck (1952) and other previous reviewers. Meta-analysis is regarded as a more precise method of reviewing research literature because it considers information that is ignored by simple box-score analyses.

For example, suppose a box-score analysis is conducted which only reports the number of significant versus insignificant results for a particular comparison. This method is biased in favor of studies with large samples, which can produce statistically significant results with smaller effect sizes. It also ignores the direction and the magnitude of nonsignificant differences. If there was a consistent nonsignificant trend running throughout these studies, then the combination of these results using a meta-analytic procedure might yield a conclusion very different from that obtained by a traditional review (Cook & Leviton, 1980).

Meta-analysis can also be regarded as a more precise method of evaluating large bodies of research than traditional methods because it can evaluate the degree to which factors of the studies interact in producing their results (Cook & Leviton, 1980). For example, the Luborsky et al. (1975) review presented a box-score summary of comparisons based on several factors of the therapy evaluated (such as group versus individual format, behavioral versus nonbehavioral therapy, therapy versus no therapy, and so on). Because of the small cell sizes which would have been produced if the interactions among these factors had been examined, Luborsky et al. described the effects of only very few of the possible interactions of these factors. Meta-analysis, on the other hand, can examine simultaneously (say, through a multiple regression analysis) the relationships between effect size and treatment factors in isolation and in combination. Hence, it can provide a more precise description of the relationships between treatment outcome and aspects of therapy.

Objectivity

Meta-analysis has also been characterized as more objective than traditional methods of conducting research reviews (Cook & Leviton, 1980). For example, reviewers conducting traditional qualitative reviews of the research literature can introduce a systematic bias, either deliberately or indeliberately, in several ways. They may neglect altogether studies with results inconsistent with their bias, exclude such studies on methodological grounds, exclude such studies as irrelevant on theoretical grounds, and interpret remaining studies in ways favorable to their own position. Although these difficulties are not necessarily present in qualitative reviews, reviewers (and readers) must always be aware of such threats to the validity of the review.

Meta-analysis is not free of the risk of reviewer bias. However, because the meta-analyst must make explicit the rules used to select and quantify the studies included in the review (Nurius & Yeaton, 1987; Strube & Hartmann, 1983), the reviewer and reader are both in better positions than in traditional reviews to detect the occurrence and minimize the influence of reviewer bias.

For example, Smith and Glass stated that their review was more objective than earlier reviews of the therapy outcome literature. They included all the controlled therapy outcome studies that they could find (including analogue studies and studies in unpublished dissertations), thereby reducing the risk of introducing bias through the selection of studies favorable to a particular position. They did not exclude studies on methodological grounds (although they did rate aspects pertinent to the quality of the design, such as the length of the follow-up and the reactivity of outcome measures), in order to reduce the risk of introducing systematic bias through the inconsistent application of design criteria, thereby eliminating studies favorable to one position while retaining studies with conclusions favorable to another position. They relied on quantitative methods, rather than on subjective qualitative judgments, to evaluate the extent to which psychotherapy is effective and the relationship between various aspects of therapy and therapy outcome.

Criticisms of the Smith and Glass Meta-analyses

Although Smith and Glass have argued in favor of the superiority of meta-analytic procedures over traditional qualitative methods of conducting reviews of large bodies of research, and although meta-analysis has been accepted as an appropriate means of evaluating large bodies of research (e.g., Cook & Leviton, 1980; Strube & Hartmann, 1983), many criticisms have been directed against the methods and conclusions of Smith and Glass. Most of these criticisms fall under the headings below.

The "Apples and Oranges" Argument

Rachman and Wilson (1980) questioned whether meta-analysis was appropriate for examining such a diverse group of studies as that reviewed by Smith and Glass (1977). Cooper (1979) noted that meta-analysis was appropriate for reviewing the research literature when the studies "share a common conceptual hypothesis" or when they "share operations for the realization of the independent or dependent variables, regardless of conceptual focus" (p. 133). Rachman and Wilson suggested that neither condition was met in the studies reviewed by Smith and Glass. "The spread in quality of experimental design, in adequacy of measurement, and in conceptual focus is so great that attempts to integrate findings across such widely divergent research are doomed to muddy the troubled waters still further" (p. 250).

Violations of the Assumptions of Meta-analysis

Gallo (1978) questioned whether the assumptions underlying meta-analysis were met in the Smith and Glass (1977) review. Landman and Dawes (1982) articulated one of the major mathematical assumptions underlying meta-analysis which was violated in the Smith and Glass meta-analyses. Meta-analysis requires that the units of analysis (effect size) be statistically independent of one another. However, the Smith and Glass (1977) review violated this assumption in five ways. Nonindependent effect sizes were included which resulted from: (a) multiple measures administered to a single subject; (b) a measure administered at different times to a single subject; (c) nonindependent scores from a single measure (such as both a global score and a subscore); (d) nonindependent, overlapping samples within a single article; and (e) nonindependent, overlapping samples across studies.

The problem of nonindependence raises the possibility that one study could contribute multiple effect sizes (which may be correlated with one another and so which do not contribute independent information) to the overall results than other, perhaps better designed studies.

Ignoring Design Quality

Smith et al. (1980) noted that the practice of excluding studies on the basis of methodological weaknesses introduces the possibility of bias through reviewers applying methodological standards inconsistently in order to select studies favorable to their own position. They therefore included all studies, regardless of quality, in order to make their meta-analysis more objective.

This practice has been severely criticized (Eysenck, 1978, 1983; Kazdin & Wilson, 1978; Rachman & Wilson, 1980; Searles, 1985). It gives as much weight to a poorly designed study as to a well-designed study. It introduces the possibility that the results of a strong study will be negated by those of a series of weak studies. Including studies of mixed quality in a meta-analysis may therefore obscure rather than clarify the findings. Eysenck (1978) used a familiar axiom to criticize this practice of using questionable data in an attempt to reach any kind of conclusion: "Garbage in—garbage out" (p. 517).

Kazdin and Wilson (1978) argued that a "series of methodologically inadequate studies that to one degree or another repeat basic errors in design and/or implementation is no better than a single inadequate study" (p. 134). Scientists have traditionally adopted this position. For example, parapsychologists have long made the "bundle of sticks" argument. That is, parapsychologists acknowledge that they do not have a single strong experiment that provides replicable results favorable to their claims. However, they note that they have many weak pieces of evidence. They then argue that, just as a bundle of sticks is stronger than a single stick in isolation, so is a series of weak results stronger than any one of the results in isolation. Parapsychologists' "bundle of sticks" argument has traditionally been rejected by most scientists.

Rachman and Wilson (1980) determined that more than one-third of the studies (144 of 375) in the Smith and Glass (1977) meta-analysis were unpublished dissertations. Although dissertation research is not necessarily different in quality from published research, it is likely that dissertation studies are of lower average quality and are of greater variability of quality than those in professional journals. To base a review on so many unpublished studies will obscure the results of the studies with the strongest designs. It is also difficult for a reader to replicate the results of a review based on so many unpublished works.

Although many scientists would agree with the criticism of meta-analysis that priority should be given to the strongest studies, this position does not provide an answer to the problem of potential reviewer bias. Smith and Glass attempted to address this criticism by rating the quality of studies and then determining empirically whether design quality was related to outcome. If such a relationship was demonstrated, then this would support the position of analyzing strong and weak studies separately. As reported above, the relationship between design quality and outcome was unclear. Whereas Smith and Glass (1977) found that effect size was significantly positively related to design quality, Smith et al. (1980) reported an insignificant relationship between outcome and design.

Alternative Interpretations of Results

The results of meta-analysis, like those of any other statistical technique, must be interpreted. Different reviewers may therefore reach different conclusions from a single set of results.

For example, Gallo (1978) examined the statistical evidence for the two major conclusions of Smith and Glass (1977): that therapy was effective and that there was little difference between the outcomes of different types of therapies. Smith and Glass reached the latter conclusion when they found that only about 10 percent of the variance in effect size was accounted for by therapy type. However, both Gallo (1978) and Strahan (1978) used the data of Smith and Glass to determine that only 10.31 percent of the variance in effect size was accounted for by the factor of Therapy versus No Therapy. In other words, Smith and Glass (1977) interpreted a 10 percent contribution to the variance of effect size as significant when it supported the claim that therapy was superior to no therapy, but they interpreted an equally large effect as insignificant in order to conclude that there was no difference between therapy types.

Gallo (1978) also showed that the finding of an average effect size of therapy of .68 is open to alternative interpretations. Although statistically significantly greater than zero, this effect size may still not be clinically significant or meaningful in a cost-benefit analysis. For example, suppose a client pays $30 per hour for 17 hours of therapy (the average number of hours of therapy in the Smith and Glass review). At the end of therapy, the client has therefore paid $510 for, on the average, an improvement of .68 of a standard deviation. Whether such an improvement is "clinically significant" may well depend on the outcome measure. If the outcome measure is life expectancy, then the improvement is tremendously significant and well worth the time and money; however, if the outcome measure is a paper-and-pencil measure of anxiety or a test of ethnocentrism, then the improvement may not be cost-effective. The conclusion of Smith and Glass (1977) that psychotherapy has an average effect size of .68 is therefore open to alternative interpretations, including that such an improvement is not clinically meaningful.

Another writer who examined the data from the Smith and Glass (1979) meta-analysis and reached a very different interpretation was Rimland (1979). Because the data reported by Smith and Glass (1977) suggest that only 10 percent of the variance in effect size is due to whether or not the client received therapy, and because Smith and Glass found that neither therapist experience nor therapy duration was related to outcome, Rimland questioned how psychotherapists can justify charging for treatment beyond a single session or requiring extensive training and licensing requirements. The title of Rimland's article suggests that he interpreted the Smith and Glass meta-analysis as sounding the "death knell" for psychotherapy.

The Control Group Problem

Smith and Glass included in their meta-analyses studies that compared one treatment to at least one other treatment or control group. The problem here is that the studies differed with respect to whether or not they included a control group and, if they did have a control group, with respect to what kind of control group they employed. For example, effect sizes for a specific type of therapy (say, desensitization) were calculated in some studies by comparing that therapy to a control condition and in other studies by comparing it to another therapy type. In some studies, effect sizes were calculated for a treatment by comparing it to a no-treatment condition, whereas in other studies its effect was determined by comparison to a placebo treatment. Thus, effect sizes across studies may not be entirely comparable.

Rachman and Wilson (1980) illustrated this difficulty. Suppose a study compared two treatments and found that they produce equal outcomes.

This may mean that the two treatments are equally effective or that they are equally ineffective. Unless the treatments are also compared to some control condition, it is impossible to determine whether either treatment has a success rate better than the spontaneous remission rate. Rachman and Wilson (1980), therefore, argued in favor of including in a research review on the effectiveness of psychotherapy only those studies that compared some form of therapy to a control condition.

Eysenck (1983) also criticized Smith et al. (1980) because of their handling of control groups. Smith et al. calculated that the average effect size of placebo treatments was .56 (significantly greater than the effect sizes of two types of therapy and not significantly less than the effect sizes of four other types of therapy). However, they evaluated therapies by comparing their effect sizes to a no-treatment condition rather than to placebo treatment. Eysenck suggested that Smith et al. evaluate psychotherapy by comparing its effectiveness to that of placebo treatment. When this is done, the effect sizes of most therapies become either statistically or clinically insignificant.

Subjective Judgments

Although Smith et al. (1980) have argued that meta-analysis is more objective than methods employed in traditional research reviews, meta-analysis does require that the reviewer make numerous judgments. Meta-analysts must judge which studies to include, what variables to examine, how to code the variables, and so on. Thus, meta-analysis involves subjective judgments, which introduces the possibility of reviewer bias.

For example, Smith and Glass (1977) assigned ten therapy types to four groups, which they identified as ego, dynamic, humanistic, and behavioral therapies. Smith and Glass compared the average effect sizes of these four groups (although they did not report this result). They then combined the therapy groups into two major classes, behavioral and nonbehavioral, and reported that behavioral therapies had a slightly higher average effect size (.80) than nonbehavioral therapies (.60). Presby (1978) criticized Smith and Glass for assigning rational-emotive therapy (RET) to the ego therapies and, later, with the nonbehavioral therapies. Albert Ellis, the developer of RET, has acknowledged the behavioral elements in his treatment (Ellis & Harper, 1975). RET is short-term, directive, problem oriented, and more similar in many respects to behavior therapy than to traditional insight-oriented therapy. Although Smith and Glass assigned RET to the nonbehavioral therapies on the basis of the ratings of 25 clinicians and counselors who had judged the similarity among the ten therapy types, many other reviewers would classify RET among the behavioral therapies. If RET is assigned to the behavioral rather than the nonbehavioral therapies, then the average effect sizes for behavioral and nonbehavioral therapy become, respectively, .83 and .58. The difference between the behavioral and nonbehavioral therapies is therefore larger if RET is classified as a behavioral therapy.

A similar situation occurred in Smith et al. (1980). They assigned therapy types to six groups and then classified these groups into three classes with the following effect sizes: Verbal (.85), Behavioral (.98), and Developmental (.42). Although Smith et al. indicated that this shows the behavioral therapies to be "clearly superior," a reanalysis of this difference, correcting for the reactivity of the outcome measures employed, found that the superiority of the behavioral over the verbal therapies became insignificant. Smith et al. classified Cognitive therapies (including RET, rational restructuring, fixed role therapy, and so on) with the Verbal therapies. Because Cognitive therapies are short-term, directive, and problem oriented, many other reviewers would have classified them among the Behavioral therapies. If Cognitive therapies are classified with the Behavioral rather than with the Verbal therapies, then the average effect sizes of the Behavioral and Verbal therapies would be, respectively, 1.03 and .71, yielding a difference between Behavioral and Verbal therapies more than double the original difference and likely to remain significant even after correcting for outcome measure reactivity. Again, this demonstrates how different subjective judgments by reviewers can lead to very different conclusions.

Another subjective judgment made by Smith and Glass that may have affected their conclusions was their rating of the reactivity of outcome measures. They rated measures completed by the therapist or client as higher in reactivity (or fakability), and measures such as physiological ratings or ratings made by judges blind with respect to the treatment status of the client as lower in reactivity. Because many studies of the effectiveness of behavioral therapy employed either client or therapist ratings of behavior change, Smith and Glass stated that the "reactivity or susceptibility to bias of the outcome measures was higher for the behavioral superclass than for the nonbehavioral superclass" (pp. 757–758).

Although it is true that ratings made by clients and therapists are more likely to be biased than physiological recordings or ratings made by blind judges, it is also true that some ratings by therapists or clients are less susceptible to bias than other ratings. To judge all ratings by therapists and clients as high in reactivity ignores the fact that therapist and client ratings vary in reliability and validity. Studies of behavioral therapy typically employ client and therapist ratings of client behavior as an index of improvement. A therapist rating (such as distance to which a phobic is willing to approach a feared object) or a client rating (such as number of cigarettes smoked or number of nights that an enuretic wet the bed) may well be high in both reliability and validity. Such ratings, although not completely free of the risk of reactive bias, can be demonstrated to have sufficient reliability (consistency, accuracy) and validity (meaningful relationship to the problem behavior which is the focus of treatment). Such behavioral ratings are also very likely to be higher in reliability and validity than therapist and client ratings of more global, abstract, or internal constructs (such as adjustment, ego strength, or insight). Rather than rate the reactivity of outcome measures simply in terms of whether a client or therapist made the ratings, another reviewer might decide to rate outcome measures according to their demonstrated psychometric properties of reliability and validity. If this were done, then one might not conclude, as did Smith and Glass, that studies of behavioral therapies employed less adequate measures than studies of nonbehavioral therapies, and so the results of the studies of behavioral therapies are more questionable.

Inconsistent Applications of Techniques

Although Smith and Glass have characterized their meta-analyses as more objective than traditional review methods because they included all studies, regardless of quality, and because they let statistical analyses rather than reviewer judgments produce their conclusions, they have still been criticized for applying their meta-analytic techniques inconsistently. For example, Smith and Glass stated that they did not exclude any studies, so as not to introduce the possibility of reviewer bias through the systematic exclusion of studies unfavorable to one's own position. However, Rachman and Wilson (1980) identified several well-known and important studies by behavior therapists that were not included in the Smith and Glass (1977) meta-analysis.

When Smith and Glass (1977) assigned ten types of therapy to the two classes of behavioral and nonbehavioral therapy, they excluded Gestalt therapy from the comparison of the two classes because of an "inadequate number of studies" (p. 757) ("8 studies showing 16 effect sizes" [p. 756]). However, they included in this comparison studies of Adlerian therapy which also yielded only 16 effect sizes. Because their unit of analysis was effect size for individual measures and not the average effect size for a study, they should have treated Adlerian and Gestalt therapy consistently. For example, if both types of therapy are included, then the average effect size of nonbehavioral therapies is .57; if both types of therapies are excluded, then the average effect size of nonbehavioral therapies is .60. In either case, the average effect size would be slightly lower than that obtained when including Adlerian and excluding Gestalt therapy.

Meta-analysis, then, although an extremely useful technique for evaluating large bodies of research literature, is not without limitations of its own. Because it enables large numbers of studies to be compared statistically and enables the statistical determination of the influence of various characteristics of studies to the overall effect, it is an extremely useful approach. However, meta-analysis, like traditional approaches to conducting research reviews, "consists of a series of complex, subjective, and sometimes arbitrary-seeming decisions" (Strube & Hartmann, 1983, p. 25). The meta-analyst, as well as the consumer of meta-analyses, should be aware of the subjective nature of many meta-analytic decisions, and so regard the conclusions of meta-analytic reviews with the same caution that one would maintain when evaluating the results of traditional reviews. If one is not aware of the potential for bias in meta-analyses, then one might easily be overwhelmed by the apparent objectivity of such quantitative summaries of large numbers of studies, what Cook and Leviton (1980) regarded as the major limitation of meta-analyses: "an unwarranted psychological sense of security" (p. 469).

Other Meta-analyses of Therapy Outcome Studies

Following the publication of the Smith and Glass meta-analyses of psychotherapy outcome studies, several other meta-analytic reviews have been conducted in attempts to improve the methodology and address the criticisms raised above.

Andrews and Harvey (1981)

The first of these was conducted by Andrews and Harvey (1981). They attempted to refine the Smith et al. (1980) meta-analysis by limiting their attention only to "persons who would normally seek psychotherapy" (p. 1204). Thus, they included only studies of neurotic patients (including phobic neuroses, depressive disorders, and emotional-somatic disorders) and studies of self- or other-referred patients (excluding analogue studies). In this way, Andrews and Harvey identified 81 studies which yielded 292 effect sizes.

After conducting a meta-analysis similar to that of Smith et al. (1980), Andrews and Harvey reached three major conclusions. First, they found that the average effect size was .72. This means that the neurotic patient who receives treatment is, on the average, superior in outcome to 76 percent of untreated neurotics. Second, therapy improvement was maintained over time. Average effect sizes at two- and nine-month follow-ups were, respectively, .82 and .71. Third, there was an insignificant relationship between therapy outcome and treatment duration. Brief therapies produced an average effect size (.76) which did not differ statistically from those of short-term (.73) or long-term (.86) treatments. Andrews and Harvey suggested that this last result was due to the fact that behavioral therapies

(.97),—significantly more effective than verbal therapies (.74) and developmental therapies (.35)—tended to treat less severe disorders with shorter treatment durations than other therapies. Thus, treatment duration was confounded with severity of disorder and type of therapy.

Searles (1985): Meta-analysis One

Searles (1985) further refined the Andrews and Harvey (1981) meta-analysis. Although Andrews and Harvey stated that they confined their attention to neurotic disorders, Searles (1985) observed that Andrews and Harvey included in their meta-analysis studies on the treatment of homosexuality, underachievement, and other problems not commonly considered as neurotic. In addition, Searles suggested that studies of somatic disorders, such as migraine headaches, should also be excluded from a meta-analysis of the treatment of neurotics. Searles also argued that studies should be included in the meta-analysis if they had a strong design. His criterion for selection of studies on the basis of design was to include only those studies that compared one or more treatments to a control condition (excluding studies that compared two or more treatments to one another, without a control group). In this way, Searles reduced the Andrews and Harvey sample to 16 studies, 8 of behavior therapy and 8 of psychodynamic therapy.

After finding that one study of psychodynamic therapy and three studies of behavior therapy had to be dropped because of insufficient data, Searles reported that the average effect size of psychodynamic therapy (.32, based on 78 effect sizes) was substantially less than that of behavior therapy (.88, based on 32 effect sizes). From this, Searles concluded that, when studies of the treatment of neurotic patients are selected for their methodological rigor, then behavior therapy "clearly accounts for most of the reported effect size" (p. 460).

Landman and Dawes (1982)

Landman and Dawes (1982) conducted a reanalysis of the Smith and Glass (1977) meta-analysis. They attempted to refine the Smith and Glass review by eliminating the problem of nonindependent effect sizes. They also sought to improve the quality of the meta-analysis by including only those studies that included a control group (excluding studies that compared one treatment to another). From the list of 375 studies examined by Smith and Glass (1977) and 93 additional studies, they randomly selected 65 studies (excluding dissertations). From this list, they identified 42 studies which employed a no-treatment or placebo control group. To control for the problem of nonindependent effect sizes, they examined separately outcome at post-treatment and at follow-up. They also found the average effect size of all measures administered at the same time to a subject, using the average effect size as the unit of analysis, rather than having the effect size for each measure as the unit of analysis as in the Smith and Glass meta-analyses.

Landman and Dawes determined that the average effect size of psychotherapy was .90. In addition, they found that the average effect size at the first follow-up period (based on 12 studies) was 1.01. Finally, they reported that the effect size of psychotherapy when compared to a no-treatment control was .80 and when compared to a placebo treatment condition was .58.

Thus, Landman and Dawes (1982) concluded that their meta-analysis supported the conclusion of Smith and Glass (1977) that psychotherapy was effective. Because their review included only studies with no-treatment or placebo control groups (and therefore were of higher average design quality than the studies reviewed by Smith and Glass), Landman and Dawes agreed with the contention of Smith and Glass that quality of design had little impact on the results of their meta-analysis. Finally, since Landman and Dawes controlled for the problem of nonindependence of effect sizes, they concluded that the mathematical problem of nonindependence had little impact on the results of the Smith and Glass meta-analysis.

Searles (1985): Meta-analysis Two

Searles (1985) again attempted to refine this refined meta-analysis. He eliminated from the Landman and Dawes (1982) meta-analysis those studies of the effectiveness of undifferentiated "counseling." These were eliminated by Searles because he did not regard these studies as involving "anything approaching psychological intervention," targeting problems such as study habits or occupational planning which are not related to neurotic disorders and are therefore not "relevant to a study of psychotherapy" (p. 459).

In this way, Searles identified 19 behavioral studies and 2 psychodynamic studies, and found that the average effect size of behavioral therapy (1.22) was again substantially higher than that of psychodynamic therapy (.27). Although Searles recognized that these results may not be interpretable because of the small number of studies of psychodynamic therapies, he noted that the Landman and Dawes review was based on a sample that virtually excluded psychodynamic therapies (and so its results should not be generalized to this kind of therapy) and emphasized the well-controlled nature of behavioral studies.

Shapiro and Shapiro (1982)

Shapiro and Shapiro (1982) conducted another meta-analysis which attempted to improve upon the methodology of Smith et al. (1980). Shapiro and Shapiro identified 143 studies which compared two therapies to one another and to a control condition (of these, only 21 were also in the Smith et al. [1980] review). This comprised a set of well-designed studies and so addressed the criticisms of the Smith and Glass meta-analyses concerning the lack of appropriate control groups. Shapiro and Shapiro also excluded from consideration studies in unpublished dissertations.

They found that psychotherapy produced an average outcome of approximately one standard deviation superior to that of untreated controls (.93 when effect sizes of individual measures were the unit of analysis; .98 when effect sizes of treatment groups were the unit of analysis). Shapiro and Shapiro also found that therapy types differed significantly in their average effect size. Average effect sizes for therapy types were as follows: Mixed Behavioral (1.42), Behavioral (1.06), Cognitive (1.00), Unclassified Behavioral (.78), Minimal (Placebo) Treatment (.71), and Dynamic/Humanistic (.40). Although Shapiro and Shapiro determined that several aspects of therapy were related to outcome (for example, individual therapy produced greater responses than group therapy), they also demonstrated that differences between treatment types were largely independent of these factors.

Prioleau, Murdock, and Brody (1983)

Prioleau, Murdock, and Brody (1983) conducted another meta-analysis which refined the technique of Smith et al. (1980). Prioleau et al. argued that the placebo control group is more appropriate than either the waiting list or no-treatment control group when examining the effectiveness of psychotherapy. They therefore identified 40 studies from those reviewed by Smith et al. (1980) that compared psychotherapy (and not behavior therapy) to a placebo control group. After discarding eight studies which were seriously methodologically flawed, Prioleau et al. compared the average effect sizes of psychotherapy and placebo groups (using the group effect size and not the measure effect size as the unit of analysis).

Prioleau et al. found that psychotherapy had an average effect size of .42 (although this was inflated by one extreme score—the median effect size was .15). They also found insignificant relationships between effect size and duration of treatment, sample size, client type (analogue versus "real"), and outcome measure (self-report versus other). Six studies that included follow-ups showed that there was no tendency for the effects of psychotherapy relative to the placebo control to increase during the follow-up period. When separating studies into those with real versus analogue patients, Prioleau et al. found that the only studies demonstrating clear effects of therapy were those that did not use real patients. From this, Prioleau et al. concluded that "the benefits of psychotherapy do not exceed those of placebo in real patients" (p. 284).

Bowers and Clum (1988)

Bowers and Clum (1988) conducted a meta-analysis of 69 treatment studies published between 1977 and 1986 which compared some form of behavior therapy to a placebo or other nonspecific treatment condition. They used the average effect size for all dependent variables as the unit of analysis. When treatment was compared to no treatment, Bowers and Clum calculated the mean effect size to be .76. When treatment was compared to a placebo or nonspecific treatment, the average effect size was .55. Finally, when a nonspecific treatment was compared to no treatment, the average effect size was .21. Thus, Bowers and Clum concluded that the effect of specific behavioral treatments was more than twice that of placebo or other nonspecific treatments.

Kazdin and Bass (1989)

Kazdin and Bass (1989) identified 120 therapy outcome studies published in five selected journals over a three-year period. Of these, 85 provided sufficient information to permit the calculation of effect sizes. In agreement with Bowers and Clum (1988), Kazdin and Bass found that the average effect size when treatment was compared to no treatment (.85) was substantially higher than when treatment was compared to some placebo or other nonspecific treatment condition (.38) or when one treatment was compared to another active treatment (.50).

In addition, Kazdin and Bass estimated the power of the statistical tests performed by the original researchers. They found that the power of comparisons of treatment to no treatment (median = .995) was substantially higher than that of comparisons of two specific treatments (median = .74). Thus, one reason why researchers to date have not provided convincing evidence for the superiority of one therapy over another may simply be that the statistical power of the tests performed to determine possible differences between treatments has been insufficient.

Matt (1989)

Matt (1989) randomly selected 25 studies from the Smith et al. (1980) meta-analysis. He had three judges independently code the effect sizes from these investigations. Matt found that these judges identified more than twice as many effect sizes per study as Smith et al. and that these judges determined mean effect sizes approximately one-half the mean effect size reported by Smith et al. These findings clearly illustrate the subjectivity involved in any meta-analysis of the literature. The judgments of individual judges can substantially affect the outcome of the review.

With the exception of Kazdin and Bass (1989), these meta-analyses were based on sets of studies which either overlapped with or were subsets of the studies in the Smith and Glass (1977; Smith et al., 1980) reviews. They demonstrate that even meta-analyses of the same or similar sets of studies can yield very different conclusions, depending on the subjective decisions made by the meta-analyst. Thus, meta-analytic reviews should be subject to the same critical examination as traditional reviews, considering the decisions made by the reviewer to select and classify studies (Brown, 1987).

Since the original Smith and Glass (1977) meta-analysis of the effectiveness of psychotherapy in general, many other reviewers have conducted meta-analyses on selected segments of the therapy outcome literature. For example, meta-analyses have been conducted to determine the effectiveness of specific treatments, such as cognitive-behavior therapy (Miller & Berman, 1983) and self-statement modification (Dush, Hirt, & Schroeder, 1983), to determine the effectiveness of treatment of specific disorders, such as tension and migraine headaches (Blanchard, Andrasik, Ahles, Teders, & O'Keefe, 1980), and to determine the relative efficacies of two or more treatments, such as psychotherapy versus drug therapy in the treatment of unipolar depression (Steinbrueck, Maxwell, & Howard, 1983) and cognitive therapy versus systematic desensitization (Berman, Miller, & Massman, 1985). Recent meta-analyses have also examined the effectiveness of psychotherapy within certain client populations, such as children (e.g., Casey & Berman, 1985; Weisz, Weiss, Alicke, & Klotz, 1987).

In fact, the literature on the effectiveness of psychotherapy with children presents an interesting parallel to the research summarized above on therapy with adults. An initial challenge to the field (Levitt, 1957) cited research showing that children who receive psychotherapy have outcomes similar to those of untreated children. This was followed by criticisms of the methodology of the initial review (e.g., Hood-Williams, 1960), other reviews which led to both favorable (e.g., Heinicke & Goldman, 1960; Hood-Williams, 1960) and unfavorable (e.g., Barrett, Hampe, & Miller, 1978; Levitt, 1963, 1971) conclusions regarding the effectiveness of therapy with children, and ultimately to more and better designed studies. Quantitative reviews using modern meta-analytic techniques have become increasingly popular (e.g., Casey & Berman, 1985; Weisz et al., 1987). However, the subjective judgments of the meta-analysts have led to very different conclusions regarding the relative efficacies of different forms of therapy. Most recently, meta-analyses have begun to address the effectiveness of specific types of treatment with children (e.g., Fuhrman & Durlak, 1989).

Summary and Conclusions

This chapter has reviewed the issue of the effectiveness of psychotherapy, focusing upon the evaluation of the empirical research conducted, particularly since Eysenck's (1952) review. Prior to the 1950s, psychotherapists evaluated therapy subjectively. They relied upon their own and their clients' impressions of the effectiveness of psychotherapy, uncontrolled descriptive reports of the effectiveness of therapy, and theoretical discussions of the mechanisms through which psychotherapy was thought to operate.

Eysenck (1952) examined the research and concluded that the uncontrolled studies conducted up to that time did not demonstrate that psychotherapy with adult neurotics had a superior outcome to untreated neurotics. He challenged the field to produce scientific evidence— controlled experimental studies—that supported the claim that psychotherapy worked. Although Eysenck's conclusion was hotly disputed, the field recognized the need for such empirical evidence of claims of therapeutic efficacy.

Since the 1950s, there has been an increasing number of controlled studies concerning the effectiveness of psychotherapy. Such a large body of empirical studies makes it difficult for a professional to critically evaluate and integrate the entire research literature. Hence, there has been a related increase in the number of reviews of the research. Because reviewers may differ in how they include and exclude, how they evaluate, and how they interpret the findings of studies, different reviewers have reached different conclusions regarding the effectiveness of therapy in general and the relative efficacies of different forms of therapy.

Since the 1970s, reviewers have employed meta-analytic techniques in an attempt to reduce the potential for bias associated with the subjective decisions made by any reviewer. Because these techniques make explicit the decisions made by a reviewer, they help both the reviewer and the reader to recognize and perhaps to moderate the potential bias. However, meta-analyses still involve many subjective judgments and so do not remove all potential for reviewer bias. Readers should be aware of the potential for bias even in meta-analytic reviews and examine them critically.

In conclusion, psychotherapists have accepted the scientific standard for the evaluation of claims concerning the effectiveness of therapy. The following consequences have resulted:

1. The field has conducted a large number of controlled therapy outcome studies. This research has contributed much to our understanding of the effects of therapy, along with the influences on and processes of therapy.

2. The quality of the controlled research has improved. In addition, the nature of the studies has become more and more specific. Rather than simply attempt to determine whether psychotherapy is effective, psychotherapy outcome studies now address whether a specific treatment is effective for a specific disorder when delivered under specific circumstances.

3. The field has developed new therapies, such as the behavioral and cognitive therapies, which are more suited to scientific evaluations than traditional therapies, and which some have concluded are more effective than the traditional therapies.

4. The field has emphasized the principle of accountability in its delivery of mental health services. For example, the *General Guidelines for Providers of Psychological Services* of the American Psychological Association (APA, 1987) lists "Accountability" as one of its major guidelines. Under this heading, providers of psychological services are instructed, "There are periodic, systematic, and effective evaluations of psychological services" (p. 8). Similarly, under another guideline, providers "are encouraged to develop and/or apply and evaluate innovative theories and procedures, to provide appropriate theoretical or empirical support for their innovations, and to disseminate their results to others" (p. 4). To illustrate this last statement, psychotherapists are further informed that their profession is "rooted in a science" (p. 4) and, as such, they must continually explore, study, and evaluate their procedures.

As a result of all of these changes, the consumer of psychotherapy benefits. The treatments offered to clients today are more likely than those of the 1940s to have an empirical foundation, and the clients have more assurance that what they are being offered actually works.

References

American Psychological Association. (1987). *General guidelines for providers of psychological services.* Washington, DC: American Psychological Association.

Andrews, G., & Harvey, R. (1981). Does psychotherapy benefit neurotic patients? A reanalysis of the Smith, Glass, and Miller data. *Archives of General Psychiatry, 38,* 1203–1208.

Barrett, C. L., Hampe, I. E., & Miller, L. C. (1978). Research on child psychotherapy. In S. L. Garfield & A. E. Bergin (Eds.), Handbook of psychotherapy and behavior change: An empirical analysis (2nd ed.) (pp. 411–435). New York: Wiley.

Bergin, A. E. (1971). The evaluation of therapeutic outcomes. In A. E. Bergin & S. L. Garfield (Eds.), Handbook of psychotherapy and behavior change: An empirical analysis (pp. 217–270). New York: Wiley.

Bergin, A. E., & Garfield, S. L. (1971). Preface. In A. E. Bergin & S. L. Garfield (Eds.), Handbook of psychotherapy and behavior change: An empirical analysis (pp. ix–xii). New York: Wiley.

Bergin, A. E., Murray, E. J., Truax, C. B., & Shoben, E. J. (1963). The empirical emphasis in psychotherapy: A symposium. Journal of Counseling Psychology, 10, 244–250.

Berman, J. S., Miller, R. C., & Massman, P. J. (1985). Cognitive therapy versus systematic desensitization: Is one treatment superior? Psychological Bulletin, 97, 451–461.

Blanchard, E. B., Andrasik, F., Ahles, T. A., Teders, S. J., & O'Keefe, D. (1980). Migraine and tension headache: A meta-analytic review. Behavior Therapy, 11, 613–631.

Bowers, T. G., & Clum, G. A. (1988). Relative contribution of specific and nonspecific treatment effects: Meta-analysis of placebo-controlled behavior therapy research. Psychological Bulletin, 103, 315–323.

Brown, J. (1987). A review of meta-analyses conducted on psychotherapy outcome research. Clinical Psychology Review, 7, 1–23.

Campbell, D. T., & Stanley, J. C. (1966). Experimental and quasi-experimental designs for research. Chicago: Rand McNally.

Cartwright, D. S. (1955). Effectiveness of psychotherapy: A critique of the spontaneous remission argument. Journal of Counseling Psychology, 2, 290–296.

Casey, R. J., & Berman, J. S. (1985). The outcome of psychotherapy with children. Psychological Bulletin, 98, 388–400.

Cook, T. D., & Leviton, L. C. (1980). Reviewing the literature: A comparison of traditional methods with meta-analysis. Journal of Personality, 48, 449–472.

Cooper, H. M. (1979). Statistically combining independent studies: A meta-analysis of sex differences in conformity research. Journal of Personality and Social Psychology, 37, 131–146.

DeCharms, R., Levy, J., & Wertheimer, M. (1954). A note on attempted evaluations of psychotherapy. Journal of Clinical Psychology, 10, 233–235.

Denker, R. (1946). Results of treatment of psychoneuroses by the general practitioner. A follow-up study of 500 cases. New York State Journal of Medicine, 46, 2164–2166.

Dush, D. M., Hirt, M. L., & Schroeder, H. (1983). Self-statement modification with adults: A meta-analysis. Psychological Bulletin, 94, 408–422.

Ellis, A., & Harper, R. A. (1975). A new guide to rational living. North Hollywood, CA: Wilshire.

Eysenck, H. J. (1952). The effects of psychotherapy: An evaluation. Journal of Consulting Psychology, 16, 319–324.

Eysenck, H. J. (1955). The effects of psychotherapy: A reply. Journal of Abnormal and Social Psychology, 50, 147–148.

Eysenck, H. J. (1960). The effects of psychotherapy. In H. J. Eysenck (Ed.), *Handbook of abnormal psychology: An experimental approach* (pp. 697–725). New York: Basic Books.

Eysenck, H. J. (1964). The outcome problem in psychotherapy: A reply. *Psychotherapy: Theory, Research and Practice, 1,* 97-100.

Eysenck, H. J. (1965). The effects of psychotherapy. *International Journal of Psychiatry, 1,* 99–142.

Eysenck, H. J. (1966). *The effects of psychotherapy.* New York: International Science Press.

Eysenck, H. J. (1978). An exercise in mega-silliness. *American Psychologist, 33,* 517.

Eysenck, H. J. (1983). Special Review: M. L. Smith, G. V. Glass, and T. I. Miller: *The benefits of psychotherapy. Behaviour Research and Therapy, 21,* 315–320.

Feifel, H., & Eells, J. (1963). Patients and therapists assess the same psychotherapy. *Journal of Consulting Psychology, 27,* 310–318.

Frank, J. (1961). *Persuasion and healing.* Baltimore: Johns Hopkins University Press.

Freud, S. (1963). Introductory lectures in psychoanalysis. In J. Strachey (Ed. and Trans.), *The standard edition of the complete psychological works of Sigmund Freud* (Vol. 16, pp. 241–489). London: Hogarth Press. (Original work published in 1917)

Freud, S. (1964). New introductory lectures on psychoanalysis. In J. Strachey (Ed. and Trans.), *The standard edition of the complete psychological works of Sigmund Freud* (Vol. 22, pp. 1–182). London: Hogarth Press. (Original work published in 1933)

Fuhrman, T. S., & Durlak, J. A. (1989, May). *Review of cognitive-behavioral therapy with maladaptive children: A meta-analysis.* Paper presented at the meeting of the Midwestern Psychological Association, Chicago, IL.

Gallo, P. S. (1978). Meta-analysis—A mixed meta-phor? *American Psychologist, 33,* 515–517.

Goldberg, C. (1986). *On being a psychotherapist.* New York: Gardner.

Gross, M. L. (1978). *The psychological society.* New York: Simon and Schuster.

Gurin, G., Veroff, J., & Feld, S. (1960). *Americans view their mental health.* New York: Basic Books.

Heinicke, C. M., & Goldman, A. (1960). Research on psychotherapy with children: A review and suggestions for further study. *American Journal of Orthopsychiatry, 30,* 483–494.

Hood-Williams, J. (1960). The results of psychotherapy with children: A revaluation. *Journal of Consulting Psychology, 24,* 84–88.

Hunt, J. M. (1952). Toward an integrated program of research on psychotherapy. *Journal of Consulting Psychology, 16,* 237–246.

Kazdin, A. E. (1986). The evaluation of psychotherapy: Research design and methodology. In S. L. Garfield & A. E. Bergin (Eds.), *Handbook of psychotherapy and behavior change* (3rd ed.) (pp. 23–68). New York: Wiley.

Kazdin, A. E., & Bass, D. (1989). Power to detect differences between alternative treatments in comparative psychotherapy outcome research. *Journal of Consulting and Clinical Psychology, 57,* 138–147.

Kazdin, A. E., & Wilson, G. T. (1978). *Evaluation of behavior therapy: Issues, evidence, and research strategies.* Cambridge, MA: Ballinger.

Knight, R. P. (1941). Evaluation of the results of psychoanalytic therapy. *American Journal of Psychiatry, 98,* 434–436.

Kris, E. (1947). Round table discussion: Problems in clinical research. *American Journal of Orthopsychiatry, 17,* 196–230.

Lambert, M. J., Shapiro, D. A., & Bergin, A. E. (1986). The effectiveness of psychotherapy. In S. L. Garfield & A. E. Bergin (Eds.), *Handbook of psychotherapy and behavior change* (3rd ed.) (pp. 157–211). New York: Wiley.

Landis, C. (1938). A statistical evaluation of psychotherapeutic methods. In S. E. Hinsie (Ed.), *Concepts and problems of psychotherapy* (pp. 155–169). London: Heinemann.

Landman, J. T., & Dawes, R. M. (1982). Psychotherapy outcome: Smith and Glass' conclusions stand up under scrutiny. *American Psychologist, 37,* 504–516.

Levitt, E. E. (1957). The results of psychotherapy with children: An evaluation. *Journal of Consulting Psychology, 21,* 189-196.

Levitt, E. E. (1963). Psychotherapy with children: A further evaluation. *Behaviour Research and Therapy, 1,* 45–51.

Levitt, E. E. (1971). Research on psychotherapy with children. In A. E. Bergin & S. L. Garfield (Eds.), *Handbook of psychotherapy and behavior change: An empirical analysis* (pp. 474–494). New York: Wiley.

Luborsky, L. (1954). A note on Eysenck's article "The effects of psychotherapy: An evaluation." *British Journal of Psychology, 45,* 129–131.

Luborsky, L., Singer, B., & Luborsky, L. (1975). Comparative studies of psychotherapies: Is it true that "everyone has won and all must have prizes"? *Archives of General Psychiatry, 32,* 995–1008.

Malan, D. H. (1973). The outcome problem in psychotherapy research: A historical review. *Archives of General Psychiatry, 29,* 719–729.

Mansfield, R. S., & Busse, T. V. (1977, October). Meta-analysis of research: A rejoinder to Glass. *Educational Researcher, 6,* 3.

Matt, G. E. (1989). Decision rules for selecting effect sizes in meta-analysis: A review and reanalysis of psychotherapy outcome studies. *Psychological Bulletin, 105,* 106–115.

Meltzoff, J., & Kornreich, M. (1970). *Research in psychotherapy.* New York: Atherton.

Miles, H. H. W., Barrabee, E. L., & Finesinger, J. E. (1951). Evaluation of psychotherapy with a follow-up study of 62 cases of anxiety neurosis. *Psychosomatic Medicine, 13,* 83–105.

Miller, R. C., & Berman, J. S. (1983). The efficacy of cognitive behavior therapies: A quantitative review of the research evidence. *Psychological Bulletin, 94,* 39–53.

Nurius, P. S., & Yeaton, W. H. (1987). Research synthesis reviews: An illustrated critique of "hidden" judgments, choices, and compromises. *Clinical Psychology Review, 7,* 695–714.

Presby, S. (1978). Overly broad categories obscure important differences between therapies. *American Psychologist, 33,* 514–515.

Prioleau, L., Murdock, M., & Brody, N. (1983). An analysis of psychotherapy versus placebo studies. *The Behavioral and Brain Sciences, 6,* 275–310.

Rachman, S. (1971). *The effects of psychotherapy.* New York: Pergamon.

Rachman, S. J., & Wilson, G. T. (1980). *The effects of psychological therapy* (2nd ed.). New York: Pergamon.

Rimland, B. (1979). Death knell for psychotherapy? *American Psychologist, 34,* 192.

Rosenzweig, S. (1954). A transvaluation of psychotherapy: A reply to Hans Eysenck. *Journal of Abnormal and Social Psychology, 49,* 298-304.

Sanford, N. (1953). Clinical method: Psychotherapy. *Annual Review of Psychology, 4,* 317-342.

Searles, J. S. (1985). A methodological and empirical critique of psychotherapy outcome meta-analysis. *Behaviour Research and Therapy, 23,* 453-463.

Shapiro, D. A., & Shapiro, D. (1982). Meta-analysis of comparative therapy outcome studies: A replication and refinement. *Psychological Bulletin, 92,* 581-604.

Shryock, R. H. (1947). *The development of modern medicine: An interpretation of the social and scientific factors involved* (2nd ed.). Madison, WI: University of Wisconsin Press.

Smith, M. L., & Glass, G. V. (1977). Meta-analysis of psychotherapy outcome studies. *American Psychologist, 32,* 752-760.

Smith, M. L., Glass, G. V., & Miller, T. I. (1980). *The benefits of psychotherapy.* Baltimore: Johns Hopkins University Press.

Steinbrueck, S. M., Maxwell, S. E., & Howard, G. S. (1983). A meta-analysis of psychotherapy and drug therapy in the treatment of unipolar depression with adults. *Journal of Consulting and Clinical Psychology, 51,* 856-863.

Strahan, R. F. (1978). Six ways of looking at an elephant. *American Psychologist, 33,* 693.

Strube, M. J., & Hartmann, D. P. (1983). Meta-analysis: Techniques, applications, and functions. *Journal of Consulting and Clinical Psychology, 51,* 14-27.

Strupp, H. H. (1963a). The outcome problem in psychotherapy revisited. *Psychotherapy: Theory, Research and Practice, 1,* 1-13.

Strupp, H. H. (1963b). The outcome problem in psychotherapy: A rejoinder. *Psychotherapy: Theory, Research and Practice, 1,* 101.

Thorne, F. C. (1952). Rules of evidence in the evaluation of the effects of psychotherapy. *Journal of Clinical Psychology, 8,* 38-41.

Watson, R. I. (1952). Research design and methodology in evaluating the results of psychotherapy. *Journal of Clinical Psychology, 8,* 29-33.

Weisz, J. R., Weiss, B., Alicke, M. D., & Klotz, M. L. (1987). Effectiveness of psychotherapy with children and adolescents: A meta-analysis for clinicians. *Journal of Consulting and Clinical Psychology, 55,* 542-549.

Wertheimer, M. (1978). Humanistic psychology and the humane but tough-minded psychologist. *American Psychologist, 33,* 739-745.

Wilder, J. (1945). Facts and figures on psychotherapy. *Journal of Clinical Psychopathology, 7,* 311-347.

Zubin, J. (1953). Evaluation of therapeutic outcome in mental disorders. *Journal of Nervous and Mental Disease, 117,* 95-111.

CHAPTER THREE

The Stability of Personality

Introduction

In 1968, Walter Mischel published a book entitled *Personality and Assessment*. This work initiated a controversy concerning one of the fundamental assumptions of personality theories, namely, the stability of personality traits. Like Eysenck's 1952 paper on the effectiveness of psychotherapy, Mischel's book became an instant classic, sparking a heated debate that continues today.

Traditional personality theories assumed that personality traits were stable across situations. Indeed, the very concept of a personality trait assumes that behavior is stable across situations. For example, Gordon Allport (1937), one of the foremost trait theorists of personality, defined a personality trait as "a generalized and focalized neuropsychic system (peculiar to the individual) with the capacity to render many stimuli functionally equivalent and to initiate and guide consistent (equivalent) forms of adaptive and expressive behavior" (p. 295). The key notions in this definition are that traits render many stimuli functionally equivalent and then initiate equivalent forms of behavior.

For example, consider a man characterized by the trait of aggressiveness. According to traditional trait theories, he will express aggression across many situations: driving an automobile aggressively, competing aggressively in both sports and career, enjoying aggressive films and jokes. Although the behaviors in which he engages across situations are different from one another (driving aggressively is quite different from enjoying aggressive films), and although the situations which elicit these behaviors are also quite different from one another, the behaviors are equivalent in that they all express aggression. The underlying trait has rendered distinct stimuli functionally equivalent and so resulted in the initiation of functionally equivalent behaviors.

Psychodynamic theories also assume that personality is stable across situations. Although psychodynamic theorists place more emphasis on the dynamics of personality (motivation, defenses) than do traditional trait theorists of personality, they assume that the underlying dynamics of personality are stable over time and so result in functionally equivalent behaviors across situations.

For example, consider a woman with underlying doubts about her femininity who employs denial of sexuality as a defense against the anxiety which the recognition of such doubts would produce. Psychodynamic theorists assume that she will deny her sexuality in many different situations. She may dress and act in a nondescript manner so as to avoid the attention of men; she may join social groups with primarily female memberships; she may respond on a word association test with words devoid of sexual connotations. Even though these behaviors (as well as the stimuli which elicit the behaviors) are quite different from one another, they are all similar in that they express the defense of denial of sexuality. Just as occurred in the example of the man with the trait of aggressiveness, this woman responded to dissimilar stimuli in functionally equivalent ways.

Although Mischel's 1968 book is noted for its stimulation of the controversy concerning the validity of the assumption of the stability of personality across situations, it was not the first work to question this assumption. As early as the 1920s, empirical investigations by Hartshorne and May (1928, 1929) and by Newcomb (1929) found little consistency in the stability across situations of specific trait behaviors (such as honesty or introversion-extroversion). In 1934, Lehmann and Witty reviewed the empirical literature up to that time which addressed the prediction of behavior from trait measures of personality and concluded that the results were "so unreliable and undependable . . . that one is led to question the actual existence of the general traits" (p. 490). Similarly, at about the time that Mischel's 1968 book appeared, other reviewers of the empirical literature (e.g., Peterson, 1968; Vernon, 1964) were also questioning the validity of the assumption of the stability of personality across situations.

Mischel's (1968) Argument

Mischel reopened the issue of the stability of personality traits with his 1968 book. In this work, he reviewed what he considered to be "representative examples" of empirical investigations of the consistency of behavior. The studies included in the review covered a range of topics, including intellectual and cognitive variables (e.g., ability, achievement, cognitive style) and personality variables (e.g., moral behavior, dependency, tolerance for ambiguity).

Mischel concluded that there was evidence of stability for the following individual characteristics: (a) intelligence, (b) cognitive style, (c) self-reported personality traits, and (d) behavior across similar situations. Because these characteristics demonstrated stability, measures of these variables would be useful in predicting behavior.

Contrary to the assumption of trait and psychodynamic theories, however, Mischel found little empirical evidence for the stability of personality traits across dissimilar situations. The evidence supported the concept of behavioral specificity to rather than generality across situations. Mischel found that "evidence for behavioral specificity across situations has been reported over and over again for personality measures since the earliest correlational studies at the turn of the century" (p. 36).

Because of the lack of evidence to support the assumption of the stability of personality across situations, Mischel questioned the utility of traits in making predictions concerning behavior across situations. Rather than rely solely on the use of traits to predict behavior, when such trait behaviors have been shown to be inconsistent across situations, Mischel advocated the inclusion of situational factors in attempts to predict behavior.

This position was welcomed by behaviorists who agreed that behavior should be explained in terms of environmental stimuli rather than as the product of internal mental constructs. Behavioral psychologists, who at this time were becoming increasingly critical of the assumptions and practices of traditional psychodynamic approaches to clinical psychology, perceived Mischel's review as another nail in the coffin of psychodynamic psychology.

However, Mischel did not advocate a strictly behavioral position. Traditional behaviorists attempted to account for behavior solely in terms of environmental stimuli. Mischel, on the other hand, recognized that some individual characteristics were stable and useful in predicting behavior. "It would be a complete misinterpretation . . . to conclude that individual differences are unimportant. . . . The real questions are not the existence of differences among individuals but rather their nature, their causes and consequences, and the utility of inferring them for particular purposes" (Mischel, 1968, p. 38).

Mischel, then, recommended that both situational and individual characteristics should be included in discussions of the causes of behavior and in attempts to predict future behavior. According to Mischel, a psychology of personality should include those variables, whether situational or personal, that have been demonstrated empirically to be related to behavior in a situation. Thus, Mischel advocated a position that has come to be known as *person-situation interactionism.*

Interestingly, Mischel's argument relates to several important phenomena in the area of social psychology. Social psychologists have found it useful to determine the causal explanations which an individual develops in order to explain his or her experiences. Such causal explanations, called *attributions,* have been shown to be related to the individual's later behavior. A bias in the way people form attributions to explain the experiences of other people has been shown to be so prevalent that it has been termed the *fundamental attribution error* (Ross, 1977). This label refers to the finding that people in general tend to overestimate the role of internal influences and to underestimate the role of external or situational influences when explaining the experiences of others.

For example, suppose an individual says something that embarrasses another guest at a party. When other people later explain this behavior, it is quite likely that they will generate explanations based on the individual's possession of negative personal characteristics (e.g., "thoughtlessness," "crudeness," "impulsivity"). However, when this individual later examines the social gaffe and attempts to explain it, it is very likely that the individual will be aware of situational influences that were unknown to the others (e.g., "fatigue," "job stress," "physical resemblance between two people whom he confused," and so on) and explain the embarrassing behavior as the result of these external factors. In general, the fundamental attribution error suggests that people overestimate the influence of internal factors when explaining the behavior of others.

Mischel's (1968) review led some writers to suggest that clinical psychologists, along with people in general, may traditionally have succumbed to the fundamental attribution error and so overemphasized the role of individual characteristics in explaining people's behavior. "By weaving what seem to be disparate and variable patient behaviors into a common, stable thread, clinicians create at least an illusion of understanding, predictability, and control" (Jordan, Harvey, & Weary, 1988, p. 93).

Another social psychological phenomenon related to Mischel's argument is the tendency for people to "blame the victim." For example, Walster (1966) demonstrated that people have a general tendency to blame the victims of negative experiences for the events that befall them. From this result, it follows that people in general—clinical psychologists included—will attribute their clients' psychological problems to the clients themselves. In this way, we should expect therapists to perceive their clients' circumstances as due, at least in part, to internal influences. Thus, we can predict that clinicians will seek out various psychological shortcomings in their clients.

Mischel's emphasis of situational factors became quite influential among psychologists of personality. For example, shortly after the publication of Mischel's book, Carlson (1971) reviewed 226 recent journal articles in the personality literature and found that 128 (57 percent) ignored subject variables altogether.

Mischel's position also became influential in areas of psychology other than personality. Parallel to Mischel's (1968) conclusion that there was only a limited relationship between personality traits and behavior, similar conclusions have been drawn concerning the relationship between behavior and individual characteristics other than personality traits. For example, Wicker (1969) reviewed the empirical literature and concluded that attitudes were only slightly related to behavior. Similarly, Mabe and West (1982) reviewed the research and concluded that there was only a modest correlation between self-reported ability and ability-related behavior. Less of the variance in predictive success was accounted for by subjects' self-ratings than by situational factors such as anonymity and instructions that one's self-evaluation would be compared to actual performance.

In addition, numerous studies have employed the analysis of variance model to examine the relative contributions of situational and personal factors to the variance of behavior. Although the results of these studies are not entirely consistent, they tend to find that the variance attributable to personal factors is less than that attributable to situations and/or to the interaction between individual and situational factors (e.g., Bowers, 1973; Endler & Magnusson, 1976b).

Criticisms of Mischel

Mischel's book sparked a heated debate. Although behaviorists and other critics of traditional psychodynamic and trait theories applauded Mischel's conclusions, adherents to these schools sought to refute Mischel's methodology and to reinterpret his results. Many vigorous criticisms of Mischel appeared in the literature. Among the most commonly expressed and strongly worded criticisms of Mischel were the following:

Nonrepresentativeness of the Research Reviewed

Mischel's review of the "representative examples" of pertinent research overlooked investigations that have found support for the assumption of the stability of personality. Several reviewers (e.g., Block, 1977; Hogan, DeSoto, & Solano, 1977; Stagner, 1976) have identified studies which demonstrate that trait behavior is stable across situations, contrary to those cited by Mischel (1968). In addition, several well-designed and more recent studies (e.g., Epstein, 1984; Small, Zeldin, & Savin-Williams, 1983) have found that certain traits show greater cross-situational consistency than had been reported by Mischel (1968). For these reasons, it would be a serious error to come away from the debate concerning the stability of personality with the mistaken idea that there is no consistency in behavior across situations.

Even Mischel (1968), contrary to the interpretations of some critics, did not go so far as to argue that, because there was no consistency in behavior across situations, then it follows that personality traits "do not exist" (Epstein, 1979, p. 1098). Mischel (1968) recognized that there was a great deal of behavioral consistency, especially in intellectual tasks and cognitive processes, in self-report measures of personality and in behaviors across similar situations. His criticism of traditional personality traits was based, not so much on the failure to find any examples of consistent trait-related behaviors, but rather on the limited utility of such personality traits in predicting behavior. Theorists who invoke traits as explanatory constructs must demonstrate empirically that they are useful in predicting behavior across situations.

Oversimplified View of Trait and Psychodynamic Theories

Another commonly expressed criticism of Mischel's 1968 book is that Mischel failed to recognize that traditional psychodynamic and trait theories of personality can account for and in fact expect behavior to demonstrate situational specificity; hence, his review does not refute either psychodynamic or trait theories of personality.

This position has been expounded by several writers. For example, Wachtel (1973) stated that "the mere fact that behavior varies from situation to situation is in no way a refutation of the psychodynamic approach" (p. 327). He then explained how contemporary psychodynamic theories can account for situational specificity in behavior.

Similarly, Alker (1972), among many other criticisms, argued that Mischel's review does not constitute a threat to sophisticated trait theories. Only the most simplistic trait theory would fail to consider how traits interact with one another. Within sophisticated trait theories, one trait may act as a moderator variable for another. In this way, the expression of one trait in a situation depends on the level of another trait. Thus, one trait may show more or less cross-situational consistency depending on the level of another trait. Both Gordon Allport (1961) and Raymond Cattell (1965), perhaps the two foremost trait theorists of personality, have developed complex trait theories which lead to some degree of situational specificity in behavior.

Because both psychodynamic and trait theories of personality expect at least some degree of situational specificity, the failure to find cross-situational consistency does not constitute a refutation of either trait or psychodynamic theories.

Again, it should be noted that Mischel did not claim that his review constituted a refutation of either psychodynamic or trait theories of personality. Mischel has repeatedly acknowledged that psychodynamic theories recognize behavioral specificity (Mischel, 1968, 1969, 1971, 1973b). His criticism of psychodynamic theories is not that they have failed to provide theoretical explanations for how their constructs lead to behavioral specificity, but rather that they have failed to demonstrate empirically that such constructs are useful in predicting behavior (Mischel, 1973b).

Similarly, Mischel (1968) recognized that sophisticated trait theories might incorporate moderator variables or other complex interrelationships among traits to account for situational specificity in behavior. Again, what such theories need to do, according to Mischel, is to demonstrate empirically the utility of such approaches for predicting behavior.

Methodological Weaknesses in the Studies Reviewed

Many of the studies cited by Mischel (1968) were poorly designed and so their results do not lend strong support for his position. Studies which improve upon the methodologies of those cited by Mischel or which are better conceived so as to test trait approaches more precisely might yield results consistent with the traditional assumption of the consistency of trait-related behavior. For example, both Seymour Epstein (1977, 1979, 1980, 1983a, 1983b) and Daryl Bem (Bem & Allen, 1974) have developed research methodologies, to be discussed later in this chapter, which they think provide stronger tests of claims of the stability of personality across situations than the studies reviewed by Mischel (1968).

One often-expressed methodological criticism has been directed against studies which have employed the analysis of variance method to determine the amount of behavioral variance that can be attributed to either situational or personal factors, or to the interaction of these factors. Many such studies have been conducted, with results typically showing that situational factors or the interaction between personal and situational factors account for at least as much of the variance as personal factors (e.g., Bowers, 1973; Endler & Magnusson, 1976b). These studies have therefore been cited by proponents of either situational or person-situation interactional models of personality.

A problem with this method that has been identified by several writers (e.g., Alker, 1972; Epstein, 1979) is that the results of the analysis of variance are applicable primarily to the population sampled and situations included in the study. By manipulating the range (and variance) of the subjects and situations, one can control the relative proportions of variance accounted for by personal and situational factors.

To illustrate this, suppose one were interested in determining the relative contributions of personal and situational factors to swimming time. The range of both subjects and situations (distances) tested will have a profound effect on the results. For example, suppose the distances tested were 50 and 55 meters. If the subjects were world class swimmers (who, presumably are quite homogeneous with respect to ability), then one would likely find a large situational effect and a small personal effect. However, if the subjects were sampled from the general public, it is likely that one would find a large personal effect and a moderate situational effect. On the other hand, suppose the distances tested were 50 and 200 meters. In this case, the range of situations is so great that, regardless of whether the subjects are average or world class swimmers, one would be likely to find a large situational effect and only a much smaller personal effect.

Numerous studies have determined that situational factors are at least as important as individual factors in contributing to the variance of some trait-related behavior. However, because such results are specific to the ranges of subjects and situations tested, and because the ranges of subjects and situations tested may not have been representative of the ranges of subjects and situations in general, these results may not generalize to other populations of subjects and situations. When evaluating such a study, it is important to question whether the ranges of subjects and situations examined are representative of the ranges of subjects and situations in "the real world."

Methodological Bias in the Studies Reviewed

Critics have also suggested that the studies cited by Mischel (1968) have a methodological bias that favors the detection of situational influences on behavior. This criticism, although related to the previous one in that it also attacks the methodological adequacy of the research, is somewhat more subtle. Rather than question the designs of individual studies on methodological or conceptual grounds, this criticism questions the exclusive use of experimental designs to investigate the issue of the stability of personality.

Cronbach (1957) discussed the roles of correlational and experimental research designs in psychology. One of the differences Cronbach noted between these two research methods is that it is easier to detect behavioral stability with a correlational design whereas it is easier to detect behavioral change with an experimental design. Cronbach (1957) also observed that psychologists who prefer experimental research tend to be unreceptive to correlational research. Thus, because many (perhaps most) psychologists prefer experimental research (biased in the direction of the detection of behavioral change), and because such psychologists tend to be unreceptive to the results of correlational research (biased in the direction of the detection of behavioral stability), psychology is biased in the direction of a situationist view of behavior (Cronbach, 1957).

This argument, developed before Mischel's (1968) book on the stability of trait-related behavior, has been repeated many times since then (e.g., Bowers, 1973; Epstein, 1979, 1980; Wachtel, 1973). These writers do not take the extreme view that psychology should accept only one type of research and reject the other, but rather that psychology should employ both methods while remaining aware of the strengths, limitations, and biases of each. In this way, situationally oriented psychologists should become aware of the correlational studies that support claims of behavioral consistency while trait psychologists should become aware of the experimental studies that demonstrate the influence of situational variables on behavior. The result can only be the development of theories of personality which include both situational and individual influences on behavior.

Mischel's (1973a) Cognitive Social Learning Theory

Mischel responded to the critics of his 1968 review with the publication (1973a) of an important paper in which he detailed an approach to personality which he called Cognitive Social Learning Theory.

In this work, Mischel corrected the misconceptions which had developed concerning his views on the influence of individual factors on behavior. Both critics of and adherents to the situationist position had frequently misinterpreted his conclusions. For example, Mischel (1968) had *not* claimed: that individual factors are unimportant (or even less important than situational influences); that there are no consistencies in behavior; that traits do not exist; or that he had refuted traditional trait and psychodynamic theories of personality. "No one suggests that the organism approaches every new situation with an empty head, nor is it questioned by anyone that different individuals differ markedly in how they deal with most stimulus conditions" (Mischel, 1973a, p. 262).

Rather, his criticism of traits was based on the inadequacy of the available empirical evidence which attempted to demonstrate that broad psychological traits were useful in predicting behavior across situations (Mischel, 1973a):

What has been questioned is the utility of inferring broad dispositions from behavioral signs as the bases for trying to explain the phenomena of personality and for making useful statements about individual behavior. The available data do not imply that different people will not act differently with some consistency in different classes of situations; they do imply that the particular classes of conditions must be taken into account far more carefully than in the past, tend to be much narrower than traditional trait theories have assumed, and for purposes of important individual decision making, require highly individualized assessments of stimulus meanings. (p. 262)

In this way, by focusing on the empirical inadequacy of trait approaches to predicting behavior across situations, Mischel challenged the field to develop new models of personality which would yield more accurate methods of predicting behavior.

Mischel's own suggestion for attempting to improve the degree to which psychologists can predict behavior across situations was to elaborate upon his previously proposed person-situation interactional model. Mischel (1973a) identified five personal variables which he believed were stable across situations and therefore useful in predicting behavior. These variables were the following:

Competencies

As Mischel (1968) had found in his earlier review, there was substantial evidence that intelligence and other general abilities were stable across situations. A measure of a particular competency is therefore likely to be a useful predictor of behavior related to the assessed ability.

Encoding Strategies

Similarly, Mischel (1968) had found that cognitive style was stable, and therefore useful in predicting behavior, across situations. *Cognitive style,* or *cognitive encoding strategy,* refers to the manner in which an individual perceives, organizes, and retrieves information. It is clear that the way in which one encodes information will be related to how one uses that information to guide behavior (e.g., Bandura, 1971). Individuals who encode an experience in different ways are likely to behave differently when faced with a comparable situation.

Expectancies

Through experience, people develop expectancies that certain behaviors are likely to lead to certain outcomes. That one's understanding of the contingencies between behavior and environmental consequences influences behavior has been well documented by Bandura (1969, 1971) and others. Such expectancies play an important role in Bandura's social learning theory.

Subjective Stimulus Values

The same stimulus may have different subjective values for two individuals. For example, if a red light is repeatedly paired with shock, a subject will eventually develop an aversive reaction to the light itself. On the other hand, if a red light is repeatedly paired with food, then the subject will develop a positive response to the light. Through one's unique conditioning (classical, instrumental, or observational), one develops unique subjective values for various stimuli. Some stimuli are favored while others are avoided. Some stimuli have large positive or negative values while others have smaller values. In this way, knowledge of an individual's subjective stimulus values enables psychologists to predict accurately how the individual will behave across situations in which the stimulus is presented as a consequence of behavior.

Self-Regulatory Systems

Individuals respond not only to environmental stimuli but also to self-imposed goals and processes. For example, Meichenbaum (1977) has described how the self-instructions of clinic patients are related to their symptomatic behaviors. Others (e.g., Mahoney, 1974) have examined how cognitive problem-solving processes are related to behavior. Indeed, these individuals have been labeled "cognitive-behaviorists" because of their interest in the relationship between cognitions and behaviors and because of their adoption of the empirical methods of behaviorism to examine cognitions. Cognitive-behaviorists have produced an extensive body of literature which shows how cognitive self-regulatory processes (e.g., self-instruction, problem-solving strategies, attribution processes) are related to and influence behavior.

These five variables, according to Mischel (1973a), represent an alternative to the traits of traditional personality theories. All five variables have been demonstrated empirically to be related to behavior across situations and are therefore personal factors which are useful in the prediction of behavior. All five variables can be regarded as cognitive in nature and, as such, are different in kind from traditional personality traits. Mischel's emphasis on the cognitive processes underlying social behavior was consistent with contemporary theoretical and empirical advances in social psychology and led him (1973a) to present them as "cognitive social learning person variables."

Mischel's (1973a) paper, then, was important in that it clarified his interactionist position and proposed a cognitive social learning model of personality. Whereas some critics and overzealous advocates of the situationist position had misinterpreted his 1968 book as suggesting that there were no consistencies in behavior and no place for personal factors in predicting behavior, Mischel now clearly stated that he thought that personal factors were important in influencing and predicting behavior. Whereas previous psychodynamic and trait theories of personality invoked traits as explanatory constructs which had only limited empirical relationships to actual behavior, Mischel now proposed using personal variables which were consistent with the empirical research in cognitive and social psychology in the 1960s and 1970s.

Research on Person-Situation Interactionism

One of the major criticisms of Mischel's (1968) book was that the studies he reviewed were methodologically weak, and so did not provide proper tests of claims of the stability of personality. Several research programs have been developed which employ innovative methodologies in efforts to test more critically claims of the consistency of personality. This section of the chapter will discuss two such programs, along with Mischel's responses to these projects.

Epstein's Research

Perhaps the most vigorous proponent of the position that improved research methodologies are necessary to demonstrate the stability of personality is Seymour Epstein (1977, 1979, 1980, 1983a, 1983b). Epstein based his criticism of Mischel on the fundamentals of psychometric theory. He suggested that many of the studies included in the review by Mischel (1968) employed measures of personality traits which had limited test reliability.

You will recall that the reliability of a test refers to its consistency or stability—the degree to which the test yields stable results over time, raters, and conditions. The reliability of a test sets an upper limit on the extent to which valid relationships can be established between the trait assessed by the test and other variables. If a test cannot measure a construct reliably, then the test cannot be used to demonstrate a valid relationship between the construct and any other variable. (Chapters Four and Five present more lengthy discussions of the criteria of reliability and validity and their relationship.)

One of the basic theorems of psychometrics is that test reliability is increased when the number of items on the test is increased. A test with modest reliability can be transformed into one with substantial reliability simply by adding test items which are comparable to the original ones. In this way, one can "shore up" the reliability of a test so that it is possible to demonstrate valid relationships between the construct measured by the test and other variables.

Epstein noted that many of the studies cited by Mischel (1968) employed trait measures with only limited reliability. Thus, at best they could demonstrate only limited relationships between the traits assessed by the measures and other trait-related behaviors. In addition, most of these studies assessed traits on only a single occasion.

Epstein suggested that one could conceive of these measures of a trait with low reliability administered on a single occasion as individual items on a test. Just as single test items must have lower reliability, and therefore fewer valid relationships to other variables, than a test which combines the items, so will measures of a trait administered on a single occasion have lower reliability and fewer valid relationships to other variables than a test which combines the individual measures.

Epstein suggested that personality researchers should employ aggregate measures of traits. That is, the trait should be measured on multiple occasions and then a measure of the trait should be derived which combines the individual assessments. This aggregate measure will be more reliable than any of the single-occasion measures and so the aggregate measure will be more useful in demonstrating valid relationships between the trait and other variables.

In his studies which employed aggregate measures of personality traits (Epstein, 1977, 1979, 1980), Epstein demonstrated more significant correlations between trait-related behaviors than was the case for single-occasion measures. Mischel (Mischel & Peake, 1982, 1983) has responded to Epstein's suggestion, acknowledging that trait measures with higher reliability are desirable and should help researchers demonstrate valid relationships between traits and other variables. However, Mischel and Peake (1982) also noted that several of the major studies included in the Mischel (1968) review did employ aggregate measures of traits (e.g., Hartshorne & May, 1928; Newcomb, 1929) and were still unable to demonstrate that trait-related behaviors were consistent across situations.

Mischel and Peake (1982) went on to critique Epstein's (1979) study which employed the aggregate method of assessment to demonstrate behavioral consistency. Mischel examined the significant correlations reported by Epstein and found that they provided little support for the assumption of the consistency of cross-situational trait-related behavior. For example, the number of telephone calls made was substantially correlated with the number of telephone calls received when both were recorded daily over a 28-day period. However, as Mischel noted, these behaviors very probably are causally related to one another and so *must* show a substantial relationship to one another; in addition, one of the behaviors is produced by someone other than the subject. Therefore, it is difficult to use the correlation between these two behaviors as evidence for cross-situational consistency in the behavior of the subject.

Finally, Mischel and Peake (1982) pointed out that there is a significant distinction between temporal consistency and cross-situational consistency, which may be masked by Epstein's use of aggregated trait measures. In his 1968 review, Mischel reported that there was considerable consistency in behavior across similar situations—what can be regarded as temporal consistency. However, this review found little evidence of cross-situational consistency. Mischel, then, is interested in the extent to which trait-related behaviors are consistent across dissimilar situations. To aggregate or combine trait measures obtained across dissimilar situations is to avoid the issue of cross-situational consistency altogether. Although it does yield a more reliable measure of the average level of the trait, it ignores the issue of the consistency of trait-related behavior across situations.

To employ Epstein's suggestion in order to examine the cross-situational consistency of trait-related behavior, one should first obtain a trait measure by aggregating over many similar situations and then determine the degree to which this measure is correlated with another trait-related behavior measured by aggregating over many situations which are similar to one another and dissimilar to the first set of situations. This uses the temporal consistency of behavior (reported by Mischel [1968]) to obtain reliable trait measures (suggested by Epstein) to then determine whether there is cross-situational consistency in trait-related behavior (the issue of interest to Mischel).

Bem's Research

Another psychologist who criticized the methodology of the studies reviewed by Mischel (1968) is Daryl Bem (Bem & Allen, 1974). Bem, a proponent of interactionist approaches to personality and a defender of Mischel's views (e.g., Bem, 1972), has been active in proposing research methodologies to overcome the weaknesses of early trait investigations (Bem & Funder, 1978).

Bem and Allen (1974) noted that trait theorists such as Gordon Allport regarded traits as idiographic rather than nomothetic. That is, according to Allport (1937), traits differ across individuals not only in how they are interrelated, but also in terms of which traits are important (and may be expressed in a particular situation). Researchers, on the other hand, typically have adopted a nomothetic approach concerning traits. That is, the trait under investigation is assumed to be important for all subjects and is further assumed to be expressed in all subjects in the same way.

Clearly, these assumptions of the nomothetic approach may not hold. Consider the following example. Two subjects exhibit equal degrees of competitiveness on the athletic field, and so a researcher rates them as equally competitive. The subjects then participate in a prisoner's dilemma task in the laboratory, with one exhibiting a high degree of competition and the other showing a high degree of cooperation. The researcher then concludes that, for these subjects, the trait of competitiveness does not show cross-situational consistency.

Is this conclusion justified? According to Allport and other idiographic trait theorists, it is not. Although these subjects demonstrated equal degrees of competitiveness in one situation, this does not mean that the interrelationships among all their traits are the same, and so they should not be expected to show equal competitiveness in all other situations. For example, these subjects may vary with respect to the trait of need for approval. The subject who is high in need for approval may, in the laboratory task, act cooperatively so as to gain the social approval of the experimenter. The other subject, low in need for approval, is not influenced to act in this way and so continues to act competitively. Thus, the difference between the two subjects' trait structures leads them to act in ways that are interpreted by the nomothetic researcher as cross-situationally inconsistent.

Similarly, the two subjects may perceive the laboratory task in different ways, and so the trait of competitiveness may be expressed differently. One competitive subject may perceive the goal of the task as to maximize the difference between the two participants' scores; hence, this subject will act in a competitive way. The other competitive subject may perceive the goal of the task to be to maximize one's own score, regardless of the score of the other participant; hence, this subject will act in a cooperative fashion. In this way, one trait can be expressed in the same situation in different ways, depending upon how the situation is perceived.

Bem and Allen (1974) suggested that the idiographic approach may be helpful in research on the cross-situational consistency of traits (and in other research as well). Although researchers may not wish to abandon the nomothetic method, it may be helpful to incorporate the idiographic method.

For example, suppose a researcher wishes to measure the trait of friendliness in terms of the degree to which a subject initiates an interaction with a confederate while sitting in a waiting room. Rather than assume that this situation taps equally into the trait of friendliness for all subjects (and risk violating the assumptions of the nomothetic approach noted above), the researcher might pre-select subjects so that only those who report that they are consistently friendly across situations are included. Subjects who are consistently friendly may be equivalent in the degrees to which the trait of friendliness is important and to which this situation may tap the trait of friendliness. Hence, these are subjects for whom the nomothetic assumptions regarding traits may hold.

Bem and Allen (1974) reported the results of such a study in which they examined the cross-situational consistency of behaviors associated with several traits, for subjects who rated themselves as high or low with respect to their consistency across situations on each trait. Bem and Allen found that subjects who described themselves as more consistent tended to exhibit more cross-situational consistency than did subjects who rated themselves as lower in consistency. In addition, they noted that, with respect to one variable, behaviors believed by the experimenters to be associated with a trait proved to be unrelated to the subjects' self-assessment of the trait.

The study by Bem and Allen (1974) was an interesting attempt to identify individuals who exhibit cross-situational consistency. However, an attempt by Mischel and Peake (1982) to replicate the work failed to produce a group that showed greater cross-situational consistency. Mischel (Mischel & Peake, 1982, 1983) has therefore expressed doubts about this "idiographic" method. Bem (1983), in turn, has responded that the primary purpose of the Bem and Allen (1974) paper was to highlight the difficulties of the nomothetic approach to trait research and not to develop a research method which would solve these difficulties.

Summary and Conclusions

The controversy associated with Mischel's 1968 book flared brightly throughout the 1970s. Although the issue of the stability of personality has certainly not been completely resolved, it is not too early to consider the impact which Mischel's book has had on the field.

Mischel's controversy has influenced the study of personality in several ways:

1. The global nature of traits in traditional psychodynamic and trait theories of personality has had to be reexamined. Although it would be a misinterpretation of Mischel's writings to claim that his 1968 review proved that "traits do not exist," it is not misleading to state that his book led the field to reconsider the broad, all-encompassing nature of traits. Contemporary psychologists often employ trait concepts in much more narrow, situation-specific contexts than had been the case prior to 1968. For example, rather than simply use the term *anxiety* in a global way, clinical psychologists today frequently distinguish among "test anxiety," "dating anxiety," "public speaking anxiety," and other specific contexts in which anxiety is experienced.

2. Cognitive social learning factors have become recognized as useful predictors of behavior. Since Mischel's 1968 book, there has been a "cognitive revolution" (Baars, 1986) in many areas of psychology. Research in social, cognitive, developmental, and clinical psychology has shown that many behaviors are associated with cognitive processes. If these cognitive

processes can be shown to be stable, then these factors will be useful in predicting behavior. Many contemporary psychologists therefore use cognitive variables, rather than traditional personality traits, as explanatory theoretical constructs.

One index of the increased reliance upon cognitive processes in clinical psychology is the rise in the school of cognitive-behaviorism. According to Hollon and Beck (1986), there has been an "explosion" of interest among clinical psychologists in cognitive theories of pathology and approaches to treatment, as evidenced by the number of influential treatises and treatment manuals, textbooks, new research journals (e.g., *Cognitive Therapy and Research*), and studies devoted to cognitive therapeutic models.

3. There has been an increase in and refinement of research methods designed to demonstrate the consistency of behavior across situations. Epstein's (1979) aggregate approach to the measurement of personality traits is only one of several innovative and potentially useful approaches to resolving Mischel's controversy. Other equally innovative and potentially useful approaches have also appeared in the research literature. For example, Bem and Allen (1974) described an idiographic method of identifying subpopulations within which behavior is more stable across situations. Bem and Funder (1978) described a "template-matching" methodology which employed both situational and individual characteristics to predict behavior across situations. Other researchers (e.g., Endler, 1976; Raush, 1976) have developed or refined statistical methods in order to assess person-by-situation interactions more accurately.

4. Interactional theories of personality have become an important, even a leading, school in the contemporary study of personality. Professional conferences have been devoted to the discussion of interactional theories of personality, with the concomitant publication of major books on the approach (e.g., Endler & Magnusson, 1976a; Magnusson, 1981; Magnusson & Endler, 1977). Whereas traditional psychodynamic and humanistic theories of personality concentrated on individual characteristics, and whereas traditional behavioral theories of psychology restricted their focus to situational influences on behavior, the person-situation interactional approach is now widely regarded as an intuitively appealing and empirically sound alternative.

References

Alker, H. A. (1972). Is personality situationally specific or intrapsychically consistent? *Journal of Personality, 40,* 1–16.

Allport, G. W. (1937). *Personality: A psychological interpretation.* New York: Holt.

Allport, G. W. (1961). *Pattern and growth in personality.* New York: Holt, Rinehart, and Winston.

Baars, B. J. (1986). *The cognitive revolution in psychology.* New York: Guilford Press.

Bandura, A. (1969). *Principles of behavior modification.* New York: Holt, Rinehart, and Winston.

Bandura, A. (1971). *Social learning theory.* New York: General Learning Press.

Bem, D. J. (1972). Constructing cross-situational consistencies in behavior: Some thoughts on Alker's critique of Mischel. *Journal of Personality, 40,* 17–26.

Bem, D. J. (1983). Further deja vu in the search for cross-situational consistency: A response to Mischel and Peake. *Psychological Review, 90,* 390–393.

Bem, D. J., & Allen, A. (1974). On predicting some of the people some of the time: The search for cross-situational consistencies in behavior. *Psychological Review,* 81, 506–520.

Bem, D. J., & Funder, D. C. (1978). Predicting more of the people more of the time: Assessing the personality of situations. *Psychological Review, 85,* 485–501.

Block, J. (1977). Advancing the psychology of personality: Paradigmatic shift or improving the quality of research? In D. Magnusson & N. S. Endler (Eds.), *Personality at the crossroads: Current issues in interactional psychology* (pp. 37–63). Hillsdale, NJ: Erlbaum.

Bowers, K. S. (1973). Situationism in psychology: An analysis and a critique. *Psychological Review, 80,* 307–336.

Carlson, R. (1971). Where is the person in personality research? *Psychological Bulletin,* 75, 203–219.

Cattell, R. B. (1965). *The scientific analysis of personality.* Chicago: Aldine.

Cronbach, L. J. (1957). The two disciplines of scientific psychology. *American Psychologist, 12,* 671–684.

Endler, N. S. (1976). Estimating variance components from mean squares for random and mixed effects analysis of variance models. In N. S. Endler & D. Magnusson (Eds.). *Interactional psychology and personality* (pp. 412-423). Washington, DC: Hemisphere.

Endler, N. S., & Magnusson, D. (1976a). *Interactional psychology and personality.* Washington, DC: Hemisphere.

Endler, N. S., & Magnusson, D. (1976b). Personality and person by situation interactions. In N. S. Endler & D. Magnusson (Eds.), *Interactional psychology and personality* (pp. 1–25). Washington, DC: Hemisphere.

Epstein, S. (1977). Traits are alive and well. In D. Magnusson & N. S. Endler (Eds.), *Personality at the crossroads: Current issues in interactional psychology* (pp. 83–98). Hillsdale, NJ: Erlbaum.

Epstein, S. (1979). The stability of behavior: I. On predicting most of the people much of the time. *Journal of Personality and Social Psychology, 37,* 1097–1126.

Epstein, S. (1980). The stability of behavior: II. Implications for psychological research. *American Psychologist, 35,* 790–806.

Epstein, S. (1983a). Aggregation and beyond: Some basic issues on the prediction of behavior. *Journal of Personality, 51*, 360–392.

Epstein, S. (1983b). The stability of confusion: A reply to Mischel and Peake. *Psychological Review, 90*, 179–184.

Epstein, S. (1984). The stability of behavior across time and situations. In R. Zucker, J. Aronoff, & A. I. Rabin (Eds.), *Personality and the prediction of behavior* (pp. 209–268). San Diego, CA: Academic Press.

Hartshorne, H., & May, M. A. (1928). *Studies in the nature of character (Vol. 1). Studies in deceit.* New York: Macmillan.

Hartshorne, H., & May, M. A. (1929). *Studies in the nature of character (Vol. 2). Studies in service and self-control.* New York: Macmillan.

Hogan, R., DeSoto, C. B., & Solano, C. (1977). Traits, tests, and personality research. *American Psychologist, 32*, 255–264.

Hollon, S. D., & Beck, A. T. (1986). Cognitive and cognitive-behavioral therapies. In S. L. Garfield & A. E. Bergin (Eds.), *Handbook of psychotherapy and behavior change* (3rd ed.) (pp. 443–482). New York: Wiley.

Jordan, J. S., Harvey, J. H., & Weary, G. (1988). Attributional biases in clinical decision making. In D. C. Turk & P. Salovey (Eds.), *Reasoning, inference, and judgment in clinical psychology* (pp. 90–106). New York: Free Press.

Lehmann, H. C., & Witty, P. A. (1934). Faculty psychology and personality traits. *American Journal of Psychology, 44*, 490.

Mabe, P. A., & West, S. G. (1982). Validity of self-evaluation of ability: A review and meta-analysis. *Journal of Applied Psychology, 67*, 280–296.

Magnusson, D. (1981). *Toward a psychology of situations: An interactional perspective.* Hillsdale, NJ: Erlbaum.

Magnusson, D., & Endler, N. S. (Eds.). (1977). *Personality at the crossroads: Current issues in interactional psychology.* Hillsdale, NJ: Erlbaum.

Mahoney, M. J. (1974). *Cognition and behavior modification.* Cambridge, MA: Ballinger.

Meichenbaum, D. (1977). *Cognitive-behavior modification: An integrative approach.* New York: Plenum.

Mischel, W. (1968). *Personality and assessment.* New York: Wiley.

Mischel, W. (1969). Continuity and change in personality. *American Psychologist, 24*, 1012–1018.

Mischel, W. (1971). *Introduction to personality.* New York: Holt, Rinehart and Winston.

Mischel, W. (1973a). Toward a cognitive social learning reconceptualization of personality. *Psychological Review, 80*, 252–283.

Mischel, W. (1973b). On the empirical dilemmas of psychodynamic approaches: Issues and alternatives. *Journal of Abnormal Psychology, 82*, 335–344.

Mischel, W., & Peake, P. K. (1982). Beyond deja vu in the search for cross-situational consistency. *Psychological Review, 89*, 730–755.

Mischel, W., & Peake, P. K. (1983). Some facets of consistency: Replies to Epstein, Funder, and Bem. *Psychological Review, 90*, 394–402.

Newcomb, T. M. (1929). *Consistency of certain extrovert-introvert behavior patterns in 51 problem boys.* New York: Columbia University, Teachers College, Bureau of Publications.

Peterson, D. R. (1968). *The clinical study of social behavior*. New York: Appleton-Century-Crofts.

Raush, H. L. (1976). Interaction sequences. In N. S. Endler & D. Magnusson (Eds.), *Interactional psychology and personality* (pp. 424–443). Washington, DC: Hemisphere.

Ross, L. (1977). The intuitive psychologist and his shortcomings: Distortions in the attribution process. In L. Berkowitz (Ed.), *Advances in experimental social psychology* (Vol. 10) (pp. 173–220). New York: Academic Press.

Small, S. A., Zeldin, R. S., & Savin-Williams, R. C. (1983). In search of personality traits: A multimethod analysis of naturally occurring prosocial and dominance behavior. *Journal of Personality, 51*, 1–16.

Stagner, R. (1976). Traits are relevant: Theoretical analysis and empirical evidence. In N. S. Endler & D. Magnusson (Eds.), *Interactional psychology and personality* (pp. 109–124). Washington, DC: Hemisphere.

Vernon, P. E. (1964). *Personality assessment: A critical survey*. New York: Wiley.

Wachtel, P. L. (1973). Psychodynamics, behavior therapy, and the implacable experimenter: An inquiry into the consistency of personality. *Journal of Abnormal Psychology, 82*, 324–334.

Walster, E. (1966). Assignment of responsibility for an accident. *Journal of Personality and Social Psychology, 3*, 73–79.

Wicker, A. W. (1969). Attitudes versus actions: The relationship of verbal and overt behavioral responses to attitude objects. *Journal of Social Issues, 25*, 41–78.

CHAPTER FOUR

Reliability and Validity of Projective Tests

Introduction

Projective personality tests represent another of the major issues on which the subjective and the objective approaches to clinical psychology have clashed. Projective tests experienced a meteoric rise in use from the 1930s through the 1950s. However, from the 1950s through the present, clinical psychologists with an objective or scientific orientation have questioned the assumptions and utility of projective methods. The purpose of this chapter is to review the conflict between the subjective and objective schools of clinical psychology with regard to the issue of projective personality tests.

Nature of Projective Tests

The term *projective test* is used to describe a class of assessment instruments which share the following characteristics:

1. Test items consist of vague or unstructured stimuli which the subject is required to organize or interpret in some way;
2. Each subject can respond to the stimuli in a unique way and so there is an unlimited number of possible responses to each test stimulus;
3. The subject's underlying personality is assumed to influence how he organizes the test stimulus and so the subject's personality is assessed through a proper interpretation of the subject's test responses.

Examples of projective tests are familiar to both students of psychology and laypersons. They include the Rorschach Inkblot Test, the

Thematic Apperception Test (TAT), and the Draw-A-Person Test (and other human figure drawing tests).

The term *projective methods* is generally attributed to L. K. Frank. Frank (1948) stated that the term was first used publicly in a paper he presented in 1939 before the New York Academy of Sciences. In addition, Frank published a paper in 1939 based on this presentation. Frank (1939) is well known for his comparison of projective tests to X-rays. Both are indirect methods of determining the internal state of an individual. In both cases, a stimulus is "passed through an individual," yielding a picture that may only dimly reflect the internal state of the individual, and so must be interpreted by a trained diagnostician. Although Frank is generally credited with introducing the term, Lindzey (1961) noted that Murray (1938) had previously used the term *projective test*. Hence, Lindzey credited Murray with the introduction of the term.

The concept of *projection* was introduced by Freud in 1895. In discussing the possible consequences of an individual being unable to master his or her internally generated sexual excitation, Freud (1895/1962) wrote: "It [the psyche] *behaves as though it were projecting that excitation outwards*" (p. 112). Here, he described projection as a basic neurotic mechanism. The neurotic individual projected an internally generated threat outward and responded to it as though it were an external threat.

Later, Freud (1896/1962) elevated projection to the status of a defense mechanism, in which the individual attributed to others his or her own threatening thoughts or feelings, as in the case of paranoia (p. 184). It is this meaning of projection as a defense mechanism which is most familiar to psychologists. As a defense mechanism, projection is an unconscious defensive process which serves to protect the individual from painful or threatening material.

It should be noted that the term *projective test* is therefore something of a misnomer, because responses to projective test stimuli are neither necessarily defensive nor unconscious (Anderson, 1951; Zubin, Eron, & Schumer, 1965). Many psychological processes in addition to projection, both defensive and nondefensive, conscious and unconscious, may influence how an individual responds to a projective test stimulus. Hence, several writers have suggested alternative terms for projective tests such as "misperception" tests (Cattell, 1951) or "apperception" tests (Bellak, 1950). However, the term *projective test* has remained the conventional label for this class of assessment instruments.

Types of Projective Tests

Although projective methods are generally regarded as a single class of assessment techniques, some effort has been devoted to the classification of different kinds of projective methods. Lindzey (1959) discussed several of the schemes that had been proposed to date in an effort to categorize projective tests. Of these, the most well known is that of Frank (1948), who divided projective tests into five subtypes: (a) Constitutive, which involve the imposition of some structure or organization onto unstructured materials (e.g., Rorschach); (b) Cathartic, which involve emotional expression or an emotional reaction to some stimulus (e.g., doll play, psychodrama); (c) Interpretative, which require the subject to assign some meaning to the test stimulus (e.g., TAT); (d) Constructive, which require the arrangement of materials into larger or more organized products (e.g., Eriksonian play); and (e) Refractive, which involve the alteration or distortion of a conventional mode of communication (e.g., handwriting).

Lindzey (1961) later proposed an alternative system of classifying projective tests, which has become quite popular. Lindzey's categories of projective methods are: (a) Association, (b) Construction, (c) Completion, (d) Choice or Ordering, and (e) Expression.

History of Projective Tests

Projective tests were introduced primarily in the first half of this century. In 1910, Whipple listed the available assessment instruments and failed to include personality as a category of psychological tests. Then, aided by the rise in the psychoanalytic theory of personality, with its emphases on psychic determinism and the role of unconscious influences, projective tests appeared on the scene and rapidly increased in both number and application. The Rorschach Inkblot Test (Rorschach, 1921/1942), TAT (Morgan & Murray, 1935), Draw-A-Person Test (Machover, 1949), Incomplete Sentences Blank (Rotter & Rafferty, 1950), and other major projective tests appeared on the scene at this time of the dominance of the psychoanalytic model.

Still, it should be noted that tests similar to the major projective tests had been used, at least intermittently, before the advent of Freudian theory. Early word association experiments were conducted by Galton in 1879 and by Wundt in 1880 (Bell, 1948). In 1905, Binet and Simon used children's verbal responses to pictures as tests of their cognitive abilities (Rabin, 1968; Zubin, Eron, & Schumer, 1965). Binet and Henri employed inkblots in an 1895 investigation of visual imagination (Bell, 1948; Rabin, 1968).

Even centuries ago, the use of and rationale underlying projective techniques had been anticipated. For example, both Rabin (1968) and Zubin et al. (1965) noted that Leonardo da Vinci had described the visual associations possible when viewing a blot made by a sponge and how such associations could serve as a spur to the imagination. Similarly, in *Hamlet*, act 3, scene ii, Shakespeare (1602/1959) had two characters describe the various animals they could perceive in a single cloud.

The initial response of clinical psychologists toward projective tests was generally favorable. For example, Aronow and Reznikoff (1973) examined 275 reviews of the Rorschach Test which appeared in the Buros *Mental Measurements Yearbooks* from 1938 to 1965. They found that the early reviews were predominantly positive, expressing optimism about the utility of the test and describing the Rorschach in very favorable terms, such as "useful and penetrating," "very subtle and significant," and "likely to be more valid . . . than . . . personality inventories" (p. 309).

One index of the field's endorsement of projective tests is the rapid increase in use of these tests. Louttit and Browne (1947) surveyed clinics regarding their use of psychological tests and found that a major change from the previous decade was the inclusion of projectives (both the TAT and Rorschach) among the most commonly used tests. Sundberg (1954) examined the references in the *Fourth Mental Measurements Yearbook* (Buros, 1951) and found that, from the years 1937 to 1951, the Rorschach Inkblot Test had become the psychological test most often cited in the professional literature. According to Buros (1970), in the years from 1939 to 1943, Rorschach references increased from 18 percent of all test references in the professional literature to a full 39.3 percent. As Macfarlane (1942) said, projective tests spread "with the rapidity of a virulent infection" (p. 405).

After the initial expansion in use and endorsement of projective techniques, clinical psychologists began to examine the scientific foundations of these instruments more thoroughly. Researchers began to question both the theoretical assumptions underlying projective techniques and the psychometric properties of the tests. An initial indifference toward scientific validation of projective tests was replaced with enthusiasm. For example, Schofield (1952) catalogued all clinical research studies in six selected journals and found that, for the third year in a row, studies of the validity of projective tests formed the single largest category of clinical research.

It should be noted that this research concerning the validity of projective tests was not conducted simply by critics of the tests. Much of the work was done by proponents of projectives who intended to demonstrate that their methods in fact had sufficient reliability and validity.

Assumptions of Projective Tests

The assumptions underlying projective personality tests are closely associated with traditional psychoanalytic personality theory. Korner (1950) identified three fundamental assumptions of projective tests:

1. All behavior manifestations are expressive of an individual's personality. This includes both the most as well as the least significant aspects of the individual's behavior. The purpose of administering a projective test, rather than simply relying upon observation of the individual's naturally occurring behavior, is to ensure that all subjects are observed in a common or standardized situation.

2. The individual taking a projective test provides information about his or her psychological makeup that the examinee would or could not give otherwise. Because the test stimuli are ambiguous, it is difficult for the examinee to determine what is the "correct" or "healthy" response. Thus, test responses reveal the subject's "true" nature rather than the nature which the subject would like the examiner to perceive.

3. Each response is brought about by a distinctive set of causal influences. This is the traditional Freudian assumption of psychic determinism—the idea that all behaviors are the result of unique underlying psychic influences. Even if an individual would consciously influence his responses to projective test stimuli (say, by responding to a TAT card by describing the plot of a movie the subject recently saw), Korner thought that the selection of this plot rather than some other story would still provide information about the individual's underlying personality.

Macfarlane and Tuddenham (1951) identified three corollaries to the assumption of psychic determinism which have often been cited as fundamental assumptions of projective techniques: (a) the projective test protocol is a sufficient sampling of the subject's behavior to warrant an accurate interpretation of his personality, (b) the determinants of each and every response are basic and general, and (c) projective tests tap personality equally in different individuals.

These corollaries are quite basic. Even if the assumptions cited by Korner (1950) are correct, the projective test user must further assume that the test yields sufficient information to warrant accurate personality interpretations, that the subject's underlying personality influences are more important than, and can be distinguished from, situational influences, and that the test works in the same way across subjects.

Although these assumptions were generally accepted by early users of projectives (e.g., Abt, 1950; Rapaport, 1942; Sarason, 1954), they came under increasing scrutiny during the 1950s. For example, Murstein (1961) identified ten assumptions commonly made about projective techniques and then reviewed the empirical evidence concerning the validity of these assumptions. He found that, at best, these assumptions had conflicting support and, at worst, they had been disconfirmed. He concluded that the results of the research conducted to date demonstrated that several beliefs about projective tests had been accepted by clinical psychologists without sufficient empirical validation. Similarly, Zubin et al. (1965) presented the assumptions of projective techniques and noted that they "have by no means been made completely explicit, nor have they all been tested" (p. 606).

Reliability and Validity as Applied to Projective Tests

In the 1950s and 1960s, then, clinical psychologists had begun to question the validity of the theoretical assumptions underlying projective tests. Similarly, by this time, the field had also begun to examine empirically the reliability and validity of projectives.

The standards which are used to evaluate psychological tests have been well known since 1954, when the American Psychological Association issued its "Technical Recommendations for Psychological Tests and Diagnostic Techniques," which was later revised and published as *Standards for Educational and Psychological Tests and Manuals* (1966).

The basic requirements for any useful test are reliability and validity. *Reliability* refers to the stability or consistency of measurements and, depending upon the nature of the construct being assessed, should be demonstrated across occasions, raters, and/or subparts of the test.

Validity refers to the accuracy of the test. It addresses the issue of whether the test is in fact measuring what it was designed to measure. Test validity is most often demonstrated by correlating test scores with independent assessments, either concurrent or subsequent, of the construct in question. In this way, the criterion-related validity of the test can be measured.

Early users of projective techniques tended to accept the utility of these instruments without empirical demonstrations of their reliability and validity. For example, Macfarlane and Tuddenham (1951) noted that, in Bell's (1948) classic book on projective tests, only 15 of 748 references to the Rorschach and only 14 of 91 references to the TAT were primarily concerned with the empirical validation of these instruments.

Although the standards of reliability and validity are now accepted by psychologists as necessary features of any useful test, early proponents of projective tests questioned whether these criteria should be employed to evaluate projective techniques. For example, Frank (1948) expressed doubts as to whether the criteria of reliability and validity were "relevant" to projective testing, because reliability and validity concern tests for which group norms are important, whereas what is important in projective testing is the description of the individual. Similarly, Symonds (1949) stated that the primary purpose of projective tests was to describe rather than to measure the individual's personality, and so the standards of reliability and validity, which are essential for measurement instruments, are not so important for projectives. Ainsworth (1951) characterized the primary function of projective tests as classification rather than measurement and identified problems with applying traditional methods of assessing test reliability and validity to projectives.

Objections to the Standard of Reliability for Projective Tests

The nature of projective tests poses several obstacles when attempting to determine their reliability. Jensen (1959) and Murstein (1963) provided useful summaries of the difficulties encountered when attempting to measure the reliability of projective tests. Their works suggest that there are five major objections raised by projective test users to the traditional approaches to the determination of the reliability of projective tests.

1. Test-retest reliability may not be appropriate for projectives. This point has been made repeatedly by proponents of projective techniques (e.g., Ainsworth, 1951; Frank, 1948; Rosenzweig, 1950) because: (a) the subject's recollection of previous responses may influence responses during the retest, (b) the "psychological experience" of the test may be influenced by situational factors, and so test-retest differences may reflect real situational differences and not test unreliability, and (c) the psychological make-up of the subject may change from one occasion to the next, and so test-retest differences may reflect real psychological differences and not test unreliability.

These objections to the measurement of the test-retest reliability of projective techniques are not given much weight by Jensen (1959) and Murstein (1963). Other tests (such as structured personality inventories or intelligence tests) must also face the issue of a subject's recalling previous responses. This has not posed an overwhelming obstacle to the test-retest reliabilities of such instruments.

In addition, projective tests have assumed that responses to test stimuli are influenced by "basic and general" personality factors. To argue that projective tests are so influenced by situational factors that it is not possible to measure their test-retest reliability speaks against either the standardization of the administration procedure or against a theoretical assumption underlying the test. Jensen (1959), Murstein (1963), and others (e.g., Eysenck, 1952; Rotter, 1954) have noted that proponents of projective tests have been inconsistent on this point. On the one hand, they hold that the test-retest reliability of projectives cannot be assessed by traditional methods but, on the other hand, they administer the same test on several occasions to a subject and use such multiple administrations to demonstrate changes in the subject's personality.

2. Split-half and related indices of internal consistency may not be appropriate for projectives. Proponents of projective tests (e.g., Piotrowski, 1937) have noted that the stimulus materials in many projective tests (e.g., Rorschach inkblots, TAT cards) are, by design, not equivalent; rather, they tap into different aspects of the subject's personality. If projective test items are not equivalent, then one should not expect the measures obtained from different items to be highly correlated with one another. Hence, measures of internal consistency should be expected to be lower for projectives than for other tests.

Jensen (1959) responded to this objection by acknowledging the correctness of the argument. Each type or measure of test reliability is concerned with a different issue. If the items of a projective test are nonequivalent, then it is indeed inappropriate to assess the test's reliability with a measure of the internal consistency of scores across items. However, Jensen also noted that, despite this argument, many scores generated by the Rorschach represent totals to which such nonequivalent items contribute and which are interpreted independently of the specific items that contributed to the scores. According to Jensen, the reliability of such scores can be estimated using split-half methods.

3. In actual practice, projective test protocols are interpreted in a configural manner; hence, reliability estimates of individual projective scales are irrelevant.

The standard reply to this objection is that the reliabilities of the elements of a configuration influence the reliability of the configuration (Jensen, 1959). If individual scale scores can be shown to be unreliable, then a configuration based on these individual scale scores will also be unreliable.

4. Projective tests are designed for the purpose of description rather than measurement (Frank, 1948; Symonds, 1949); hence, traditional estimates of test reliability are not appropriate for projectives. For example, Frank (1939, 1948) compared projective techniques to X-rays. By passing the projective test material "through" the individual, we obtain a "picture" of the internal state of the individual. The test result is a picture or a description, rather than a numerical measurement. In this way, Frank argued that traditional

methods of estimating test reliability are not appropriate for such qualitative assessments.

Jensen (1959) responded to this objection by noting that interjudge reliability is essential for both X-rays and projective tests. These techniques require that a trained diagnostician evaluate the test results to determine whether certain pathological signs are present or absent and to combine these signs in some way so as to arrive at a summary evaluation of the subject. For both X-rays and projective tests, then, it is crucial that test users can demonstrate that judges agree on the presence/absence of these signs as well as on the meaning of these signs.

5. It is not necessary to demonstrate the reliability of projective tests, because these tests have already been shown to be valid, and a valid test must be reliable. This objection is based on practical grounds. Proponents of projective tests (e.g., Goldfried, Stricker, & Weiner [1971]) have argued that, if the validity of these tests has already been established, then it becomes a moot point to go back and demonstrate their reliability.

Jensen's (1959) reply to this argument was straightforward. First, it is not accepted by all psychologists that projective tests are valid. Second, if both the reliability and validity of projective tests are in question, then it will generally be simpler to conduct studies to examine their reliability than their validity. Reliability studies are usually easier to conduct than validity studies. If a projective test is found to have inadequate reliability, then there is no need to conduct the more complex validation study.

Objections to the Standard of Validity for Projective Tests

Ainsworth (1951) and others (e.g., Blatt, 1975; Karon, 1968; Little, 1959; Macfarlane, 1942; Meehl, 1959) have similarly addressed the difficulties associated with the demonstration of the validity of projective tests. These difficulties can be summarized as follows.

1. It is difficult to select an adequate criterion to demonstrate the criterion-related validity of projective tests. According to Klopfer and Taulbee (1976), this has been the single greatest obstacle to the demonstration of the validity of projectives. Because projective tests are designed to tap into the underlying dynamics of personality, the proper criterion for the demonstration of criterion-related validity should be another measure of these underlying dynamics. The problem here is that no other adequate measures of these dynamics may be available.

A common procedure in validation studies is to determine the correlation between the projective test score and some measurable criterion (e.g., presenting symptomatology, response to psychotherapy). Although such research is essential, it is more an examination of the construct validity (which concerns the relationship between the test's measure of a psychological construct and other, theoretically related variables) than the criterion-related validity of the instrument.

Proponents of projective tests raise these arguments to show the difficulty of demonstrating the criterion-related validity of projective tests. They then argue that a lack of evidence in favor of the criterion-related validity of projectives is the result of this methodological difficulty, and not the result of an inherent lack of validity.

Critics of projective tests, on the other hand, agree that it is difficult to select an adequate criterion to measure the criterion-related validity of projectives, but they then conclude that the problem is with projective tests themselves. Science, after all, requires that its constructs be at least indirectly measurable, and that its statements be falsifiable (Hempel, 1966). If the constructs measured by projective techniques cannot be measured in other ways or if their theoretical relationships to other variables cannot be tested, then they should not be included in a science of psychology.

2. The studies of the validity of projective tests are methodologically weak. Much of the research on the psychometric properties of projective techniques is limited by design flaws such as the following:

a. The tests are administered, scored, and interpreted by individuals who do not have sufficient training or experience in their use. These studies may demonstrate the poor validity of projective tests when used by such examiners, but they do not speak to the psychometric properties of projectives when used by trained or experienced practitioners.

b. The tests are used for purposes other than those for which they were originally designed. If a study attempts to determine the relationship between a projective test score and some inappropriate criterion (e.g., performance in graduate school), then we should expect the result to be a failure to demonstrate the validity of the instrument. The reason, however, is the inadequate criterion and not the actual invalidity of the test.

c. The tests are used in ways other than those in which they are employed in actual practice. For example, advocates of projective tests report that, in actual practice, projective tests are not scored blindly with respect to other information about the subject and that individual subscale scores are not interpreted independently of other scores. If studies of the psychometric properties of projective tests employ such features, then their results are limited to these nonrepresentative uses of the tests and should not be generalized to projective tests as they are used in actual practice.

Proponents of projective tests have identified such methodological limitations in the studies of the psychometric properties of projectives and, when these studies fail to support the validity or reliability of projectives, argued that the results are due to the design flaws and not to inherent psychometric failings of the tests. Critics of projective tests recognize these design flaws, but do not consider them to be sufficient justification for the absence of evidence of reliability and validity. That it is difficult to demonstrate the validity of a test does not excuse the lack of empirical demonstrations of validity.

Reviews of the Reliability and Validity of Projective Tests

Even after granting that projective tests may have a set of unique problems in determining their psychometric properties, clinical psychologists, even strong proponents of projectives (e.g., Bell, 1948), recognized that the standards of reliability and validity applied for projectives and had to be demonstrated in order for these tests to be considered useful. For example, in a discussion of projective techniques, Tomkins (1947) stated that the "acid test" of any assessment technique is its usefulness in making successful predictions. Similarly, Exner (Exner & Weiner, 1982), one of the leading advocates of the Rorschach Inkblot Test, strongly recommended that Rorschach users base their interpretations on empirically validated research, characterizing the intuitive approach to the interpretation of the Rorschach as a "ouija-board" approach, which is "often professionally embarrassing" (p. 9).

Schofield's (1950a, 1950b, 1951, 1952) reviews of research in clinical psychology suggested that the turning point for the empirical examination of the validity of projective tests occurred in the late 1940s. Schofield (1950a) examined the publications in four journals in clinical psychology from 1946 to 1948 and reported that fewer than 20 percent of the journal articles contained empirical research. He categorized this research and found that studies concerning the validation of projective techniques comprised only 7.1 percent of the total number of empirical clinical studies. His later reviews (1950b, 1951, 1952), however, found that the number of empirical studies in clinical psychology was rising, that these studies increasingly examined the validity of the field's methods and assumptions, and that, in each of the years from 1949 to 1951, examination of the validity of projective tests was the single largest category of clinical research—a full 21.0 percent of the total number of clinical studies in the year 1951.

From this period to the present, an enormous amount of attention has been devoted to the empirical evaluation of the reliability and validity of projective tests. The literature on projective tests is far too vast to review exhaustively here (for example, the *Ninth Mental Measurements Yearbook* [Buros, 1985] indicated that there were 4,644 published works to date on the Rorschach). What follows is a brief overview of several of the major efforts to review the research evidence concerning the reliability and validity of projective tests.

Reviews of Projective Tests in General

Throughout the 1950s, chapters in the *Annual Review of Psychology* (Butler & Fiske, 1955; Cronbach, 1956; Kelly, 1954; Rotter, 1953; Wittenborn, 1957) repeatedly noted the negative evidence (or, at best, the lack of positive evidence) for the reliability and validity of projectives. Kelly's (1954) conclusion is typical: "All evidence points to the fact that much of current practice involves the use of tests and techniques for which there is almost no evidence of predictive validity for the relevant criterion" (p. 306).

At this time many other reviews were conducted of the empirical evidence concerning the psychometric properties of projective tests. The following are representative of the conclusions drawn by the reviewers:

• "The results of most of the projective test validity studies were negative" (Rotter, 1954, p. 273)

• "There is no satisfactory evidence for any of the numerous claims made for these devices" (Eysenck, 1958, p. 120)

• "The published evidence on projective techniques indicates that they have either zero or, at best, very low positive effective validity indexes" (Little, 1959, p. 287)

• "No general conclusion concerning reliability is possible even with respect to any particular technique. The reported reliabilities are usually lower than is considered acceptable in the case of objective tests " (Jensen, 1959, p. 133)

• "There are few outcomes or behaviors which [the clinician] can safely predict on the basis of present scientific evidence. Therefore, . . . he is forced to avoid the use of tests, or else to use them rashly without sufficient evidence. Either result is unfortunate!" (Suinn & Oskamp, 1969, p. 138)

Although the reviews cited above are by no means exhaustive, they reflect clinical psychology's increasing awareness of the lack of empirical evidence for the reliability and validity of projective techniques. Also, it should be noted that the reviews of this period were not uniformly negative. For example, Rabin (1951) reported that, in his opinion, the Rorschach test had been shown to possess adequate validity.

However, most psychologists, even those who advocated the use of projectives and who believed that, ultimately, these tests are valid, voiced concerns over the lack of empirical evidence to support the reliability and validity of projectives. For example, Levy (1950) wrote of human figure drawings that "the technique of analyzing drawings is without sufficient experimental validation, rarely yields unequivocal information, and frequently misleads the unwary into plausible misstatements about the person whose drawings are being studied" (pp. 257–258). Of the TAT, Holt (1951) wrote: "It should be stated in all frankness that neither the reliability nor the validity of the method of interpretation advocated in the chapter has been rigorously tested . . ." (p. 223).

Reviews of Individual Projective Tests

Specific projective tests did not fare much better. Several major projective techniques, including the Rorschach Inkblot Test, TAT, and human figure drawings, have been the focus of major research reviews. A selection of representative reviews of these instruments follows.

Rorschach Inkblot Test

Cronbach (1949) conducted an influential review of early studies of the reliability of the Rorschach. Cronbach found so many methodological and statistical errors in these studies that he concluded that few of the findings of these studies could be trusted.

Schofield (1952) reported that, of 38 tests of the validity of the Rorschach from 1949 to 1951, 26 (68.4 percent) yielded negative results (and the positive results included some which Schofield [1951] characterized as having only "borderline" significance). Similarly, Ellis (1952) reported that, of 12 recent studies of the relationship between the Rorschach and personality inventories, only two produced significant results.

Windle (1952) reviewed the research on the prognostic validity of psychological tests and concluded, with regard to the Rorschach, that the evidence "failed to disclose any very encouraging concordance among studies for any diagnostic category" (p. 464). Eysenck (1952) examined the evidence concerning the reliability of the Rorschach and concluded that "the literature here is in such a confused state that it is almost impossible to derive any agreed conclusions" (p. 164).

Zubin (1954) examined research concerning the reliability and validity of the Rorschach and concluded that the Rorschach had failed with respect to both criteria. He suggested that clinicians shift their focus from the perceptual to the content aspect of the Rorschach and use the Rorschach as a structured interview. Later, Zubin et al. (1965) could not find sufficient evidence to alter this conclusion. They wrote that "the clinical status of the Rorschach technique, based on an evaluation of research evidence, is not wholly satisfactory, despite claims to the contrary" (p. 239).

Jensen (1959) found that, in general, split-half estimates of the reliability of the Rorschach are higher than test-retest estimates, and that interrater estimates only rarely appeared in the literature. He also found that, in general, estimates of Rorschach reliability are highly variable.

Holzberg (1960) examined evidence concerning the reliability of the Rorschach. For each approach to the measurement of reliability, Holzberg found either that insufficient efforts had been made to assess reliability or that research results were too conflicting to permit a final conclusion to be drawn.

In this review, Holzberg provided an interesting apology for the lack of evidence in support of the interrater reliability of the Rorschach. He noted that "it is possible for judges to emphasize different aspects of the record, and yet all of these aspects may be valid" (p. 373). He later wrote that "the Rorschach method cannot be isolated from the interpreter, the Rorschach and the psychologist being one integral methodology" (p. 374). In a scientific discussion, such statements should be regarded with caution. Once such statements enter a theoretical system, it is possible to explain any disconfirming result as due to the inadequacy of the individual who conducted the test. In other words, the system becomes irrefutable—what Popper (1963) considered a "pseudoscience" rather than a science.

Suinn and Oskamp (1969) examined the predictive validity of projectives over the period from 1950 to 1965. With regard to the Rorschach, they concluded: "At most, the studies reviewed here have established the *selective validity* of certain Rorschach indices. . . . However, its all-too-common use as an all-purpose trait predictor, diagnostic indicator, and global personality descriptor is not justified by any scientific evidence presently available" (pp. 124–125).

Goldfried et al. (1971) examined research on the reliability and validity of the Rorschach and concluded that the evidence supported the use of the instrument as a means of assessing both perceptual and verbal responses—indices directly representative of behavior. However, they did not support the interpretation of the content of test responses in order to obtain a symbolic representation of behavior. This approach, according to Goldfried et al., is particularly susceptible to "errors of measurement and the persistence of illusory correlation" (p. 396).

Exner (1974, 1978; Exner & Weiner, 1982) developed a new scoring system for the Rorschach which he described as capable of obtaining high interscorer agreement. Research on the reliability of the Exner system (Exner, 1978; Exner & Weiner, 1982) has demonstrated that it has moderate to high test-retest reliability in both adult and adolescent populations and for both patients and nonpatients.

Peterson (1978) examined recent studies of the Rorschach and questioned whether it had sufficient predictive validity to justify its continued use in clinical practice.

Parker (1983) conducted a meta-analysis of 39 studies of the reliability and validity of the Rorschach, which appeared in the *Journal of Personality Assessment* from 1971 to 1980. Parker found that, when a priori hypotheses with previous empirical support or sufficient theoretical foundations are tested, then research tends to support both the reliability (rs > .83) and the validity (rs > .45) of the Rorschach.

More recently, Parker, Hanson, and Hunsley (1988) conducted a meta-analysis of studies of the reliability and validity of the Rorschach, MMPI, and WAIS which were published in two journals over a twelve-year period. On the basis of four findings, they estimated the reliability (including both interrater and internal consistency) of the Rorschach to be .86; from two findings, they calculated the stability (test-retest reliability) of the Rorschach to be .85. From five studies, they estimated that the convergent validity of the Rorschach was .41. In general, Parker et al. found that the reliability and validity of the Rorschach were acceptable and were not appreciably lower than those of the other tests.

Piotrowski (1965), a strong proponent of projective tests, recognized the weak empirical support for the Rorschach, and explained that practitioners may have been using the test in ways other than those for which the test was originally developed. According to Piotrowski, Herman Rorschach (1921/1942) initially developed the test for strictly theoretical purposes—to study perception and the related processes of sensation, memory, and association. Piotrowski stated that Rorschach himself had expressed caution about the use of the inkblot test for making diagnoses or for other purposes. Thus, if the Rorschach test is being used for purposes for which it was not intended, then it is not surprising that empirical tests fail to support its validity.

In summary, the Rorschach Inkblot Test has generated an enormous literature since its publication in 1921. Although efforts by Exner (1974, 1978; Exner & Weiner, 1982) and Parker (1983) have shown that particular scales of the Rorschach can be scored and interpreted with adequate reliability and validity, many of the empirical evaluations of the Rorschach have yielded negative results. Practitioners who employ this test should use it in a narrow fashion, testing specific hypotheses for which the research literature provides empirical support. The traditional global use of the Rorschach should be regarded with caution.

Thematic Apperception Test (TAT)

Another major projective test is the TAT. Following its introduction by Morgan and Murray (1935), the TAT rapidly rose in popularity so that, from 1948 to 1951, the TAT was the fourth most frequently cited psychological test and the second most frequently cited projective test, after the Rorschach (Sundberg, 1954). As was the case with the Rorschach, reviews of the empirical evidence concerning the reliability and validity of the TAT have repeatedly shown that its clinical use has far outdistanced its scientific status.

Early supporters of the TAT recognized that its empirical adequacy had not been sufficiently documented. For example, although Tomkins (1947) stated that he believed that the validity of the TAT had been demonstrated, he later (1949) acknowledged that the empirical evidence was not consistently supportive. Similarly, Bell (1948) reported that, in his opinion, the TAT was accepted by clinical psychologists more on the basis of their own experience with the test and not on the basis of a scientific evaluation of the instrument. Holt (1951), one of the foremost proponents of the TAT, described his approach to the scoring and interpretation of the TAT, but acknowledged that "neither the reliability nor the validity of the method . . . has been rigorously tested" (p. 223).

The most influential reviews of the TAT from this period may well be those of Lindzey (1952), Jensen (1959), and Murstein (1963).

Lindzey (1952) identified ten assumptions underlying the TAT and reviewed the research evidence concerning the validity of each. Although Lindzey found that these assumptions varied in their support (from those which were confirmed by empirical studies, through those which had contradictory findings or relatively no empirical attention, to those which were disconfirmed), he suggested that further research attention was warranted with regard to all of the assumptions of the TAT.

Jensen (1959) found that, of the more than 700 publications to date on the TAT, only a few concerned its reliability. He reviewed these studies and found that their estimates of the reliability of the TAT were quite variable, with many below the level of acceptability of any measurement instrument.

Murstein (1963) reviewed the evidence on the reliability of the TAT and concluded that its test-retest reliability was "very low but significant" (p. 140), that its internal consistency was "quite low" (p. 148), and that its interscorer reliability was "mediocre" (p. 148). He also examined research on the validity of the TAT and concluded that "these studies yield evidence of statistical validity of the TAT. The values reported, however, seem too low to be of practical utility" (p. 282).

Many other evaluations of the TAT have been conducted, often yielding such negative results. The following conclusions are representative of the evaluations of the TAT:

• "It does not appear that objective criteria have been found through which the TAT can be of prognostic use" (Windle, 1952, p. 467)

- "It is not possible to regard the TAT as a valid instrument of personality assessment, as such" (Zubin et al., 1965, p. 462)

- "Contrary to its original rationale, the TAT stories seem to reflect overt personality trends, rather than covert or unconscious dynamics. The greatest success of the TAT seems to be in predicting *interpersonal* behaviors, particularly aggressive, hostile, or acting-out traits" (Suinn & Oskamp, 1969, pp. 127-128)

- "[there is not] a cohesive body of knowledge about the TAT or its application to personality evaluation" (Dana, 1972, p. 458)

Swartz (1978) reached one of the most negative conclusions in the literature concerning the TAT. After examining recent studies on the TAT, Swartz questioned "the ultimate usefulness of an instrument that yields such mixed results after 40 years of investigation" (p. 1130).

It should be noted that not all of the evaluations of the TAT have been negative. For example, Harrison's (1965) review of the research on the TAT found that the reliability of the instrument was quite good, with most estimates of interjudge reliability above .70. He also concluded that "there is impressive evidence that the technique possesses intrinsic validity" (p. 597).

In summary, research on the TAT has not consistently supported either the psychometric properties or the theoretical assumptions of the test. Although some scoring systems can be used reliably, the clinical validity of these systems remains to be demonstrated. Even when certain scoring systems for the TAT are found to have adequate reliability and validity, it is not clear that these systems are used by clinicians in actual practice. For example, Klopfer and Taulbee (1976), strong proponents of projective tests, recognized that "the objective scoring systems that have been developed for the TAT are almost totally absent in routine clinical use" (p. 554). Thus, as with the Rorschach, clinicians who employ the TAT should do so in a conservative fashion, restricting their use of the test to a narrow range of hypotheses which have been shown to have empirical support.

Draw-A-Person

Another major projective test is the Draw-A-Person (DAP). Machover (1949) reported that she had found Goodenough's Draw-a-Man Test, which had originally been developed to assess intelligence, to be a rich source of clinical material. She described numerous hypotheses concerning the relationship between an individual's personality dynamics and the characteristics of his or her human figure drawings. In this book, Machover did not consider the reliability of the DAP. However, she did think that the validity of the instrument had been demonstrated in the clinical examination of "thousands of drawings." She also alluded to validation studies that supported the use of the instrument but did not cite any data in support of the validity of the DAP.

Levy (1950) examined the evidence on the projective method of interpreting figure drawings and concluded that "the technique of analyzing drawings is without sufficient experimental validation, rarely yields unequivocal information, and frequently misleads the unwary into plausible misstatements about the personality of the person whose drawings are being studied" (pp. 257–258).

Perhaps the most influential evaluations of the DAP are Swenson's reviews (1957, 1968). Swensen (1957) examined empirical studies from 1949 to 1956 on Machover's hypotheses concerning the DAP. Although he found that "some evidence supports the use of the DAP as a rough screening device, and as a gross indicator of 'level of adjustment'" (p. 463), he also concluded that the evidence "does not support Machover's hypotheses about the meaning of human figure drawings. . . . More of the evidence directly contradicts her hypotheses than supports them" (p. 460).

Swensen (1968) later updated his review to include research through 1966. He reported that there was now sufficient evidence for the reliability of global ratings of adjustment derived from the DAP but that the reliability and validity of single signs continued to be low. He concluded that "the use of the structural and content signs on the DAP for clinical assessment is not likely to provide any improvement in the clinicians' judgmental accuracy" (p. 40).

Another major review of the research on the DAP was that of Roback (1968). He examined research of the DAP from 1949 to 1967 and found that the evidence generally failed to support Machover's hypotheses.

Harris (1972) reviewed the recent literature on the DAP and noted the questionable validity of the instrument. He also addressed the unreliability of the signs or indicators of the DAP due to the variability across drawings and the confound of artistic ability.

In summary, reviews of the research evidence on the use of human figure drawings to assess personality have not yielded favorable evaluations. The clinical practice of interpreting personality from characteristics of a client's drawing must therefore be regarded with extreme caution.

Summary

The 1950s and 1960s saw numerous efforts to examine the reliability and validity of projective techniques. These efforts were by no means universal in their failure to support projectives. Still, it is fair to say that they severely questioned the reliability and validity, and therefore the utility, of projective techniques. The following trends ran through this literature:

1. Many studies demonstrated that projective techniques were low in reliability and validity.
2. When projectives were found to have adequate psychometric properties, these results often failed to generalize to other studies.
3. Even when the reliability or validity of projective tests was established, the possibility of using a more cost-effective alternative was raised. For example, Goldfried et al. (1971), although generally supportive of the Rorschach, wrote: "Considering the usual 1.5–2 hours taken for administration and scoring, it seems only reasonable to admit that the Rorschach may not always be the most practical measure" (p. 6).

The Changing Status of Projective Tests

As a result of the critical examination of projective tests throughout the 1950s and 1960s, the status of projective tests experienced a dramatic change. Whereas these tests had previously occupied a favored position in the armamentarium of clinical tools, following 1950 they came to be regarded with much more caution and skepticism. This change can be illustrated both by the attitudes of psychologists toward projective tests and the use of projective tests in research and applied settings.

Attitudes of Psychologists toward Projective Tests

As discussed above, research reviews on the psychometric properties of projective tests consistently questioned the reliability and validity of these instruments. Even though many clinicians remained faithful to projective techniques, the field as a whole viewed these tests less favorably. For example, Aronow and Reznikoff (1973) examined the published reviews of books on the Rorschach from 1938 to 1965. They found that, although the early reviews tended to be optimistic and enthusiastic about this instrument, later reviews tended to be quite pessimistic, citing inadequate research support, difficulties in scoring and interpretation, and problems with its theoretical foundation.

Zubin et al. (1965), following their review of the research on projectives, questioned whether "it is time to give up" (p. 609) on them. Similarly, McReynolds (1968) reported that "many psychologists appear ready to reject the approach as inherently unsatisfactory" (p. 8).

Even strong advocates of projective tests recognized the crisis that these tests were facing (e.g., Hertz, 1970; Holt, 1967; Weiner, 1972). One index of the status of projective tests, even among their proponents, is that the members of the Society for Projective Techniques and Personality Assessment voted in 1970 to remove the term "Projective Techniques" from their name (Ames, 1970). The following year, the *Journal of Projective Techniques and Personality Assessment* was renamed the *Journal of Personality Assessment*.

Surveys of academic clinical psychologists have shown that Rorschach instructors believe that further research, especially on the scoring, interpretation, and validity of the Rorschach is important (Jackson & Wohl, 1966). These surveys have also shown that academic clinicians tend to see projective tests as declining in importance and the clinical use of projectives as unsupported by research (Piotrowski & Keller, 1984a; Thelen, Varble, & Johnson, 1968). However, these surveys all found that academic clinical psychologists support the continued training of doctoral candidates in the major projective techniques.

A survey of directors of APA-approved clinical internships provided similar results (McCully, 1965). McCully found that internship directors reported a decline in intern interest in projectives but that they supported the continued training of clinical psychology students in projective techniques.

Use of Projective Tests

Mills (1965) conducted a review of the use of projective tests in research published from 1947 to 1964 in the *Journal of Projective Techniques and Personality Assessment*. He reported that the top three projective techniques (respectively, the Rorschach, TAT, and human figure drawings) remained stable throughout the entire period, but that other projectives (such as the Szondi, Make-A-Picture, and Mosaic) greatly declined in use over this period.

Crenshaw, Bohn, Hoffman, Matheus, and Offenbach (1968) reviewed the use of projective tests in ten journals from 1947 to 1964. They agreed with Mills (1965) on which projective tests were used most frequently and which had experienced significant declines in usage. However, Crenshaw et al. also reported the peak periods of use for the major projectives. They found that research use had peaked for the Rorschach in 1954, for the TAT in 1955, and for human figure drawings in 1955.

Buros initiated several series (*Mental Measurements Yearbook, Tests in Print, Personality Tests and Reviews*) which reviewed and attempted to cite all published works which used various psychological tests. Examination of these works reveals that the number of publications per year on the major projective techniques (Rorschach, TAT, DAP) continued to rise from their introduction through the early 1970s, when they all experienced a decline. Buros also reported the total number of references that cited psychological tests. From this information, one can then calculate the percentage of references to psychological tests that cited a specific test in the entire universe of references. Table 4–1 presents these percentages for the Rorschach, TAT, and Machover DAP. This table indicates that the peak use of these major projectives, relative to the field's use of all psychological tests, occurred in the period from 1953 to 1959.

Although projective tests have not gained the psychometric respectability sought by their followers, the research use of projectives has declined, and the field's general attitude toward these tests has become more negative and skeptical, projective tests continue to be used frequently in clinical practice. Surveys of clinicians in a variety of applied settings have shown that projective tests are widely used, and that the same projectives used most frequently in the 1940s (Rorschach, TAT) are the most frequently used today (Louttit & Browne, 1947; Lubin, Larsen, & Matarazzo, 1984; Lubin, Larsen, Matarazzo, & Seever, 1985; Lubin, Wallis, & Paine, 1971; Sundberg, 1961). Surveys of private practitioners (Hinkle, Nelson, & Miller, 1968) as well as clinicians in community mental health centers (Brown & McGuire, 1976; Piotrowski & Keller, 1978, 1989) have agreed that projective tests are still in frequent use by clinicians.

TABLE 4–1 • *Percentage of References in the Mental Measurements Yearbook Citing the Rorschach, TAT, and Machover DAP*

Volume	Year	Rorschach	TAT	DAP
9	1985	1.30	.84	.37
8[a]	1978	2.16	1.39	.32
7[b]	1972	6.02	3.26	.44
6	1965	9.20	4.80	.11
5	1959	16.65	4.46	.60
4	1953	14.00	2.94	.29
3	1949	13.14	—	—
2	1941	9.71	—	—

[a]Includes data from Buros, O. K. (1974). *Tests in print II.*
[b]Includes data from Buros, O. K. (1970). *Personality tests and reviews.*

Even though these surveys have demonstrated that the use of projectives may vary across type of agency (Lubin et al., 1985; Sell & Torres-Henry, 1979) and theoretical orientation (Piotrowski & Keller, 1984b; Piotrowski, Sherry, & Keller, 1985), all have agreed that projective methods are still used frequently today and that psychologists recommend their continued use. Although psychologists now use many alternatives to projective tests, they have not stopped using projective techniques altogether.

Summary and Conclusions

In summary, then, the following generalizations can be drawn concerning clinical psychology's views toward and uses of projective psychological tests.

1. Since the 1950s, the field has become increasingly concerned with the psychometric properties of projective tests. This, by the way, is also true of other methods of psychological assessment. The American Psychological Association (1966) formalized the criteria which must be met by any useful psychological test. Projective techniques, like other tests, must be judged in terms of the degree to which they are both reliable and valid.

2. In general, the reliability and validity of projective methods have not been demonstrated to be as high as is desirable in psychological tests.

This generalization, of course, must quickly be qualified. An examination of the vast research literature on projective tests indicates that the following exceptions must be recognized: (a) there are some methods of scoring and interpreting a projective test that are more reliable and valid than other methods; (b) a projective test may be more reliable and valid for some purposes or within some populations than others; and (c) there are some projective tests that are more reliable and valid than other projective tests. Still, even after granting these qualifications, it is fair to conclude that the reliability and validity of projective tests are lower than proponents of these tests expected.

3. Along with increased caution and skepticism regarding projective techniques, there has been an increase in the field's use of and reliance on alternative methods of assessment. Since the 1950s, clinical psychology has devoted an increasing amount of attention to behavioral assessment, structured personality testing, and cognitive assessment. Many new structured tests, as well as coding systems for making behavioral observations, have appeared in the literature over the past several decades.

4. Projective tests have remained popular among practicing clinicians, despite the increased emphasis on alternative methods and the negative evaluations of projectives.

Even psychologists who do not accept the psychodynamic assumptions underlying projective techniques can use them in several nontraditional ways. For example, a clinician might use a projective test as an "ice-breaker" to help establish rapport with an uncommunicative client, to observe client behavior in an ambiguous situation, or to conduct a semi-structured interview.

5. Because the reliability and validity of projective tests are often found to be lower than is desirable for useful tests, psychologists should exercise caution when using these techniques and use them in narrower and more conservative ways than they have been used in the past. Projective techniques should be employed in ways which have been supported by the research literature, and not in a global or all-encompassing fashion. They should be used to address specific issues for which they have been shown to be valid.

Goldfried et al. (1971) and Exner and Weiner (1982) are among the many advocates of projective tests who recommend that clinical psychologists should use these instruments conservatively, employing scoring systems with demonstrated reliability and making empirically validated interpretations.

Unfortunately, research evidence does not always show that psychologists use projective instruments in this way. For example, Exner and Exner (1972) surveyed clinical psychologists and found that, among all Rorschach users, approximately one in five does not score responses at all and that, among those who do score Rorschach responses, about four in five "personalize" the scoring. According to Exner and Exner, such diversity is of little use in developing a "better understanding of the reliability or validity of the Rorschach" (p. 408).

In summary, the status of projective tests has changed dramatically over the last several decades. Once the major tool in the clinical psychologist's armamentarium of assessment devices, projective tests were examined empirically and found to be lacking in the basic psychometric properties required of all useful tests. Following a period of severe criticism, which included predictions of the demise of projectives and their replacement with alternative methods, projective tests continue to be used today, albeit in more limited and less global ways than in the past.

References

Abt, L. E. (1950). A theory of projective psychology. In L. E. Abt & L. Bellak (Eds.), *Projective psychology: Clinical approaches to the total personality* (pp. 33–66). New York: Knopf.

Ainsworth, M. D. (1951). Some problems of validation of projective techniques. *British Journal of Medical Psychology, 24,* 151–161.

American Psychological Association. (1966). *Standards for educational and psychological tests and manuals.* Washington, DC: American Psychological Association.

Ames, L. B. (1970). Projecting the future of a projective technique. *Journal of Projective Techniques and Personality Assessment, 34,* 359–365.

Anderson, H. H. (1951). Human behavior and personality growth. In H. H. Anderson & G. L. Anderson (Eds.) *An introduction to projective techniques* (pp. 3–25). New York: Prentice-Hall.

Aronow, E., & Reznikoff, M. (1973). Attitudes toward the Rorschach test expressed in book reviews: A historical perspective. *Journal of Personality Assessment, 37,* 309–315.

Bell, J. E. (1948). *Projective techniques: A dynamic approach to the study of the personality.* New York: Longmans, Green.

Bellak, L. (1950). On the problems of the concept of projection. In L. E. Abt & L. Bellak (Eds.), *Projective psychology: Clinical approaches to the total personality* (pp. 7–32). New York: Knopf.

Blatt, S. J. (1975). The validity of projective techniques and their research and clinical contribution. *Journal of Personality Assessment, 39,* 327–343.

Brown, W., & McGuire, J. M. (1976). Current psychological assessment practices. *Professional Psychology, 7,* 475–484.

Buros, O. K. (1951). *The fourth mental measurements yearbook.* Highland Park, NJ: Gryphon Press.

Buros, O. K. (1970). *Personality tests and reviews.* Highland Park, NJ: Gryphon Press.

Buros, O. K. (1985). *The ninth mental measurements yearbook.* Highland Park, NJ: Gryphon Press.

Butler, J. M., & Fiske, D. W. (1955). Theory and techniques of assessment. *Annual Review of Psychology, 6,* 327–356.

Cattell, R. B. (1951). Principles of design in "projective" or misperception tests of personality. In H. H. Anderson & G. L. Anderson (Eds.), *An introduction to projective techniques* (pp. 55–98). New York: Prentice-Hall.

Crenshaw, D. A., Bohn, S., Hoffman, M. R., Matheus, J. M., & Offenbach, S. G. (1968). The use of projective methods in research: 1947–1965. *Journal of Projective Techniques and Personality Assessment, 32,* 3–9.

Cronbach, L. J. (1949). Statistical methods applied to Rorschach scores: A review. *Psychological Bulletin, 46,* 393–429.

Cronbach, L. J. (1956). Assessment of individual differences. *Annual Review of Psychology, 7,* 173–196.

Dana, R. H. (1972). Review of the TAT. In O. K. Buros (Ed.),*The seventh mental measurements yearbook* (pp. 457–460). Highland Park, NJ: Gryphon Press.

Ellis, A. (1952). Recent research with personality inventories. *Journal of Consulting Psychology, 17,* 45–49.

Exner, J. E. (1974). *The Rorschach: A comprehensive system.* New York: Wiley.

Exner, J. E. (1978). *The Rorschach: A comprehensive system (Vol. 2). Current research and advanced interpretation.* New York: Wiley.

Exner, J. E., & Exner, D. E. (1972). How clinicians use the Rorschach. *Journal of Personality Assessment, 36,* 403–408.

Exner, J. E., & Weiner, I. B. (1982). *The Rorschach: A comprehensive system (Vol. 3). Assessment of children and adolescents.* New York: Wiley.

Eysenck, H. J. (1952). *The scientific study of personality.* London: Routledge and Kegan Paul.

Eysenck, H. J. (1958). Personality tests: 1950–1955. In G. W. T. H. Fleming and A. Walk (Eds.), *Recent progress in psychiatry* (Vol. 3). (pp. 118–159). New York: Grove Press.

Frank, L. K. (1939). Projective methods for the study of personality. *Journal of Psychology, 8,* 389–409.

Frank, L. K. (1948). *Projective methods.* Springfield, IL: Charles C. Thomas.

Freud, S. (1962). On the grounds for detaching a particular syndrome from neurasthenia under the description "anxiety neurosis." In J. Strachey (Ed. and Trans.), *The standard edition of the complete psychological works of Sigmund Freud* (Vol. 3, pp. 90–115). London: Hogarth Press. (Original work published 1895)

Freud, S. (1962). Further remarks on the neuro-psychoses of defense. In J. Strachey (Ed. and Trans.), *The standard edition of the complete psychological works of Sigmund Freud* (Vol. 3, pp. 162–185). London: Hogarth Press. (Original work published 1896)

Goldfried, M. R., Stricker, G., & Weiner, I. B. (1971). *Rorschach handbook of clinical and research applications.* Englewood Cliffs, NJ: Prentice-Hall.

Harris, D. B. (1972). Review of the DAP. In O. K. Buros (Ed.), *The seventh mental measurements yearbook* (pp. 401–405). Highland Park, NJ: Gryphon Press.

Harrison, R. (1965). Thematic apperceptive methods. In B. B. Wolman (Ed.), *Handbook of clinical psychology* (pp. 562–620). New York: McGraw-Hill.

Hempel, C. G. (1966). *Philosophy of natural science.* Englewood Cliffs, NJ: Prentice-Hall.

Hertz, M. R. (1970). Projective techniques in crisis. *Journal of Projective Techniques and Personality Assessment, 34,* 449–467.

Hinkle, J. E., Nelson, S. E, & Miller, D. (1968). Psychological test usage by psychologist psychotherapists in private practice. *Psychotherapy: Theory, Research, and Practice, 5,* 210–213.

Holt, R. R. (1951). The Thematic Apperception Test. In H. H. Anderson & G. L. Anderson (Eds.), *An introduction to projective techniques* (pp. 181–229). New York: Prentice-Hall.

Holt, R. R. (1967). Diagnostic testing: Present status and future directions. *Journal of Nervous and Mental Disease, 144,* 444–465.

Holzberg, J. D. (1960). Reliability re-examined. In M. A. Rickers-Ovsiankina (Ed.), *Rorschach psychology* (pp. 361–379). New York: Wiley.

Jackson, C. W., & Wohl, J. (1966). A survey of Rorschach testing in the university. *Journal of Projective Techniques and Personality Assessment, 30,* 115–134.

Jensen, A. R. (1959). The reliability of projective techniques: Review of the literature. *Acta Psychologica, 16,* 108–136.

Karon, B. P. (1968). Problems of validities. In A. I. Rabin (Ed.), *Projective techniques in personality assessment: A modern introduction* (pp. 85–111). New York: Springer.

Kelly, E. L. (1954). Theory and techniques of assessment. *Annual Review of Psychology, 5,* 281–310.

Klopfer, W. G., & Taulbee, E. S. (1976). Projective tests. *Annual Review of Psychology, 27,* 543–567.

Korner, A. F. (1950). Theoretical considerations concerning the scope and limitations of projective techniques. *Journal of Abnormal and Social Psychology, 45,* 619–627.

Levy, S. (1950). Figure drawing as a projective test. In L. E. Abt & L. Bellak (Eds.), *Projective psychology: Clinical approaches to the total personality* (pp. 257–297). New York: Knopf.

Lindzey, G. (1952). Thematic Apperception Test: Interpretive assumptions and related empirical evidence. *Psychological Bulletin, 49,* 1–25.

Lindzey, G. (1959). On the classification of projective techniques. *Psychological Bulletin, 56,* 158–168.

Lindzey, G. (1961). *Projective techniques and cross-cultural research.* New York: Appleton-Century-Crofts.

Little, K. B. (1959). Problems in the validation of projective techniques. *Journal of Projective Techniques, 23,* 287–290.

Louttit, C. M., & Browne, C. G. (1947). The use of psychometric instruments in psychological clinics. *Journal of Consulting Psychology, 11,* 49–54.

Lubin, B., Larsen, R. M., & Matarazzo, J. D. (1984). Patterns of psychological test usage in the United States: 1935–1982. *American Psychologist, 39,* 451–454.

Lubin, B., Larsen, R. M., Matarazzo, J. D., & Seever, M. (1985). Psychological test usage patterns in five professional settings. *American Psychologist, 40,* 857–861.

Lubin, B., Wallis, R. R., & Paine, C. (1971). Patterns of psychological test usage in the United States: 1935–1969. *Professional Psychology, 2,* 70–74.

Macfarlane, J. W. (1942). Problems of validation inherent in projective techniques. *American Journal of Orthopsychiatry, 12,* 405–410.

Macfarlane, J. W., & Tuddenham, R. D. (1951). Problems in the validation of projective techniques. In H. H. Anderson & G. L. Anderson (Eds.), *An introduction to projective techniques* (pp. 26–54). New York: Prentice-Hall.

Machover, K. (1949). *Personality projection in the drawing of a human figure.* Springfield, IL: Charles C. Thomas.

McCully, R. S. (1965). Current attitudes about projective techniques in APA approved internship training centers. *Journal of Projective Techniques and Personality Assessment, 29,* 271–280.

McReynolds, P. (1968). *Advances in psychological assessment.* Palo Alto, CA: Science and Behavior Books.

Meehl, P. E. (1959). Structured and projective tests: Some common problems in validation. *Journal of Projective Techniques, 23,* 268-272.

Mills, D. H. (1965). The research use of projective techniques: A seventeen year survey. *Journal of Projective Techniques and Personality Assessment, 29,* 513–515.

Morgan, C. D., & Murray, H. A. (1935). A method for investigating fantasies: The thematic apperception test. *Archives of Neurology and Psychiatry, 34,* 289–306.

Murray, H. A. (1938). *Explorations in personality.* New York: Oxford University Press.

Murstein, B. I. (1961). Assumptions, adaptation level, and projective techniques. *Perceptual and Motor Skills, 12,* 107–125.

Murstein, B. I. (1963). *Theory and research in projective techniques: Emphasizing the TAT.* New York: Wiley.

Parker, K. (1983). A meta-analysis of the reliability and validity of the Rorschach. *Journal of Personality Assessment, 47*, 227–231.

Parker, K. C. H., Hanson, R. K., & Hunsley, J. (1988). MMPI, Rorschach, and WAIS: A meta-analytic comparison of reliability, stability, and validity. *Psychological Bulletin, 103*, 367–373.

Peterson, R. A. (1978). Review of the Rorschach. In O. K. Buros (Ed.), *The eighth mental measurements yearbook* (pp. 1042–1045). Highland Park, NJ: Gryphon Press.

Piotrowski, C., & Keller, J. W. (1978). Psychological test usage in Southeastern outpatient mental health facilities in 1975. *Professional Psychology, 9*, 63–67.

Piotrowski, C., & Keller, J. W. (1984a). Psychodiagnostic testing in APA-approved clinical psychology programs. *Professional Psychology: Research and Practice, 15*, 450–456.

Piotrowski, C., & Keller, J. W. (1984b). Attitudes toward clinical assessment by members of the AABT. *Psychological Reports, 55*, 831–838.

Piotrowski, C., & Keller, J. W. (1989). Psychological testing in outpatient mental health facilities: A national study. *Professional Psychology, 20*, 423–425.

Piotrowski, C., Sherry, D., & Keller, J. W. (1985). Psychodiagnostic test usage: A survey of the Society for Personality Assessment. *Journal of Personality Assessment, 44*, 115–119.

Piotrowski, Z. (1937). The reliability of Rorschach's Erlebnistypus. *Journal of Abnormal and Social Psychology, 32*, 439–445.

Piotrowski, Z. A. (1965). The Rorschach inkblot test. In B.B. Wolman (Ed.), *Handbook of clinical psychology* (pp. 522–561). New York: McGraw-Hill.

Popper, K. R. (1963). *Conjectures and refutations.* New York: Harper and Row.

Rabin, A. I. (1951). Validating and experimental studies with the Rorschach method. In H. H. Anderson & G. L. Anderson (Eds.), *An introduction to projective techniques* (pp. 123–146). New York: Prentice-Hall.

Rabin, A. I. (1968). Projective methods: An historical introduction. In A. I. Rabin (Ed.), *Projective techniques in personality assessment: A modern introduction* (pp. 3–17). New York: Springer.

Rapaport, D. (1942). Principles underlying projective techniques. *Character and Personality, 10*, 213–219.

Roback, H. B. (1968). Human figure drawings: Their utility in the clinical psychologist's armamentarium for personality assessment. *Psychological Bulletin, 70*, 1–19.

Rorschach, H. (1942). *Psychodiagnostics: A diagnostic test based on perception* (P. Lemkau & B. Kronenburg, Trans.). New York: Grune and Stratton. (Original work published 1921)

Rosenzweig, S. (1950). Idiodynamics in personality theory with special reference to projective methods. *Psychological Review, 58*, 213–223.

Rotter, J. B. (1953). Clinical methods: Psychodiagnostics. *Annual Review of Psychology, 4*, 295–316.

Rotter, J. B. (1954). *Social learning and clinical psychology.* New York: Prentice-Hall.

Rotter, J. B., & Rafferty, J. E. (1950). *Manual: The Rotter incomplete sentences blank.* New York: Psychological Corporation.

Sarason, S. B. (1954). *The clinical interaction: With special reference to the Rorschach.* New York: Harper.

Schofield, W. (1950a). Research trends in clinical psychology. *Journal of Clinical Psychology, 6,* 148–152.

Schofield, W. (1950b). Research in clinical psychology: 1949. *Journal of Clinical Psychology, 6,* 234–237.

Schofield, W. (1951). Research in clinical psychology: 1950. *Journal of Clinical Psychology, 7,* 215–221.

Schofield, W. (1952). Research in clinical psychology: 1951. *Journal of Clinical Psychology, 8,* 255–261.

Sell, J. M., & Torres-Henry, R. (1979). Testing practices in university and college counseling centers in the United States. *Professional Psychology, 10,* 774–779.

Shakespeare, W. (1959). *Hamlet.* In L. B. Wright (Ed.), *The Folger Library general reader's Shakespeare.* New York: Washington Square Press. (Original work published 1602)

Suinn, R. M., & Oskamp, S. (1969). *The predictive validity of projective measures: A fifteen-year evaluative review of the research.* Springfield, IL: Charles C. Thomas.

Sundberg, N. D. (1954). A note concerning the history of testing. *American Psychologist, 9,* 150–151.

Sundberg, N. D. (1961). The practice of psychological testing in clinical services in the United States. *American Psychologist, 16,* 79–83.

Swartz, J. D. (1978). Review of the TAT. In O. K. Buros (Ed.), *The eighth mental measurements handbook* (pp. 1127–1130). Highland Park, NJ: Gryphon Press.

Swensen, C. H. (1957). Empirical evaluations of human figure drawings. *Psychological Bulletin, 54,* 431–466.

Swensen, C. H. (1968). Empirical evaluations of human figure drawings: 1957–1966. *Psychological Bulletin, 70,* 20–44.

Symonds, P. M. (1949). *Adolescent fantasy: An investigation of the picture-story method of personality study.* New York: Columbia University Press.

Thelen, M. H., Varble, D. L., & Johnson, J. (1968). Attitudes of academic clinical psychologists toward projective techniques. *American Psychologist, 23,* 517–521.

Tomkins, S. S. (1947). *The thematic apperception test.* New York: Grune and Stratton.

Tomkins, S.S. (1949). The present status of the Thematic Apperception Test. *American Journal of Orthpsychiatry, 19,* 358–362.

Weiner, I. B. (1972). Does psychodiagnosis have a future? *Journal of Personality Assessment, 36,* 534–546.

Whipple, G. M. (1910). *Manual of mental and physical tests.* Baltimore: Warwick and York.

Windle, C. (1952). Psychological tests in psychopathological prognosis. *Psychological Bulletin, 49,* 451–482.

Wittenborn, J. R. (1957). The theory and technique of assessment. *Annual Review of Psychology, 8,* 331–356.

Zubin, J. (1954). Failures of the Rorschach technique. *Journal of Projective Techniques, 18,* 303–315.

Zubin, J., Eron, L. D., & Schumer, F. (1965). *An experimental approach to projective techniques.* New York: Wiley.

CHAPTER FIVE

The Reliability of Diagnosis

Introduction

The issue of the reliability of psychiatric diagnosis emerged as a significant challenge to clinical psychologists in the 1950s and exerted a strong influence on clinical research and practice in the succeeding decades. The issue remains vital today, with numerous ongoing research efforts devoted to the improvement of diagnostic reliability. This chapter will examine the concept of reliability, one of the criteria used to evaluate the usefulness of a classification system; review the history of the field's attention to the problem of diagnostic reliability; and introduce the current version of the diagnostic system used by the mental health profession.

It is interesting that, although psychologists have invested tremendous effort in attempting to improve diagnostic procedures, there have been significant challenges, even from within the field, to the very practice of diagnosis. Before reviewing efforts to evaluate and improve the reliability of diagnosis, it will be useful to consider the criticisms that have been raised against the practice of diagnosis. Responses to these criticisms will help illustrate the purposes of diagnosis.

Criticisms of Diagnosis

Two major criticisms have been directed against the practice of psychiatric diagnosis: (a) diagnostic labels can harm a client; and (b) diagnostic labels serve little purpose in the treatment of a client.

The first of these criticisms is largely associated with the humanistic school of psychology, which holds that all people are unique individuals (Allport, 1961). When one assigns a diagnostic label to a client, one ignores information concerning the unique aspects of the individual. A diagnostic label is, therefore, necessarily less accurate than an individualized description of a client.

In addition, humanistic psychology posits that any practice which limits an individual or which leads one to treat another as less than a unique individual is "dehumanizing" and, therefore, harmful. Thus, according to this school, diagnostic labels are not only less accurate than an individualized interpretation of the client, but they may also harm the client.

The harm caused by diagnostic labels has been alleged to come about in several ways. First, a diagnostic label may carry negative connotations. If members of the general public associate undesirable characteristics (such as "dangerous," "unable to hold a job," or "untrustworthy") with a particular label, then they may treat labeled individuals in a prejudicial fashion. Job opportunities, housing options, social relationships, and other important aspects of living may be adversely affected, either directly or indirectly, by the stigma of diagnostic labels. Goffman (1963), for example, has attempted to document the cost of such labels.

Another cost of labels is the perceptual bias they induce in others. A general principle that has been well documented in the areas of social, cognitive, and sensory psychology is that expectations influence perceptions (Myers, 1989). Expectations can also, unfortunately, influence the perceptions by clinical observers of one who has been labeled.

A classic study by Temerlin (1968) demonstrated this. Temerlin audiotaped an interview with an actor who presented himself in a somewhat anxious but otherwise normal manner. The interview was then presented to clinicians under different instructional sets. One group was informed that the individual was being interviewed for a job. Another group was told that this interview was with an interesting client who "looks neurotic but actually is quite psychotic." A third group heard the reverse suggestion. The clinicians then monitored the interview and assigned a diagnostic label to the interviewee.

Temerlin found that clinicians' expectations significantly affected their ratings of pathology and final diagnoses. Clinicians who had been told that the actor was psychotic assigned more severe diagnoses to him than did clinicians who had been told that this was an individual being interviewed for a job. Although no subject in the control conditions assigned a psychotic label to the target, 15 of 25 psychiatrists and 7 of 22 clinical psychologists assigned psychotic diagnoses to the individual who had been labeled psychotic.

A follow-up study by Temerlin and Trousdale (1969) showed that the same effect occurred in the judgments of student subjects. In general, both direct suggestion (labeling the interviewee as psychotic) and indirect suggestion (introducing the tape as an employment versus a clinical interview) significantly affected the judgments of clinicians and nonclinicians.

Another way in which a diagnostic label may harm an individual is that a label may persist after having outlived its usefulness. A diagnostic label may originally be accurate and helpful in understanding the nature and causes of and in developing a treatment program for a disorder. However, once the condition responds to treatment and the diagnostic label no longer fits the individual, the label may linger, continuing to carry the stigma associated with the label.

Rosenhan (1971) conducted a study which, among other interesting findings, demonstrated the tenacity of diagnostic labels. In this study, normal individuals presented themselves to psychiatric hospitals, reporting that they heard voices saying, "thud," "hollow," and "empty." Rosenhan found that these pseudopatients were invariably admitted to the hospitals, usually with the diagnosis of schizophrenia. Once in the hospital, the pseudopatients acted normally. They also kept records of their interactions with hospital staff and the nature of their treatment. For those individuals admitted with the diagnosis of schizophrenia, the discharge diagnosis was typically "schizophrenia, in remission." This label means that the diagnostician continued to think that the pseudopatient had the condition of schizophrenia, although the individual was symptom-free at the present. Thus, the initial label persisted, despite the hospital staff's observation of, on average, about three weeks of nonschizophrenic behavior.

A final way in which diagnoses have been alleged to harm the labeled individual is through a "self-fulfilling prophecy." Scheff (1966, 1974) has argued that the patient label leads people to expect certain behaviors from the patient. According to Scheff, people will reinforce the patient for label-consistent behaviors and punish the patient for label-inconsistent behaviors. In this way, patient behaviors are maintained by the responses of others. Scheff argued that, even if the label was initially incorrect, such treatment may actually elicit patient-like behavior from the labeled individual. In this way, the diagnostic label, even though initially inaccurate, becomes accurate over time.

Rosenthal (1966) has summarized the results of many research efforts which support the claim that self-fulfilling effects occur in a variety of experimental contexts. Although Barber (1976) and others have criticized this research, it is still important to recognize that the self-fulfilling effect in the context of diagnostic labeling is possible. People may selectively reinforce patients in such a way as to exaggerate, maintain, and even produce patient-like behaviors.

The second major criticism of psychiatric diagnosis is the claim that it serves little purpose in determining the treatment of a client. Representatives of the major schools of psychology—psychoanalysis, humanism, and behaviorism—have argued that diagnoses are not useful because they do not specify which treatment should be provided. For example, psychoanalysts have argued that psychiatric labels do not sufficiently characterize a patient's personality dynamics and so are not useful in developing psychoanalytically oriented treatments. Noyes (1953) presented this position, noting that "a classificatory diagnosis is less important than a psychodynamic study of the personality" and that psychiatry "should be interested in processes, not labels" (p. 159).

Humanists agreed. Rogers (1951), for example, argued against the use of psychiatric labels because they were not helpful in identifying specific treatments—clients would be treated similarly regardless of their diagnosis—and so did not provide sufficient benefits to offset their dehumanizing effects. Hence, Rogers thought that psychiatric diagnosis was unnecessary.

The criticism that psychiatric diagnosis does not serve a useful purpose was made perhaps most strongly by representatives of the behavioral school. Behaviorists have traditionally attended to the empirical validation of their claims more than have either humanists or psychoanalysts. Thus, behaviorists questioned the utility of psychiatric diagnoses on empirical grounds.

Yates (1970) presented the behavioral position when he wrote that "with but a few exceptions, the search for a diagnostic label is completely futile (since it has no etiological or treatment implications) except for research purposes . . ." (p. 7). According to the behaviorists, because diagnoses had not been demonstrated to be significantly related to specific treatments, the scientific value of diagnoses had not yet been established.

This second criticism of psychiatric diagnosis addressed the practical limitation that diagnoses may not be helpful in selecting a patient's treatment. Thus, this criticism assumes that one function of diagnosis is to assist in identifying effective treatments for clients. To respond to this, as well as the first criticism identified above, it will be helpful to consider the functions of diagnosis.

Functions of Diagnosis

Diagnosis plays the same role in psychopathology as does classification in any science (Woodruff, Goodwin, & Guze, 1974). Diagnosis enables the diagnostician both to communicate with other professionals and to make predictions about the associated and future characteristics of the clients (Woodruff et al., 1974). More specifically, diagnosis conveys information and permits professionals to make predictions about the client's symptomatology, etiology, pathophysiology, treatment, and prognosis (Spitzer, Sheehy, & Endicott, 1977).

Psychiatric labels, therefore, provide a common vocabulary of descriptive labels—a diagnostic nomenclature. Professionals benefit from the availability of a diagnostic nomenclature in that they are able to communicate clearly and concisely. Instead of having to describe every symptom of every client, a psychologist need only use a diagnostic label and others will quickly understand a large amount of information concerning the client.

In addition, a diagnosis enables professionals to make predictions about a client, thereby enabling them to consider possible etiological factors; to examine possible pathophysiological models; to select appropriate treatments; and to anticipate prognoses. Without the use of such diagnostic labels, psychologists would not be able to rely on the accumulated wisdom of the field's clinical and research experience, and would have to "reinvent" psychology for each and every client.

When evaluating psychiatric diagnoses, one must consider both their costs and their benefits. The criticism that diagnostic labels may harm a client must be weighed against their potential benefit to the client. A label may carry a stigma, persist past its usefulness, influence others to interpret the client's behaviors in a way consistent with the label, and even lead others to treat the client in such a way as to elicit abnormal behavior from him. However, the label may also help a clinician to identify the initial cause of the condition, to understand the current processes that maintain the disorder, and to select the most effective treatment for the condition. When evaluating diagnosis in this way, many clinicians recognize that the potential benefits of diagnoses outweigh their risks.

Of course, this does not eliminate the possible risks of labels. The diagnostician should use diagnoses in such a way as to minimize their potential risks. Clinicians should use labels in such a way as to avoid dehumanizing clients. They should base their diagnoses on objective evidence in order to minimize the potential of subjective perceptual bias. They should periodically reconsider diagnostic decisions to determine whether they remain accurate. They should communicate the labels to clients and to the general public in such a way as to minimize the possibility of a social stigma associated with lack of education about or misunderstanding of the nature of the condition.

Standards for Evaluating the Utility of Diagnoses

Before moving on to a review of research on the utility of psychiatric diagnoses, it will be necessary to consider briefly the criteria which are used to evaluate any classification system.

Validity

Classification and measurement are basic operations in science. Simpson (1961), a zoologist, discussed the role of classification in science. According to Simpson, the study of classification has three primary areas: Taxonomy (the theoretical study of classification), Classification (the process of forming groups), and Identification (the method of assigning subjects to categories).

A science will only be able to advance after it has achieved substantial progress in classification. The science must develop a classification system that has distinctions that are both real and important; that is, the distinctions between categories must be empirically demonstrable and associated with other variables pertinent to the science. Assignment of objects to categories will enable the scientist to make accurate statements about the associated characteristics and predictions about the future conditions of the object. This is referred to as the *validity* of the classification system.

Diagnosis in psychopathology is analogous to classification in other sciences. A valid diagnostic system makes distinctions between patients that are both real and important. The system includes diagnostic categories demonstrably distinct from one another (that is, patients in these categories actually differ from one another on a variety of empirical variables). The diagnostic categories in the system also differ from one another along dimensions that are important for the field of psychopathology. For example, patients with different diagnostic labels must actually differ on "meaningful" dimensions (such as causal factors, effective treatments, psychological or physiological correlates, and so on) and not on dimensions which are of little relevance (such as astrological sign or skin color).

Reliability

In addition to validity, a useful classification system must also be *reliable*. That is, the methods used to classify objects must be developed to the degree that substantial agreement will be achieved by different observers. No matter how real the distinctions of a classification system are, if scientists cannot achieve a high degree of agreement when using it, then the system will not be useful. In fact, if the system has insufficient reliability, it cannot be shown to possess validity.

Psychological tests and measurements have three important types of reliability. The first is interrater reliability, or the degree to which two judges who assess a subject simultaneously (or who are presented with the same information concerning the subject) arrive at a common assessment of the individual. When discussing psychiatric diagnosis, this type of reliability is crucial. A diagnostic system must demonstrate interrater reliability in order to be useful. If two or more diagnosticians cannot consistently agree on a common diagnosis, then it will be difficult to conduct research that may identify the causes, correlates, or effective treatments of a disorder.

A second important type of reliability is the degree to which assessments of an individual on two or more occasions are in agreement. This has been termed *test-retest reliability*. This type of reliability is also important in a discussion of psychiatric diagnosis. It is quite common for patients to be diagnosed at different times—during different episodes of a disorder or at different stages of a single episode. In order for the diagnostic system to be useful, a patient's condition must be recognized consistently across time.

It should be noted that test-retest reliability may be somewhat less critical for psychiatric diagnoses than interrater reliability. After all, it is possible that inconsistent diagnoses across time are due to actual changes in the patient's condition. It is possible that a patient may actually exhibit different disorders on different occasions. Hence, test-retest unreliability of diagnoses must be evaluated in the light of both the interval between diagnostic occasions (the greater the interval, the more likely that the patient's condition actually changed), the persistence of the disorder in question (some disorders such as schizophrenia and personality disorders have a chronic course whereas others such as adjustment disorders have a time-limited course), and other factors that may be related to the duration of the patient's disorder (for example, many behavior disorders in children have a relatively brief course, possibly due to maturational effects).

A third type of reliability is the degree to which subsections of a psychological test agree with one another—internal consistency. This type of reliability, however, is more important in psychological testing than in psychiatric diagnosis, and so will not be discussed further in this chapter.

The Relationship between Reliability and Validity

It is an old adage in test and measurement theory that reliability is a prerequisite for validity—that the reliability of a test or classification system places an upper limit on the validity that can be achieved with the test. It is easy to see how this principle applies to a psychiatric diagnostic system.

Suppose, for example, there are two equally prevalent mental disorders called X and Y. Suppose further that conditions X and Y each have a single necessary and sufficient cause, factors A and B, respectively, which can be assessed with perfect reliability. Finally, suppose that the differential diagnosis of conditions X and Y is not completely reliable, with any diagnostician agreeing with the "True" diagnosis on 80 percent of the cases of each disorder, but disagreeing on the other 20 percent of the cases. The measure of the reliability for this example is .60 [(.80 x .80) – (.20 x .20)].

Now assume that a researcher conducts a study of the relationship between disorders X and Y and causal factors A and B, using a single diagnostician to identify the disorders. Because factors A and B are necessary and sufficient causes of the disorders, the observed relationship between factors A and B and disorders X and Y will also have a correlation coefficient of .60. Because this correlation concerns the relationship between a disorder and a cause, it can be regarded as a validity coefficient. The reliability coefficient of .60 places a ceiling of .60 on validity coefficients which are measured in studies conducted under similar circumstances (e.g., base rates, diagnostic procedures, and so on).

In reality, psychiatric disorders may not each have a single necessary and sufficient cause. Instead, they may have causes which are necessary but not sufficient, or vice versa. They may have causes in common or multiple causes that interact in complex ways. In addition, the reliability of the measurement of causal factors may not be perfect. Thus, when conducting actual reliability and validity studies, one should expect to observe a decrease from obtained reliability coefficients to the validity coefficients.

Early Studies of Diagnostic Reliability

As discussed throughout this book, clinical psychologists began to subject their theories and practices to intensive empirical examination in the mid-1900s. Just as the field began to determine empirically the effectiveness of psychotherapy and the reliability and validity of projective test results, so did it begin to assess the reliability of its diagnostic systems. By the 1950s, clinical psychologists recognized that the reliability of a label established limits on the validity of any claims that could be made about a disorder. If a condition could not be assessed reliably, than the validity of claims concerning the relationships between that condition and other variables— including causes, effective treatments, and associated features—could not be established.

One of the first to draw attention to the importance of a reliable diagnostic system was E. B. Wilson. In a paper delivered in 1927 before the American Psychiatric Association, Wilson (cited in Doering & Raymond, 1934) advocated the improvement of psychiatric definitions, measuring techniques, and classification systems so that there would be closer agreement between observers. He also distinguished between and recognized the importance of both interrater and test-retest reliability for psychiatric assessments.

Although Wilson emphasized the importance of a reliable diagnostic system in 1927, empirical investigations of diagnostic reliability did not appear for some time. One of the earliest efforts to determine the reliability of psychiatric assessments was that of Doering and Raymond (1934). They examined both test-retest and interrater reliability for a variety of psychological characteristics (e.g., personality traits, somatic etiology). Although Doering and Raymond did not assess reliability for diagnostic categories, they reported that the pooled observations of a group of judges could be used with as much confidence as the observations of any one judge. This work is notable in that it may be the first systematic effort to measure the reliability of psychiatric assessments.

Another early study was conducted by Elkin (1947). Elkin examined the agreement between the interpretations made by 39 social scientists of a life-history document. Although Elkin's analysis of the results was qualitative rather than quantitative and so cannot be compared directly to later studies of diagnostic reliability, it is interesting that he concluded that there was "little consensus among the analysts in their judgments and interpretations" of the material (p. 109).

These initial investigations were soon followed by better designed and more systematic studies. The early studies of the reliability of psychiatric diagnosis employed three methodologies. One method was to compare the frequency with which diagnostic labels were employed across patient groups. If the patient groups could be assumed to be similar, then a demonstration that diagnosticians employed diagnostic categories with different frequencies across groups could be used to support the claim that the diagnosticians differed in how they employed the diagnostic system— an indirect test of diagnostic reliability.

Another method had patients assessed by different diagnosticians. This method permits the investigator to determine the degree of agreement between the diagnosticians—interrater reliability.

A third method was to determine the degree of agreement between diagnoses assigned to the same patient at different times—test-retest reliability.

Frequency of Use of Diagnostic Categories

One of the earliest empirical studies of diagnostic reliability was that of Boisen (1938). Boisen compared the relative proportions of schizophrenic subtypes across the state mental hospitals of three states (Illinois, Massachusetts, and New York) and across eight mental hospitals in a single state (Illinois). Boisen reported extremely wide variation both across states and across hospitals within a single state. For example, the proportion of hebephrenic schizophrenics ranged from 15.5 to 45 percent across states and from 11 to 76 percent across hospitals within a single state. Because it is not likely that the actual frequencies of schizophrenic subtypes vary so widely across states or regions within a state, these results were interpreted by Boisen as evidence of the "inadequacy of our present system of classification" (p. 235).

Similar studies were conducted by others. For example, Mehlman (1952) compared the frequencies of use by psychiatrists of broad diagnostic distinctions (organic versus psychogenic; manic-depressive versus schizophrenic) for 1,879 male and 2,157 female inpatients. For both diagnostic distinctions in both sexes, Mehlman found that individual psychiatrists differed significantly in the frequencies with which they employed each label. This result is consistent with that of Boisen (1938) and is especially significant because all the diagnosticians and patients in this study were at a single mental hospital.

Another similar result was reported by Pasamanick, Dinitz, and Lefton (1959). They examined the diagnoses assigned to 538 consecutively admitted female patients to three wards of a mental hospital, comparing the frequencies of diagnoses across three wards (one of which had three different administrators during the course of the study). They found that, despite the fact that patients assigned to different wards exhibited no demographic differences, there was a statistically significant difference in the frequencies with which diagnoses were used across wards. For example, the diagnosis of schizophrenia ranged from 23 to 36 percent of the patients across wards. In addition, Pasamanick et al. found that the frequencies of use of diagnostic labels were significantly different within a single ward across the periods during which the ward was administered by different psychiatrists. For example, the diagnosis of schizophrenia varied from 22 to 67 percent of the patients in the ward, across the three ward administrators.

A later study by Wilson and Meyer (1962) found somewhat more positive results. They examined the frequencies of use of seven diagnostic categories assigned to 128 patients on four wards of a mental hospital with those assigned to 166 patients in the same hospital during the following year. In this study, the diagnoses assigned to patients in the second year were made by a psychiatrist who was unaware of the distribution of the diagnoses in the previous year. Wilson and Meyer found a high degree of agreement between the distributions of diagnoses across the two groups of patients and they concluded that this was evidence of the existence of the disorders in the classification system and for the consistency of diagnosis.

An important series of studies, conducted in the late 1960s, demonstrated that there were substantial inconsistencies in the ways that American and British psychiatrists diagnosed mental disorders. Sandifer, Hordern, Timbury, and Green (1968) filmed diagnostic interviews with 30 patients and later showed these films to groups of psychiatrists in North Carolina, London, and Glasgow. They found that cross-national differences exceeded within-national differences in diagnosis, with the greatest cross-national differences occurring in the following ways: North Carolina diagnosticians used the label *neurotic*, Glasgow psychiatrists employed the label *personality disorder*, and both groups of British psychiatrists used the label *manic-depressive* more than did the others.

Katz, Cole, and Lowery (1969) showed a videotape of a female patient to 42 American and 32 English psychiatrists. They found that the American psychiatrists were about evenly divided in labeling the subject schizophrenic, neurotic, or personality disordered, whereas a majority of the English psychiatrists labeled her as having a personality disorder, and none of the English psychiatrists called her schizophrenic.

Kendall, Cooper, Gourlay, and Copeland (1971) showed tapes of diagnostic interviews with eight patients to groups of American and British psychiatrists. They found a substantial disagreement between the two groups of diagnosticians, primarily due to the American psychiatrists overusing the label of schizophrenia. They concluded that "the concept of schizophrenia held on the east coast of the United States now embraces what in Britain would be regarded as depressive illness but also substantial parts of several other diagnostic categories—manic illness, neurotic illness and personality disorder" (p. 129).

These studies, then, demonstrated that the frequencies of diagnosis differ significantly across countries, across states, across hospitals within a single state, across wards in a single hospital, across time within a single ward, and across psychiatrists in a single hospital. Because the sample sizes of many of these studies were large and because it is difficult to explain why there should be actual differences between patient populations across the groups that were compared, these studies supported the claim that the diagnostic system was being used differently across diagnosticians. In this way, these studies are evidence of poor diagnostic reliability.

Test-Retest Reliability

Another type of study designed to assess diagnostic reliability examined the test-retest reliability of psychiatric diagnosis. An early example of this kind of study is Masserman and Carmichael (1938). They evaluated 114 inpatients one year after their discharge from a hospital and reported a marked change in 41 patients' symptoms and classification. Similarly, the specification of the subclass of schizophrenia changed for 12 of 18 cases. In other words, diagnostic test-retest reliability over a one-year period was low. Although the cause for the low reliability may have been actual changes in the conditions of the patients, Masserman and Carmichael concluded that the "original diagnostic groupings of our patients as made by our psychiatric staff had been in gross error in many cases, or that the nosological concepts that had been used were themselves of little prognostic, therapeutic or heuristic value" (p. 928).

Goldfarb (1959) selected case records of 100 veterans who had been assessed by one of four psychologists for service-connected psychiatric disabilities. He then presented these cases (modified so that judges could not determine the patient's or the initial evaluator's identity) to the psychologists to be assigned to one of five broad diagnostic categories. Goldfarb found, on average, only 60 percent agreement between judges' initial and subsequent evaluations. When the psychologists assessed all cases two weeks later, there was, once again, only a 60 percent average rate of intra-rater reliability.

Interrater Reliability

Most early studies of diagnostic reliability attempted to determine the interrater reliability of diagnostic labels. Ash (1949) conducted what may have been the first effort to measure interrater reliability for diagnostic labels. (Eysenck reported that, early in his career, he suggested that the interrater reliability psychiatric diagnosis be assessed in his hospital [1972]. This suggestion met with both shock and resistance, and so he did not publicly pursue the project.) Ash had 52 White male patients evaluated by either two or three psychiatrists (all three attended a joint interview with the client and either two or three conducted a physical examination of the client) who assigned diagnoses independently. For major categories (such as mental deficiency, psychosis, neurosis, psychopathic personality, and predominant personality characteristics), Ash found that all three psychiatrists agreed in 45.7 percent of the cases and that two of the three agreed on from 57.9 to 67.4 percent of the cases. For 60 specific categories within the major categories, all three psychiatrists agreed on 20 percent of the cases and two of the three agreed on from 31.4 to 43.5 percent of the cases.

Seeman (1953) examined the degree to which 56 medical students, following a series of lectures on descriptive psychiatry, agreed on the diagnoses of six patients with known conditions. Seeman found that 223 of the 336 diagnoses were correct, supporting not only the reliability or agreement of the diagnoses but also the validity (or accuracy) of the diagnoses.

Hunt, Wittson, and Hunt (1953) compared the agreement on diagnosis of 794 naval personnel who were evaluated for their suitability for the service both at a precommissioning installation and at a naval hospital. They reported that there was 54 percent agreement on broad diagnostic categories (psychosis, neurosis, and personality disorder) and 32 percent agreement on specific diagnoses within these categories.

Foulds (1955) had 18 consecutively admitted patients to a psychiatric hospital evaluated by two psychiatrists who assigned labels from a list of seven categories with 11 subcategories. Foulds constructed a scale to assess the similarity of any two diagnostic labels from these lists. Foulds reported that the two diagnosticians agreed with one another substantially more than would be expected by chance alone, thereby supporting the interrater reliability of this diagnostic system.

Schmidt and Fonda (1956) examined the agreement between the diagnoses assigned to 426 patients in the first and third weeks of their stay in a state mental hospital. Using broad diagnostic categories (organic, psychotic, personality disorder), they found 84 percent agreement. For 91 specific diagnoses within these categories, they found 55 percent agreement, with agreement varying according to the diagnosis from 6 percent to 80 percent (with agreement nearly absent in cases involving personality and neurotic disorders).

Goldfarb (1959) reported the interrater reliability of four psychologists who assigned 100 veterans to five broad diagnostic categories on the basis of a review of case records. He reported an average rate of agreement of only 60 percent between any two diagnosticians.

Norris (1959) compared the diagnoses of 6,263 patients seen first during a brief stay in an observation unit and then a few weeks later at a mental hospital. She found a 60 percent agreement rate for diagnoses, which varied across categories from an 80 percent agreement rate for organic psychoses through a 54 percent agreement rate for neuroses to a 43 percent agreement rate for character and behavior disorders.

Kreitman, Sainsbury, Morrissey, Towers, and Scrivener (1961) had two psychiatrists evaluate within one week of each other 90 consecutive referrals to a psychiatric service. Each judge assigned only a single label from a list of 11 possible disorders to a patient. They found 63 percent agreement on the diagnosis, with low agreement (28 percent) for neurotic conditions and high agreement for organic (75 percent) and psychotic (61 percent) conditions. Kreitman et al. also found good interrater agreement on other aspects of the patient's condition, such as the duration, family history, previous episodes, symptoms, and recommended treatment of the condition.

Beck, Ward, Mendelson, Mock, and Erbaugh (1962) had two psychiatrists diagnose 153 outpatients within a short interval. They found a 70 percent agreement rate on general categories (psychosis, neurosis, character disorder) and a 54 percent agreement rate on specific diagnoses.

Sandifer, Pettus, and Quade (1964) had ten psychiatrists attend a diagnostic session with each of 91 inpatients. They found that nine or ten out of ten diagnosticians agreed on 30 of the 91 cases, that from six to eight out of ten agreed on 32 of the cases, and that from three to five agreed on the remaining 29 cases. They calculated an overall agreement rate of 57 percent, which varied across categories, ranging from 74 percent agreement on schizophrenia through 56 percent agreement on neurosis to 13 percent agreement on paranoid disorder.

These early studies on the interrater reliability of psychiatric diagnosis, although not entirely consistent in their findings, do exhibit several patterns:

1. Diagnostic reliability is higher for general or broad categories (such as neurosis, psychosis, personality disorder) than for specific labels within categories (e.g., schizophrenia versus manic-depression; depressive neurosis versus anxiety neurosis).
2. Diagnostic reliability is lower for the categories of neurosis and personality disorders than for other categories (psychosis, organic, mental deficiency).
3. Despite occasional findings that interrater reliability is high, there are sufficient negative findings to support the position that diagnostic reliability is only tentative, and that further work needs to be done to increase the reliability of psychiatric diagnosis.

Reviews of Early Studies of Diagnostic Reliability

Two early reviews (Beck, 1962; Kreitman, 1961) of this research agreed that, despite the positive findings reported in the literature, additional research was needed so as to improve the reliability of psychiatric diagnosis. Kreitman identified the variables that may influence diagnostic reliability and recommended a systematic analysis of them. The variables he identified as being related to diagnostic reliability include: (a) variables related to the psychiatrist (such as training, experience, theoretical orientation); (b) variables related to the examination (such as the setting, purpose, and methods of the examination); (c) variables related to the nomenclature (such as the system of classification employed); (d) variables related to the patient (such as diagnosis, severity, socioeconomic status [SES]); and (e) manner of analysis (the statistical method used to determine agreement).

In addition, Beck (1962) identified the methodological flaws in the studies conducted to date and recommended improved designs for future reliability studies. According to Beck, the following methodological problems limited these early studies:

1. Several studies employed a small sample size (Ash, 1949; Foulds, 1955; Seeman, 1953), thereby limiting the power and generalizability of the results.

2. Several studies employed diagnosticians with varying degrees of training or experience (Schmidt & Fonda, 1956; Seeman, 1953), lowering the expected degree of agreement between clinicians and limiting the generalizability of the results to the population of experienced diagnosticians.

3. Several studies examined the agreement between diagnoses made under vastly different conditions (including the amount of information available about a patient), thereby limiting the degree to which one can expect the diagnoses to be consistent. For example, the second diagnostician in the Norris (1959) study may have been aware of and influenced by the initial diagnosis. The initial diagnosis in the Hunt et al. (1953) study was made by examining clinical records and not by a direct examination of the patient, which was included in the follow-up diagnosis.

4. The diagnostic systems employed were not consistent across studies.

5. The method of measuring interrater agreement was not consistent across studies. For example, Foulds (1955) developed a scale for determining the similarity between two diagnoses. This scale was developed expressly for use in this study and so had no prior demonstrations of either reliability or validity.

6. In some studies, administrative purposes may have influenced the diagnostic process. For example, patients in the Hunt et al. (1953) study were being evaluated for the purpose of determining their suitability for continued military service. In this situation, it is possible that the results of the diagnostic evaluation were influenced by this administrative goal.

7. The interval between evaluations was not consistent. For example, the interval between the initial and follow-up evaluations in the Hunt et al. (1953) study was unspecified and so may have been inconsistent across patients. In some studies (e.g., Ash, 1949; Beck et al., 1962; Sandifer et al., 1964), the diagnosticians made their assessments simultaneously or nearly simultaneously. In other studies (e.g., Hunt et al., 1953; Norris, 1959; Schmidt & Fonda, 1956), there was an interval of at least one week between evaluations. Thus, this latter group of studies should be expected to find lower interrater reliability than the first group, because it is possible that the condition of the patient underwent at least some change in the test-retest interval.

Beck (1962) recommended that further studies of diagnostic reliability follow these guidelines: (a) they should employ the most recent version of the standard nomenclature; (b) the diagnosticians should have sufficient and comparable training and experience; (c) the conditions for assessing the patient should be uniform; (d) the time interval between evaluations should be brief and held constant; (e) the diagnostic process should be independent of administrative considerations.

Zubin (1967) published another important review of the research to date on the reliability of diagnosis. Zubin classified the research according to the type of reliability examined (test-retest, interrater, and frequency of use of diagnoses) and concluded that none of these approaches had successfully demonstrated the reliability of diagnosis. As a result of the many investigations with negative or inconsistent results, Zubin remarked that "there is widespread dissatisfaction with current diagnostic procedures" (p. 394).

Another major work from this period was the review of Spitzer and Fliess (1974). Spitzer, Cohen, Fliess, and Endicott (1967) had previously identified what had been perhaps the major methodological weakness of the early studies of diagnostic reliability—inconsistent and inadequate statistical methods used to estimate the degree of interrater agreement. Both Kreitman (1961) and Beck (1962), in their reviews of this literature, had identified as a major problem the different measures of agreement employed by researchers across the studies. For example, some employed a measure of overall agreement (the number of diagnoses in agreement with one another divided by the total number of diagnoses made). Others used the proportion of specific agreement for a disorder (defined as the proportion of cases agreed upon, ignoring all cases which both diagnosticians agree do not have the disorder).

Although these measures appeal to common sense and are relatively simple to calculate, they ignore the possibility of two diagnosticians agreeing with one another for some cases on the basis of chance alone. This is especially a problem when, as in the study by Ash (1949), the base rates of the various disorders in the sample are not of comparable magnitudes. It is desirable to have a measure of the degree of interobserver agreement that takes into account, not simply the number of agreements, but the number of agreements higher than the expected number of agreements on the basis of chance alone.

The Kappa Coefficient

Cohen (1960) introduced the Kappa coefficient (K) for exactly this purpose. This coefficient can be interpreted as the percent of observed agreements greater than the chance level, divided by the number of possible nonchance agreements.

An example will illustrate the differences among the different methods of measuring interobserver agreement. Suppose two observers each diagnose 100 patients and assign them to one of two diagnostic categories as presented in Figure 5-1.

It is easy to see from this example that, even though the overall rate of agreement is relatively high (.70) and the rate of specific agreement is high for Disorder B (.77), the K coefficient is low (.35). Because both diagnosticians identify the majority of patients as having Disorder B, there is a relatively high rate of agreement expected on the basis of chance alone.

Spitzer and Fliess (1974) reanalyzed the data from six of the early studies of the interrater reliability of psychiatric diagnosis, using K as the measure of agreement. In this way, they determined the rate of interrater agreement while eliminating the influence of chance agreements. Spitzer and Fliess found that the mean K coefficient across studies for major diagnostic categories ranged from a high of .77 (organic brain syndrome) to a low of .32 (personality disorders). Other mean K coefficients for major diagnostic categories were calculated as follows: schizophrenia (.57), affective disorder (.41), neurosis (.40), psychophysiological disorder (.38), and mental deficiency (.72).

Spitzer and Fliess concluded that: (a) there is no diagnostic category for which diagnostic reliability is uniformly high across studies; (b)

FIGURE 5–1 • *Differences among Three Measures of Interrater Agreement*

		Observer 1 Diagnoses		
		A	B	Totals
Observer 2 Diagnoses	A	20	10	30
	B	20	50	70
	Totals	40	60	100

Rate of Overall Agreement: $(20 + 50)/100 = .70$
Rate of Specific Agreement:
  Diagnosis A: $20/[.5 (30 + 40)] = .56$
  Diagnosis B: $50/[.5 (70 + 60)] = .77$
Chance Agreement: $[(30 \times 40) + (70 \times 60)]/100 = 54$
K = (Observed Agreement – Chance Agreement)/(Possible Nonchance Agreement)
  $= (70 - 54)/(100 - 54) = .35$

diagnostic reliability is satisfactory only for mental deficiency, organic brain syndrome, and alcoholism; (c) diagnostic reliability is fair for both psychosis and schizophrenia; and (d) diagnostic reliability is poor for the rest of the diagnostic categories.

Following the review of Spitzer and Fliess (1974), K coefficients have been routinely reported as a measure of the interrater reliability of diagnostic categories. However, several criticisms of the K coefficient have been published. Maxwell (1977) and Carey and Gottesman (1978) noted that the K coefficient assumes that error (mislabeling Disorder X as Y, and vice versa) is completely random when, in actual practice, it may well be the case that one kind of error is more likely than the other. For this reason, Maxwell (1977) and Janes (1979) argued for the use of a random error coefficient, rather than K, as a measure of interrater reliability.

Carey and Gottesman (1978) and McGorry, Copolov, and Singh (1989) also noted that it is possible to place too much emphasis on diagnostic reliability at the expense of validity. Although reliability is demonstrated prior to validity, reliability is sought so that validity can be established. If one focuses strictly on the reliability of a diagnostic system and ignores the contexts in which its validity will be examined, then one is misusing the criterion of reliability.

For example, when investigating a diagnostic system, one must make sure that reliability is established in the same population and using the same procedures that will be used in subsequent studies of diagnostic validity. If the frequency of a disorder varies between reliability and validity studies, because of differences in the populations studied or procedures employed, then one can encounter interesting paradoxes.

Carey and Gottesman (1978) presented examples of several such situations. By varying the frequencies of disorders from reliability to validity studies, Carey and Gottesman demonstrated that: (a) validity can exceed reliability; (b) higher reliability for one diagnostic system over another does not guarantee higher validity for that system; and (c) higher reliability for one diagnostic system over another in one population does not ensure higher reliability for that system in another population.

The conclusion drawn from these examples is clear: reliability is not an end in itself, but must be considered as a means of establishing validity. When investigating diagnostic reliability, one must ensure that the procedures employed and the populations studied are comparable to those in the subsequent studies of the validity of the diagnostic system. If studies of reliability have poor generalizability, then a demonstration of reliability provides little real progress, but may create the "false impression of advances in solving problems of nomenclature and taxonomy" (Carey & Gottesman, 1978, p. 1459).

Efforts to Develop More Reliable
Diagnostic Systems

Following these early demonstrations of the unreliability of psychiatric diagnosis, the field recognized the necessity of developing a diagnostic system with demonstrable reliability. "One of the reasons that diagnostic classification has fallen into disrepute among some psychiatrists is that diagnostic schemes have been largely based upon a priori principles rather than upon systematic studies" (Robins & Guze, 1970, p. 107).

Ward, Beck, Mendelson, Mock, and Erbaugh (1962) suggested that a major influence on diagnostic unreliability was the diagnostic system itself. They followed up the diagnostic reliability study of Beck et al. (1962) by asking psychiatrists to identify the causes of diagnostic disagreements. Ward et al. found that the majority of the diagnostic disagreements (62.5 percent) were attributed to inadequacies of the nosological system rather than to inconsistencies on the part of the patient (5 percent) or errors or inconsistencies by the diagnosticians (32.5 percent). Although there may well have been a self-serving bias on the part of these psychiatrists to attribute diagnostic unreliability to something other than their own actions (e.g., Blashfield, 1984), this study helped to focus attention on the inadequacy of the existing diagnostic system.

Mental health professionals soon acknowledged the need for a more detailed, objective, and reliable diagnostic system. Clinical psychologists recognized that reliability was an essential prerequisite for the establishment of valid statements concerning the cause, prognosis, and response to treatment of mental disorders. Zubin, Salzinger, Fleiss, Gurland, Spitzer, Endicott, and Sutton (1975) summed up the position of clinical psychologists quite well: "[In DSM-II] diagnostic stereotypes are described under each category. The task of the diagnostician then becomes one of selecting the diagnostic category in which the stereotype most closely resembles the characteristics of the patient being diagnosed. In addition, the standard nomenclature includes many categories for which there is little validity . . ." (pp. 645–646).

The 1970s saw an increase in the number of studies devoted to developing new diagnostic criteria that would enable mental health professionals to diagnose mental disorders with high reliability. The most notable developments in this regard are the Research Diagnostic Criteria (RDC) of Feighner, Robins, Guze, Woodruff, Winokur, and Munoz (1972), and the revisions of the RDC by Spitzer, Endicott, and Robins (1978).

Research Diagnostic Criteria

Feighner et al. (1972) established diagnostic criteria for 15 psychiatric disorders from the results of a series of studies on both inpatients and outpatients. Unlike the *Diagnostic and Statistical Manual of Mental Disorders* (2nd ed.) (DSM-II; American Psychiatric Association, 1968), which developed diagnostic criteria for psychiatric conditions based on the "best clinical judgment and experience" of a committee and its consultants, Feighner et al. developed their criteria through a systematic series of studies over five stages: (a) clinical descriptions; (b) laboratory studies; (c) delimitation from other disorders; (d) follow-up studies; and (e) family studies. These studies were intended to establish the validity of the psychiatric conditions (by demonstrating that they run in families and do not develop into other conditions), to identify the fundamental symptoms of psychiatric disorders, and to develop methods of distinguishing among various disorders.

Several features of Feighner's RDC are significant.

1. RDC clearly described the symptoms which were associated with a diagnosis. RDC specified the severity of symptoms associated with a condition and identified the minimum number of symptoms necessary for the assignment of a diagnostic label. RDC also distinguished between those symptoms which were necessary for a diagnosis and those which, although not necessary, could be indicative of a disorder.

2. RDC included information concerning the course of a condition in its diagnostic rules. For example, age of onset, premorbid adjustment, and duration of symptoms were considered in the diagnostic criteria for various disorders.

3. RDC incorporated exclusion criteria. That is, RDC not only indicated those symptoms which, if present, indicated a particular disorder, but also identified symptoms (and other conditions) which excluded a diagnosis from further consideration.

4. RDC included a residual category, "Undiagnosed Psychiatric Illness," to be used with individuals who were thought to have a psychiatric condition but for whom none of the specific diagnoses was found to be appropriate. Although this category would by definition contain a heterogeneous group of patients and so could only be found to have poor validity relationships with etiological or treatment variables, its inclusion would reduce the heterogeneity of other diagnostic categories and so would help eliminate the practice of using a specific diagnosis as a "wastebasket" to which patients, who did not clearly meet the criteria of other diagnostic categories, would be assigned.

The Feighner criteria were more clearly defined—more operational—than those of previous diagnostic systems, and so they could be expected to enhance the reliability and, consequently, the validity of diagnosis. This is exactly what Feighner and others found.

Feighner et al. (1972) reported the results of several efforts to assess the reliability of the RDC. In a study of 314 psychiatric emergency room patients, rates of agreement between two of four diagnosticians ranged from 86 to 95 percent. In a study of 87 psychiatric inpatients, two diagnosticians achieved an agreement rate of 92 percent. When patients from these two studies were evaluated at later times, initial diagnoses agreed with subsequent diagnoses in, respectively, 93 and 92 percent of the cases.

Other investigations were soon conducted to evaluate the reliability of the RDC. Helzer, Clayton, Pambakian, Reich, Woodruff, and Reveley (1977) used a structured interview, based on Feighner's RDC, to diagnose 101 newly admitted patients to a psychiatric hospital and to reassess these patients 24 hours later. The average K coefficient for the 12 diagnostic categories employed with these patients was .66. Helzer et al. concluded that, with few exceptions, the K coefficients obtained in this study are higher than those reported in previous research. They attributed this increase in reliability to the use of operational criteria.

Schedule for Affective Disorders and Schizophrenia

Spitzer et al. (1978) elaborated upon and modified Feighner's criteria. Their purpose was to develop diagnostic criteria which would yield homogenous groups of clients and which would meet with the acceptance of diagnosticians. Like Feighner et al. (1972), Spitzer et al. (1978) attempted to build their criteria upon a research foundation and, if no empirical evidence was available, to maximize the operationalism of the criteria. Spitzer and his colleagues developed a structured interview, the Schedule for Affective Disorders and Schizophrenia (SADS), to assist the diagnostician in gathering the information required to evaluate a client.

Spitzer et al. (1978) reported the results of several studies of the reliability of their diagnostic criteria. In two studies of the interrater reliability of diagnoses made by joint interviewers (or an interviewer and observer), K coefficients were found to range, respectively, from .75 to .97 and from .68 to 1.00. In a study of the test-retest reliability of diagnoses made by different diagnosticians over a one- to two-day interval, K coefficients ranged from .40 to 1.00. Spitzer et al. noted that these reliability coefficients tended to be higher than those found in studies of earlier diagnostic criteria. They also noted that the K coefficients they found to be low tended to occur for diagnostic categories which were used only infrequently. Thus, a small number of disagreements in these categories would lead to a substantial decrease in *K*.

Spitzer et al. (1978) also investigated a lifetime version of the SADS (SADS-L). They found high interrater reliability when the SADS-L was administered to first-degree relatives of patients (*K*s ranged from .46 to 1.00). They also found high agreement between diagnoses of previous psychiatric episodes based on all available information and those based only on the SADS-L (*K*s ranged from .63 to 1.00).

Spitzer et al. concluded by stating emphatically that the use of operational criteria in psychiatric diagnosis is "an idea whose time has come." They reviewed the benefits of a reliable diagnostic system and expressed amazement that the field was so slow to attempt to develop such a system.

The time had indeed come for the development, application, and appreciation of operational criteria for psychiatric diagnoses. Andreason, Grove, Shapiro, Keller, Hirschfeld, and McDonald-Scott (1981) demonstrated that the SADS-L could be used with substantial reliability in nonpatient populations. Helzer, Robins, Croughan, and Welner (1981) found that a structured diagnostic interview designed to be used for both research and clinical purposes had high interrater reliability when used by psychiatrists or lay interviewers (in fact, the average *K* coefficient for two lay interviewers, .62, was somewhat higher than that obtained with two psychiatrists, .52). Maier, Philipp, and Buller (1988) reported that diagnoses derived from structured interviews had higher interrater reliability and higher validity (agreement with a diagnosis based on all available information) than diagnoses based on nonstructured (traditional) interviews.

These and many other investigations have supported the reliability, validity, and utility of diagnoses based on an operational set of criteria.

DSM-III

The American Psychiatric Association continued the movement toward the development of more operational criteria for diagnoses with the publication of the *Diagnostic and Statistical Manual of Mental Disorders* (3rd edition) (DSM-III; American Psychiatric Association, 1980).

Characteristics

The DSM-III, modeled after the work of Feighner et al. (1972) and Spitzer et al. (1978), represented a significant change from the previous edition of the diagnostic manual. DSM-III clearly specified the symptoms associated with each disorder. Like Feighner's RDC, DSM-III operationalized the criteria required for the assignment of psychiatric diagnoses and included exclusion criteria.

In addition, DSM-III introduced a multiaxial system of diagnosis. Clinical syndromes are assigned to Axis I. Personality and developmental disorders are assigned to Axis II. (Axis II conditions develop relatively early in life and have a persistent course. Thus, these diagnoses carry the implicit assumptions that the client, when diagnosed, has been experiencing symptoms for a long time and that the client's present level of functioning does not represent a significant decline from previous levels of functioning.) Physical disorders related to the client's psychological condition are identified on Axis III. Axes IV and V receive, respectively, ratings of the client's recent psychosocial stressors and highest level of adaptive functioning.

The purposes of this multiaxial system were to increase the reliability of diagnosis and to include more useful information about the client. For example, using DSM-III, a clinician should, when appropriate, diagnose both the client's clinical syndrome and personality disorder. Although clinicians using earlier diagnostic systems may well have assigned both diagnoses to a client, many clinicians may have assigned only one diagnosis, perceiving the other as a secondary problem. DSM-III clearly endorses the practice of diagnosing both the clinical and the personality disorder, and so should increase both the interrater reliability and the utility of such diagnoses.

Axes IV and V also add information which is useful in understanding and treating the individual client. The prognosis of many psychological disorders is related to the severity of precipitating stressors and the client's premorbid adjustment. For example, schizophrenia has a better prognosis when the patient exhibited higher premorbid adjustment and when it develops following a severe stressor than when a stressor is absent (Willerman & Cohen, 1990). Assessment of the client's psychosocial stressors and premorbid adjustment provides useful information in treating the episode and in formulating predictions about the future course of the disorder. The client's unique history is incorporated into the diagnosis and so DSM-III, more than previous diagnostic systems, avoids the possible dehumanizing effects of treating all patients within a diagnostic category in an identical fashion.

Reliability

Initial investigations of the reliability of DSM-III diagnoses were quite favorable. Spitzer, Forman, and Nee (1979) found that the average K coefficients of Axis I and Axis II conditions were, respectively, .78 and .61 in a study of interrater reliability, and .66 and .54 in a study of test-retest reliability. Similarly, Spitzer and Forman (1979) reported that Axes IV and V had substantial reliability, with mean interrater K coefficients of .62 and .80, respectively, and mean test-retest K coefficients of .58 and .69. Hyler, Williams, and Spitzer (1982) investigated the interrater reliability between two clinicians who diagnosed a client based on interviews and on examinations of case records. They found that the average interrater K coefficients for interviews and case examinations were, respectively, .67 and .47.

In all of these studies, interrater diagnostic reliability was consistently higher than had been achieved with earlier diagnostic systems. Because diagnostic reliability is a prerequisite for diagnostic validity, the development of DSM-III was viewed by many psychologists as a sign that research based on DSM-III diagnoses would improve both understanding of the causes of disorders and effectiveness in treating disorders. In addition, the fact that these studies were conducted with many diagnosticians across several clinical settings speaks to the external validity or generalizability of the enhanced reliability of DSM-III to actual practice.

Criticisms

Despite the initial demonstrations of enhanced reliability of DSM-III diagnoses, DSM-III met with several criticisms. For example, Spitzer et al. (1979) acknowledged that reliability was only "fair" for several conditions, including Schizoaffective Disorder, Chronic Minor Affective Disorder (Dysthymic Disorder), and the Personality Disorders.

In addition, Kutchins and Kirk (1986) identified several problems with the early studies of diagnostic reliability using DSM-III. For example, diagnostic reliability was determined for some categories using only a very small number of patients. Although the average K coefficients in these studies were substantial, estimates of K for specific categories (usually the categories with few patients) were often quite low.

In addition, Kutchins and Kirk (1986) noted that these early reports were brief, and so did not describe the methodological procedures used to ensure that data contamination (where one diagnostician may have information concerning another's diagnosis) or data selection (where diagnostician's data may have been selected for inclusion in the report in a nonrandom, possibly biased way) did not occur. Kutchins and Kirk (1986) concluded that the early claims that DSM-III leads to enhanced diagnostic reliability have not been sufficiently demonstrated.

Other conceptual criticisms were directed against DSM-III. Vaillant (1984) noted that psychoanalytically oriented psychologists were dissatisfied with DSM-III's lack of recognition of the underlying psychological processes which they believe are important in the development and maintenance of disorders. Vaillant also criticized DSM-III's presentation of childhood disorders in a static, cross-sectional fashion, rather than incorporating a dynamic developmental viewpoint.

Schacht and Nathan (1977) and Harris (1979) criticized DSM-III's broadening of the range of the concept of "mental disorders," especially in the area of childhood disorders. For example, DSM-III included conditions such as reading, articulation, and arithmetic disabilities in the psychiatric nomenclature. Although these conditions may require the attention of educational and psychological specialists, psychologists must be wary of the possible adverse effects of labeling such children as having "mental disorders."

Waterhouse, Fein, Nath, and Snyder (1987) identified several additional criticisms that had been directed against DSM-III's section on childhood disorders:

1. Critics have claimed that not all childhood disorders are represented in DSM-III. For example, neither "masked depression" nor "symbiotic psychosis," two diagnoses traditionally employed with children, appear in DSM-III.

2. Criteria for distinguishing between subcategories of disorders are not clear. This makes the use of such distinctions difficult to apply and may detract from the reliability of the system. For example, DSM-III classified conduct disorders along two dimensions: Socialized/Undersocialized and Aggressive/Nonaggressive. This results in a four-way structure for subclassifying Conduct Disorders, which practitioners may find difficult to use reliably.

3. Studies have found the diagnostic reliability of DSM-III's childhood disorders to be lower than that of many adult disorders. For example, Mattison, Cantwell, Russell, and Will (1979) and Werry, Methven, Fitzpatrick, and Dixon (1983) found that claims of the enhanced reliability of DSM-III diagnoses were not supported for childhood disorders. Similarly, Vitiello, Malone, Buschle, Delaney, and Behar (1990) observed a median K coefficient of only .34 for interrater agreement for DSM-III childhood disorders and concluded that diagnostic reliability for these conditions remained "poor."

4. Empirically derived systems of classifying childhood disorders were not incorporated into DSM-III. For example, Achenbach (1982) has developed an important and influential scheme for classifying childhood disorders as either internalizing or externalizing. Achenbach (1980) criticized DSM-III for its failure to include his and other empirically developed classification systems for childhood disorders.

Another section of DSM-III that has met with strong criticism is its section on Personality Disorders (Cooper, 1987; Frances, 1980; Frances & Widiger, 1987; Siever & Kendler, 1987). The major criticisms of this section of DSM-III include the following:

1. The diagnostic criteria for the various Personality Disorders are inconsistent. For example, some of the Personality Disorders are defined on the basis of monothetic criteria (symptoms which must be present), whereas others are assessed on the basis of polythetic criteria (a specified number of a larger set of symptoms must be present).

2. The lists of symptoms associated with the various Personality Disorders exhibit significant overlap. In some cases, it is possible for a patient with one personality disorder to share more symptoms with a patient with a different personality disorder than with a patient with the same diagnosis. Such overlap across categories and heterogeneity within categories limits the reliability of differential diagnosis of the DSM-III Personality Disorders and so limits the degree to which valid relationships can be established between personality disorders and etiological factors or effective treatments.

3. Because of the criticisms cited above, the diagnostic reliability of Personality Disorders is lower than that of other DSM-III disorders. For example, Spitzer et al. (1979) found that the diagnostic reliability of the DSM-III Personality Disorders was only "fair," with mean K coefficients of .61 and .54, respectively, for interrater and test-retest reliability.

4. DSM-III diagnoses Personality Disorders on an "all-or-none" basis, whereas traditional theories typically regarded these conditions as continuous or dimensional constructs, to be considered disorders only when they exceeded some threshold.

Despite these criticisms, the status of DSM-III remained high among diagnosticians. Spitzer, Williams, and Skodol (1983) edited a volume which included data and reviews from researchers and clinicians from 18 nations. Responses to DSM-III were largely favorable. Similarly, a survey of diagnosticians from over 50 countries (Mezzich, Fabrega, Mezzich, & Coffman, 1985) found that DSM-III was used by most respondents and was perceived as more useful than ICD-9, an alternative psychiatric classification system (World Health Organization, 1978).

It is easy to understand ready acceptance of DSM-III. Its operational criteria increased ease of use and interrater reliability. Its multiaxial system encouraged the diagnostician to assess both clinical and personality disorders and to include individualized information relating to the client's premorbid functioning and psychosocial stressors. Its research foundation acknowledged that additional improvements in the system would be made as major findings appear in the literature.

DSM-III-R

In 1987, the American Psychiatric Association published the *Diagnostic and Statistical Manual of Mental Disorders* (3rd edition—revised) (DSM-III-R; American Psychiatric Association, 1987). DSM-III-R retained the essential features of DSM-III: its multiaxial rating system, operationalism, and research foundation. The revisions were primarily aimed at incorporating the results of recent research and were not intended to alter the conceptual structure of the system. For example, whereas DSM-III permitted the clinician to diagnose the condition Attention Deficit Disorder (ADD) either with or without Hyperactivity, DSM-III-R recognized that only few children received the diagnosis of ADD without Hyperactivity and so relabeled ADD as Attention Deficit Hyperactive Disorder (ADHD). Similarly, DSM-III identified the condition Agoraphobia as an Anxiety Disorder distinct from Panic Disorder. DSM-III-R, however, restructured its system to include Agoraphobia as a subcategory of Panic Disorder, because recent research has shown that Agoraphobia is typically preceded by and so may be a consequence of Panic Disorder (American Psychiatric Association, 1987).

In maintaining the conceptual framework of DSM-III, however, DSM-III-R retained DSM-III's weaknesses as well as its strengths. For example, Cantwell and Baker (1988) identified three criticisms of DSM-III which could be directed against DSM-III-R as well: (a) both DSM-III and DSM-III-R emphasize the empirical description of disorders but fail to provide a theoretical framework which would help in the classification or understanding of mental disorders, (b) DSM-III and DSM-III-R adopt a categorical approach to classifying disorders and so have difficulty in handling dimensional constructs, and (c) DSM-III and DSM-III-R overextend the concept of mental disorders, including learning and developmental disabilities as mental disorders when many educational specialists and psychologists prefer to distinguish these from mental disorders.

DSM-III-R continued to attempt to improve the reliability of diagnosis. For example, several changes were made in the way in which DSM-III-R dealt with Personality Disorders. DSM-III-R decreased the degree of overlap of symptoms for the various personality disorders, and standardized the criteria for their diagnosis (Widiger, Frances, Spitzer, & Williams, 1988). These modifications should increase the ease of use and the diagnostic reliability of the personality disorders.

Initial efforts to investigate the diagnostic reliability of DSM-III-R have been successful. For example, Volkmar, Bregman, Cohen, and Cicchetti (1988) compared the reliability of DSM-III and DSM-III-R criteria for the diagnosis of autism. They reported that the two systems had similarly high interrater reliability for the diagnosis of autism and that interrater reliability coefficients for the assessment of individual criteria of autism were, with both systems, primarily in the "excellent" range. Volkmar et al. reported that the DSM-III-R criteria for autism were somewhat broader than DSM-III criteria, and so DSM-III-R should increase the sensitivity of the diagnosis of autism (i.e., increase the probability of a true positive) while decreasing the specificity of the diagnosis of autism (i.e., increase the probability of a false positive).

Silverman and Nelles (1988) developed a semi-structured interview for the diagnosis of childhood anxiety disorders based on DSM-III/DSM-III-R criteria. Whereas previously reported estimates of the interrater reliability of these disorders were "unacceptable," Silverman and Nelles found overall K coefficients of .84 and .83 for childhood anxiety disorders based on, respectively, child and parent interviews.

Although such early efforts are encouraging, a great deal of work remains to be done in order to demonstrate the reliability of DSM-III-R diagnoses and then to determine the validity of these diagnoses in terms of useful relationships between etiological factors and effective treatments.

Summary and Conclusions

The issue of the reliability of psychiatric diagnosis, like the other issues discussed in this book, became the focus of intensive investigation in the mid-1900s when the mental health field began to question the empirical foundations of its theory and practice. Although early investigations (1930s–1940s) of this issue were characterized by numerous methodological and statistical flaws, they succeeded in establishing the issue as one which demanded the attention of the professional community. As the methodological rigor of studies of diagnostic reliability improved (1950s–1960s), it became increasingly clear that the reliability of traditional psychiatric diagnosis was lower than the field expected it to be. What was worse, diagnostic reliability was also lower than was necessary to make valid statements regarding the associated features, etiological factors, and effective treatments of disorders. For this reason, later studies (1970s–1980s) were devoted to the development of more reliable diagnostic systems.

In summary, the following conclusions can be drawn from clinical psychology's empirical investigation of the reliability of psychiatric diagnosis:

1. As reliability is a prerequisite for validity, a reliable diagnostic system is essential. In order for clinical psychology to be able to demonstrate valid statements concerning a disorder (such that it has a particular cause or responds to a specific treatment), the field must first be able to diagnose the

condition reliably. Although there can be problems when reliability is pursued as a goal apart from validity (e.g., when reliability is established in different populations or using different diagnostic procedures than will be used in validity studies), diagnostic reliability must be established for any newly defined clinical disorder or newly developed diagnostic procedure.

2. Clinical psychology has developed methodological and statistical procedures for the determination of diagnostic reliability. The field has recognized that both interrater reliability and test-retest reliability are crucial for the establishment of the validity of statements concerning clinical disorders. In addition, methodological standards have been developed for studies of both types of diagnostic reliability.

Similarly, statistical procedures have been developed for the measurement of diagnostic reliability. Most significant has been the development of the K coefficient to measure the rate of agreement on diagnostic categories, above that expected by chance alone. Although there have been criticisms of the K coefficient, and alternative statistics proposed to measure interrater agreement, current practice among clinical psychologists supports the use of K. For any newly defined clinical disorder or method of diagnosing a clinical condition, the field expects that the rate of interrater reliability be reported using the K coefficient.

3. Psychiatry and clinical psychology developed a new diagnostic system—DSM-III (and, later, DSM-III-R)—in order to enhance the reliability of diagnosis. This diagnostic system differed from previous systems in terms of its operationalism. According to DSM-III (and DSM-III-R), diagnostic criteria are more precise than ever before. Diagnostic criteria now include the number, duration, and severity of symptoms. For some disorders, monothetic symptoms (symptoms necessary for a particular diagnosis) are specified. For many disorders, exclusion criteria must be met. In general, research has shown that the new diagnostic system is indeed more reliable than earlier diagnostic systems.

4. Psychiatry and clinical psychology recognize more than ever before the importance of a research-based diagnostic system. DSM-III was, more than previous editions, based on research efforts to develop a more reliable diagnostic system. The authors of DSM-III explicitly stated that they had attempted to base their diagnostic criteria on what the best research had found to be reliable methods of diagnosing mental disorders and that they would revise the system as new research results came in. The revised system, DSM-III-R, appeared only seven years later and was modified largely on the basis of recent research. The field continues to conduct research in efforts to improve the reliability of diagnosis and plans to continually revise the diagnostic system on the basis of such research.

References

Achenbach, T. M. (1980). DSM-III in light of empirical research on the classification of child psychopathology. *Journal of the American Academy of Child Psychiatry, 19,* 395–412.

Achenbach, T. M. (1982). *Developmental psychopathology* (2nd ed.). New York: Wiley.

Allport, G. W. (1961). *Pattern and growth in personality.* New York: Holt, Rinehart and Winston.

American Psychiatric Association. (1968). *Diagnostic and statistical manual of mental disorders* (2nd ed.). Washington, DC: American Psychiatric Association.

American Psychiatric Association. (1980). *Diagnostic and statistical manual of mental disorders* (3rd ed.). Washington, DC: American Psychiatric Association.

American Psychiatric Association. (1987). *Diagnostic and statistical manual of mental disorders* (3rd ed.—revised). Washington, DC: American Psychiatric Association.

Andreason, N. C., Grove, W. M., Shapiro, R. W., Keller, M. B., Hirschfeld, R. M. A., & McDonald-Scott, P. (1981). Reliability of lifetime diagnosis: A multicenter collaborative perspective. *Archives of General Psychiatry, 38,* 400–405.

Ash, P. (1949). The reliability of psychiatric diagnoses. *Journal of Abnormal and Social Psychology, 44,* 272–276.

Barber, T. X. (1976). *Pitfalls in human research: Ten pivotal points.* New York: Pergamon.

Beck, A. T. (1962). Reliability of psychiatric diagnoses: 1. A critique of systematic studies. *American Journal of Psychiatry, 119,* 210–216.

Beck, A. T., Ward, C. H., Mendelson, M., Mock, J. E., & Erbaugh, J. K. (1962). Reliability of psychiatric diagnoses: 2. A study of consistency of clinical judgments and ratings. *American Journal of Psychiatry, 119,* 351–357.

Blashfield, R. K. (1984). *The classification of psychopathology: Neo-Kraepelinian and quantitative approaches.* New York: Plenum.

Boisen, A. T. (1938). Types of dementia praecox—A study in psychiatric classification. *Psychiatry, 1,* 233–236.

Cantwell, D. P., & Baker, L. (1988). Issues in the classification of child and adolescent psychopathology. *Journal of the American Academy of Child and Adolescent Psychiatry, 27,* 521–533.

Carey, G., & Gottesman, I. I. (1978). Reliability and validity in binary ratings: Areas of common misunderstanding in diagnosis and symptom ratings. *Archives of General Psychiatry, 35,* 1454–1459.

Cohen, J. A. (1960). A coefficient of agreement for nominal scales. *Educational and Psychological Measurement, 20,* 37–46.

Cooper, A. M. (1987). Histrionic, narcissistic, and compulsive personality disorders. In G. L. Tischler (Ed.), *Diagnosis and classification in psychiatry: A critical appraisal of DSM-III* (pp. 290–299). Cambridge: Cambridge University Press.

Doering, C. R., & Raymond, A. F. (1934). Reliability of observation in psychiatric and related characteristics. *American Journal of Orthopsychiatry, 4,* 249–257.

Elkin, F. (1947). Specialists interpret the case of Harold Holzer. *Journal of Abnormal and Social Psychology, 42,* 99–111.

Eysenck, H. J. (1972). *Psychology is about people.* New York: Library Press.

Feighner, J. P., Robins, E., Guze, S. B., Woodruff, R. A., Winokur, G., & Munoz, R. (1972). Diagnostic criteria for use in psychiatric research. *Archives of General Psychiatry, 26,* 57–63.

Foulds, G. A. (1955). The reliability of psychiatric and the validity of psychological diagnoses. *Journal of Mental Science, 101,* 851–852.

Frances, A. (1980). The DSM-III personality disorders section: A commentary. *American Journal of Psychiatry, 137,* 1050–1054.

Frances, A., & Widiger, T. A. (1987). A critical review of four DSM-III personality disorders: Borderline, avoidant, dependent, and passive-aggressive. In G. L. Tischler (Ed.), *Diagnosis and classification in psychiatry: A critical appraisal of DSM-III* (pp. 269–289). Cambridge: Cambridge University Press.

Goffman, E. (1963). *Stigma: Notes on the management of spoiled identity.* Englewood Cliffs, NJ: Prentice-Hall.

Goldfarb, A. (1959). Reliability of diagnostic judgments made by psychologists. *Journal of Clinical Psychology, 15,* 392–396.

Harris, S. L. (1979). DSM III—Its implications for children. *Child Behavior Therapy, 1,* 37–46.

Helzer, J. E., Clayton, P. J., Pambakian, R., Reich, T., Woodruff, R. A., & Reveley, M. A. (1977). Reliability of psychiatric diagnosis. II. The test/retest reliability of diagnostic classifications. *Archives of General Psychiatry, 34,* 136–141.

Helzer, J. E., Robins, L. N., Croughan, J. L., & Welner, A. (1981). Renard diagnostic interview: Reliability and procedural validity in physicians and lay interviewers. *Archives of General Psychiatry, 38,* 393–398.

Hunt, W. A., Wittson, C. L., & Hunt, E. B. (1953). A theoretical and practical analysis of the diagnostic process. In P. H. Hoch & J. Zubin (Eds.), *Current problems in psychiatric diagnosis* (pp. 53–65). New York: Grune and Stratton.

Hyler, S. E., Williams, J. B. W., & Spitzer, R. L. (1982). Reliability in the DSM-III field trials. *Archives of General Psychiatry, 39,* 1275–1278.

Janes, C. L. (1979). Agreement measurement and the judgment process. *Journal of Nervous and Mental Disease, 167,* 343–347.

Katz, M. M., Cole, J. O., & Lowery, H. A. (1969). Studies of the diagnostic process: The influence of symptom perception, past experience, and ethnic background on diagnostic decisions. *American Journal of Psychiatry, 125,* 109–119.

Kendall, R. E., Cooper, J. E., Gourlay, A. J., & Copeland, J. R. M. (1971). Diagnostic criteria of American and British psychiatrists. *Archives of General Psychiatry, 25,* 123–130.

Kreitman, N. (1961). The reliability of psychiatric diagnosis. *Journal of Mental Science, 107,* 876–886.

Kreitman, N., Sainsbury, P., Morrissey, J., Towers, J., & Scrivener, J. (1961). The reliability of psychiatric assessment: An analysis. *Journal of Mental Science, 107,* 887–908.

Kutchins, H., & Kirk, S. A. (1986). The reliability of DSM-III: A critical review. *Social Work Research and Abstracts, 22,* 3–12.

Maier, W., Philipp, M., & Buller, R. (1988). The value of structured clinical interviews. *Archives of General Psychiatry, 45,* 963–964.

Masserman, J. H., & Carmichael, H. T. (1938). Diagnosis and prognosis in psychiatry: With a follow-up study of the results of short-term general hospital therapy of psychiatric cases. *Journal of Mental Science, 84,* 893–946.

Mattison, R., Cantwell, D. P., Russell, A. T., & Will, L. (1979). A comparison of DSM-II and DSM-III in the diagnosis of childhood disorders. *Archives of General Psychiatry, 36,* 1217–1222.

Maxwell, A. E. (1977). Coefficients of agreement between observers and their interpretation. *British Journal of Psychiatry, 130,* 79–83.

McGorry, P. D., Copolov, D. L., & Singh, B. S. (1989). The validity of the assessment of psychopathology in the psychoses. *Australian and New Zealand Journal of Psychiatry, 23,* 469–482.

Mehlman, B. (1952). The reliability of psychiatric diagnoses. *Journal of Abnormal and Social Psychology, 47,* 577–578.

Mezzich, J. E., Fabrega, H., Mezzich, A. C., & Coffman, G. A. (1985). International experience with DSM-III. *Journal of Nervous and Mental Disease, 173,* 738–741.

Myers, D. G. (1989). *Psychology* (2nd ed.). New York: Worth.

Norris, V. (1959). *Mental illness in London.* London: Chapman and Hall.

Noyes, A. P. (1953). *Modern clinical psychiatry* (4th ed.). Philadelphia: Saunders.

Pasamanick, B., Dinitz, S., & Lefton, M. (1959). Psychiatric orientation and its relation to diagnosis and treatment in a mental hospital. *American Journal of Psychiatry, 116,* 127–132.

Robins, E., & Guze, S. B. (1970). Establishment of validity in psychiatric illness: Its application to schizophrenia. *American Journal of Psychiatry, 126,* 107–111.

Rogers, C. R. (1951). *Client-centered therapy.* Boston: Houghton Mifflin.

Rosenhan, D. L. (1971). On being sane in insane places. *Science, 179,* 250–258.

Rosenthal, R. (1966). *Experimenter effects in behavioral research.* New York: Appleton-Century-Crofts.

Sandifer, M. G., Hordern, A., Timbury, G. C., & Green, L. M. (1968). Psychiatric diagnosis: A comparative study in North Carolina, London and Glasgow. *British Journal of Psychiatry, 114,* 1–9.

Sandifer, M. G., Pettus, C., & Quade, D. (1964). A study of psychiatric diagnosis. *Journal of Nervous and Mental Disease, 139,* 350–356.

Schacht, T., & Nathan, P. E. (1977). But is it good for psychologists? Appraisal and status of DSM III. *American Psychologist, 32,* 1017–1025.

Scheff, T. J. (1966). *Being mentally ill: A sociological theory.* Chicago: Aldine.

Scheff, T. J. (974). The labeling theory of mental illness. *American Sociological Review, 39,* 444–452.

Schmidt, H. O., & Fonda, C. P. (1956). The reliability of psychiatric diagnosis: A new look. *Journal of Abnormal and Social Psychology, 52,* 262–267.

Seeman, W. (1953). Psychiatric diagnosis: An investigation of interperson reliability after didactic instruction. *Journal of Nervous and Mental Disease, 118,* 541–544.

Siever, L. J., & Kendler, K. S. (1987). An evaluation of the DSM-III categories of paranoid, schizoid, and schizotypal personality disorders. In G. L. Tischler (Ed.), *Diagnosis and classification in psychiatry: A critical appraisal of DSM-III* (pp. 300–320). Cambridge: Cambridge University Press.

Silverman, W. K., & Nelles, M. A. (1988). The anxiety disorders interview schedule for children. *Journal of the American Academy of Child and Adolescent Psychiatry, 27*, 772–778.

Simpson, C. G. (1961). *Principles of animal taxonomy*. New York: Columbia University Press.

Spitzer, R. L., Cohen, J., Fliess, J. L., & Endicott, J. (1967). Quantification of agreement in psychiatric diagnosis. *Archives of General Psychiatry, 17*, 83–87.

Spitzer, R. L., Endicott, J., & Robins, E. (1978). Research diagnostic criteria: Rationale and reliability. *Archives of General Psychiatry, 35*, 773–782.

Spitzer, R. L., & Fliess, J. L. (1974). A re-analysis of the reliability of psychiatric diagnosis. *British Journal of Psychiatry, 125*, 341–347.

Spitzer, R. L., & Forman, J. B. W. (1979). DSM-III field trials: II. Initial experience with the multiaxial system. *American Journal of Psychiatry, 136*, 818–820.

Spitzer, R. L., Forman, J. B. W., & Nee, J. (1979). DSM-III field trials: I. Initial interrater diagnostic reliability. *American Journal of Psychiatry, 136*, 815–817.

Spitzer, R. L., Sheehy, M., & Endicott, J. (1977). DSM-III: Guiding principles. In V. M. Rakoff, H. C. Stancer, & H. B. Kedward (Eds.), *Psychiatric diagnosis* (pp. 1–24). New York: Brunner/Mazel.

Spitzer, R. L., Williams, J. B. W., & Skodol, A. E. (Eds.). (1983). *International perspectives on DSM-III*. Washington, DC: American Psychiatric Press.

Temerlin, M. K. (1968). Suggestion effects in psychiatric diagnoses. *Journal of Nervous and Mental Disease, 47*, 349–353.

Temerlin, M. K., & Trousdale, W. W. (1969). The social psychology of clinical diagnosis. *Psychotherapy: Theory, Research, and Practice, 6*, 24–29.

Vaillant, G. E. (1984). The disadvantages of DSM-III outweigh its advantages. *American Journal of Psychiatry, 141*, 542–545.

Vitiello, B., Malone, R., Buschle, P. R., Delaney, M. A., & Behar, D. (1990). Reliability of DSM-III diagnoses of hospitalized children. *Hospital and Community Psychiatry, 41*, 63–67.

Volkmar, F. R., Bregman, J., Cohen, D. J., & Cicchetti, D. V. (1988). DSM-III and DSM-III-R diagnoses of autism. *American Journal of Psychiatry, 145*, 1404–1408.

Ward, C. H., Beck, A. T., Mendelson, M., Mock, J. E., & Erbaugh, J. K. (1962). The psychiatric nomenclature: Reasons for diagnostic disagreement. *Archives of General Psychiatry, 7*, 198–205.

Waterhouse, L., Fein, D., Nath, J., & Snyder, D. (1987). Pervasive developmental disorders and schizophrenia occurring in childhood: A review of critical commentary. In G. L. Tischler (Ed.), *Diagnosis and classification in psychiatry: A critical appraisal of DSM-III* (pp. 335–368). Cambridge: Cambridge University Press.

Werry, J. S., Methven, R. J., Fitzpatrick, J., & Dixon, H. (1983). The interrater reliability of DSM-III in children. *Journal of Abnormal Child Psychology, 11*, 341–354.

Widiger, T. A., Frances, A., Spitzer, R. L., & Williams, J. B. (1988). The DSM-III-R personality disorders: An overview. *American Journal of Psychiatry, 145*, 786–795.

Willerman, L. & Cohen, D. B. (1990). *Psychopathology*. New York: McGraw-Hill.

Wilson, M. S., & Meyer, E. (1962). Diagnostic consistency in a psychiatric liaison service. *American Journal of Psychiatry, 119,* 207–209.

Woodruff, R. A., Goodwin, D. W., & Guze, S. B. (1974). *Psychiatric diagnosis.* New York: Oxford University Press.

World Health Organization. (1978). *Mental disorders: Glossary and guide to their classification in accordance with the ninth revision of the international classification of diseases.* Geneva: World Health Organization.

Yates, A. J. (1970). *Behavior therapy.* New York: Wiley.

Zubin, J. (1967). Classification of the behavior disorders. *Annual Review of Psychology, 18,* 373–406.

Zubin, J., Salzinger, K., Fleiss, J. L., Gurland, B., Spitzer, R. L., Endicott, J., & Sutton, S. (1975). Biometric approach to psychopathology: Abnormal and clinical psychology—statistical, epidemiological, and diagnostic approaches. *Annual Review of Psychology, 26,* 621–671.

CHAPTER SIX

Clinical versus Statistical Prediction

Introduction

The change in clinical psychology discussed throughout this book is illustrated perhaps most clearly in the issue of the relative accuracies of clinical and statistical prediction. These terms refer to the two major approaches clinicians use when attempting to learn about and help a client. The clinical method involves learning as much as one can about the individual, constructing some abstract model to explain the individual's psychological functioning, and using this model to derive predictions concerning the individual's future functioning (e.g., response to one treatment versus another, likelihood of becoming violent).

The statistical method, on the other hand, involves classifying the individual among similar cases. Empirical techniques are then used to determine how this class of similar cases has behaved in the past. Then, it is assumed that the case in point will behave similarly to members of the comparison group, and so a prediction is derived for the individual which is based on the group's behavior.

The clinical method, then, involves the analysis of the individual apart from others and aims at understanding the individual. The methods used to make predictions do not rely on empirical studies of similar cases, but instead rest upon the meaningful understanding of the individual.

On the other hand, the statistical method involves the assignment of the individual to a group of similar cases. There is no attempt to "understand" the case as an individual; rather, it is assumed that the individual will behave in the future as has the related group of cases.

Predictions are based, not on an understanding of the individual, but on empirical analyses of groups.

The rivalry between these two approaches in clinical psychology has been long and heated. For example, in the introduction to his book *Clinical versus Statistical Prediction*, Meehl (1954) presented four lists of adjectives which have been used to describe the two approaches. Proponents of the clinical method describe it using such honorific terms as "dynamic, global, meaningful, holistic" (p. 4), whereas opponents derogate it as "primitive, prescientific, sloppy, uncontrolled" (p. 4). Similarly, devotees of the statistical approach praise it as "rigorous, scientific, precise, careful" (p. 4), while critics regard it as "pedantic, fractionated, trivial, forced" (p. 4).

It should be noted that the debate over the relative merits of qualitative and quantitative methods of analysis is not unique to clinical psychology. Disciplines from as wide a range as botany to musicology, linguistics to classical studies, have all experienced similar rivalries. Allport (1942), for example, cited the terms introduced by five philosophers or scientists to characterize the two approaches, ultimately selecting Windelband's terms *idiographic* and *nomothetic* to describe, respectively, the clinical and statistical methods. Nor is the debate one which started in clinical psychology with the publication of Meehl's 1954 book. As early as the 1920s, psychologists debated the relative merits of the clinical (Viteles, 1925) and statistical (Freyd, 1925) positions.

The clinical approach is associated most strongly with the psychoanalytic and humanistic schools of psychology. Freud, for example, relied on case studies both to develop and to support his proposals regarding personality theory and psychotherapy. His intention was to develop a system that could postdict (or explain after the fact) behavior, rather than predict future behavior. Following Freud, psychoanalysts have continued to rely on case studies and the clinical method more than on statistical analyses of large group studies.

Allport, a leading humanist, is also closely associated with the clinical method. Although Allport (1937, 1942) argued that both the idiographic and nomothetic methods were important and should be integrated in the study of personality, it is clear that he believed that the idiographic method was more useful in personology. "The only way to make a certain prediction of effect from cause is to study the life in which the causes operate, and not a thousand other lives. This is not to deny that actuarial prediction has its place (in dealing with masses of cases); it is good so far as it goes, but idiographic prediction goes further" (Allport, 1942, p. 157).

The statistical method relies on empirical techniques to generate predictions. These include actuarial (experience) tables, which tabulate the outcomes of previous cases as a function of selected variables. To generate a prediction for a new case requires simply the classification of the individual along these variables. A good example of the use of such actuarial tables is in the determination of automobile insurance premiums, where the prediction of risk is made as a function of variables such as driver age, age and make of car, previous driving history, and so on. Another and more sophisticated method of generating statistical predictions is the technique of statistical regression. Based on knowledge of the correlations between a criterion variable (i.e., what one is trying to predict) and a set of predictor variables, it is possible to generate an equation that enables one to predict optimally the criterion from the predictors.

Two early advocates of the statistical over the clinical method of predicting behavior were Lundberg (1941) and Sarbin (1941, 1942, 1944). Both argued that clinical prediction was essentially an informal type of statistical prediction. After all, clinical judgments are based on previous experience with similar types of individuals. Statistical regression equations are by definition the optimal formulas for predicting a criterion variable. Therefore, clinicians are doomed to failure if they use informal methods in an attempt to surpass the accuracy of mathematical predictions. Because the statistical formula generates the optimal prediction equation and because clinicians are attempting to use similar, albeit informal and unsystematic, methods to predict future behavior, clinicians would do well to use the statistical method.

Meehl's Reviews

Meehl's (1954) book focused attention on the issue of the relative accuracies of the two forms of prediction. Although earlier writers, such as Allport and Sarbin, had argued in favor of one approach or the other, Meehl's book summarized the arguments for both positions, evaluated them, and reviewed the empirical studies to date that compared the two forms of prediction. Meehl's book is perhaps best known for the results of his empirical review, which stirred a controversy just as had Eysenck's (1952) paper on the effectiveness of psychotherapy. His evaluations of the arguments of Allport and Sarbin concerning clinical and statistical prediction are also incisive and valuable.

Meehl criticized Allport for maintaining that *"psychological causation is always personal and never actuarial"* (Allport, 1942, p. 157). Allport gave the example of predicting recidivism in delinquents. If we know that 80 percent of delinquents from broken homes are recidivists, it does not follow that a single delinquent from a broken home has an 80 percent probability of becoming a recidivist. Probability is based on a frequentist notion of repeated trials. The delinquent of interest represents only a single trial! The individual either will or will not become a recidivist, and so has either a 100 or a zero percent chance of becoming a recidivist. Allport suggested that if we knew all of the variables that are related to recidivism in delinquents and then assessed these in the case in point, we would be able to predict the delinquent's outcome with near certainty.

According to Meehl, Allport's position might be interpreted by some as implying that all inferences based on class membership are invalid. Yet there is an inconsistency in Allport's position. He agreed that, if all of the predictors of recidivism in delinquents were known, then one could predict outcome with near certainty. However, this is basically a form of statistical prediction. If Allport accepts a statistical formula based on a multiple regression coefficient of .99 (i.e., near certainty), then why not accept one with a coefficient of .90? If he accepts this, then why not one with a coefficient of .80? Or .70? In principle, there is no difference between accepting actuarial predictions that yield .99 and .70 accuracies; the difference is one of accuracy of outcome and not one of the assumptions underlying or the methods used to generate the predictions.

Meehl agreed with Allport that there are times when a clinician should discard an actuarial prediction table in favor of a clinical prediction. For example, a variable may be so rare that it has not been included in any regression formulas based on previous observations, yet it may be so potent that, when it does occur, it overturns completely any regression equation based on other variables. In this case, a clinician may justifiably modify or discard altogether the equation. However, Meehl did not think it would be appropriate to discard all prediction based on class membership. Else, one would have to abandon all prediction!

Meehl also addressed at length the position of Sarbin concerning clinical prediction. Sarbin argued that all clinical prediction was based on previous observations and experiences, and so clinical prediction was a form of unsystematic or informal statistical prediction. Since statistical prediction yields the optimal method for combining predictor variables, clinical prediction cannot possibly surpass statistical prediction in accuracy.

Meehl's major criticism of this position was based on Reichenbach's (1938) distinction between the contexts of "discovery" and "justification." In the advancement of science, one engages in both of these activities. In the discovery stage, one makes observations and then develops formulations in an initial attempt to account for the observations. This stage certainly permits and even encourages the making of unique observations and the development of original hypotheses. However, after one has developed such hypotheses, one then proceeds to the context of justification. Here, the rules of evidence are quite rigorous and hypotheses must pass empirical tests before they are accepted.

Meehl argued that, when clinicians are operating in the context of discovery, they are not simply acting as informal statisticians, combining incoming data according to previous formulas. Rather, they are acting in a creative way, observing unique combinations of data, formulating original hypotheses, and generating predictions about the client based on these conceptualizations. Certainly, Meehl recognized that clinicians must submit their formulations to empirical evaluation if they wished to claim that the principles generalized to others and that such evaluations would require statistical prediction. However, when clinicians are operating in Reichenbach's context of discovery, Meehl strongly disagreed with Sarbin that they are informal actuaries.

Perhaps the most influential and controversial section of Meehl's (1954) book is the chapter that reviewed the empirical comparisons of the two methods of making predictions. Meehl reviewed the research to date and located those studies which compared directly the accuracies of clinical and statistical prediction. These studies concerned the prediction of various outcomes, such as success in training programs, recidivism, and recovery from psychosis. Meehl found 16 to 20 studies (depending upon one's standards for inclusion as relevant) *"in all but one of which the predictions made actuarially were either approximately equal or superior to those made by a clinician"* (p. 119).

Meehl (1965) later noted that the one exception in favor of clinical prediction employed a dubious statistical analysis which resulted in the inflation of the reported test statistic, and so he regarded this initial set of studies as unanimous in the finding that statistical prediction always equalled or surpassed clinical prediction.

Meehl (1954) recognized that this initial set of studies was flawed. He anticipated the criticisms of later opponents of statistical prediction by identifying five major difficulties with these studies.

Variability in the Training and Experience of the Clinicians

Little was known about the skill and qualifications of the clinicians who made the clinical predictions. For example, in some of the studies, the "clinician" was a military officer or a graduate student rather than an experienced psychologist or psychiatrist. It is not clear whether results obtained with such "clinicians" will generalize to real-world clinicians who may have different levels of training and experience.

Lack of Cross-Validation

Some studies did not use cross-validation procedures when applying statistical regression methods. A statistical regression formula is generated to produce the optimal prediction equation. Any set of data, including the one used to generate the prediction equation, includes some random error. Because the regression formula is the optimal prediction equation for the data at hand, the formula will not recognize the random error as error but instead will incorporate it so that the accuracy of prediction in the sample is optimized. When such a formula is used to make predictions in an independent sample, the equation will not be as successful as in the initial sample. The random errors in the second sample are different from those in the first and so must detract from the accuracy of the predictions.

Before using any regression formula, one should cross-validate it by applying it to a sample independent of the one used to generate it. Those studies that did not use a cross-validated regression formula, then, were biased in favor of statistical prediction. Their regression equations were, by definition, optimal and could not be surpassed by a clinician using the same predictors. Meehl noted this problem, but he also considered that it was balanced somewhat by the fact that several of the studies used prediction formulas which employed something other than the optimal empirical weights from regression equations.

Failure to Identify or Use Expert Judges

According to Meehl, most of these studies only reported the accuracy of clinicians as a group, not the accuracy of individual judges. It is possible that, even though clinicians as a group are not as accurate as statistical methods, individual clinicians may surpass the formulas. The study of such experts would be beneficial—to determine how they make such accurate judgments and to train other clinicians to make judgments in the same way. Unless studies report the accuracy of clinicians individually along with their mean performance, it is impossible to determine if any clinicians can outperform the computer.

Failure to Consider Clinicians' Confidence

Most of these early studies did not assess the confidence of the clinician. It may be the case that clinicians' predictions are accurate when they have high confidence in their judgments and that they only make clinical predictions in the real world when their confidence is high. If so, it is not appropriate to generalize to clinical judgments in actual practice from studies where clinicians are forced to make judgments. (Since Meehl's identification of the importance of this issue, the relationship between the confidence in and accuracy of a clinical judgment has been the focus of many investigations. This research will be discussed in Chapter Seven.)

Failure to Control the Amount of Information Used

According to Meehl, in many of these early studies the amount of information actually being used by the clinicians was unknown. For example, if clinicians are presented with 40 figures for a subject, representing personality, intelligence, and achievement test scores, it may not be clear how many of these scores are actually considered by the clinicians to form their final judgments. Similarly, if clinicians are presented with a case history or a transcript of a projective test protocol, it is not clear how much of this information they actually use. For one to compare the relative accuracies of clinical and statistical prediction and conclude that one method is more accurate, one must consider equivalent amounts of information with each method. Because of the difficulty involved in determining how much information the clinician is using, objective comparisons of the two prediction methods are difficult.

Meehl updated his box-score comparison of the empirical studies of clinical and statistical prediction on several occasions. It should be noted, however, that these later presentations were brief, and included neither lists of references nor discussions of individual studies. In 1957, Meehl reported that, in 27 studies which compared the two methods, statistical prediction was always found to be equal (10 studies) or superior (17 studies) to clinical prediction. In 1965, Meehl found that, in the approximately 50 studies which compared the two methods, statistical prediction was always equal (about one-third) or superior (about two-thirds) to clinical prediction. In 1986, Meehl noted that, of almost 90 studies, no more than 6 suggested even a weak tendency for clinical prediction to surpass statistical prediction.

Most recently, Meehl (Dawes, Faust, & Meehl, 1989) reported that, of almost 100 comparative studies of the two forms of prediction in the social sciences, statistical prediction equalled or surpassed clinical prediction in virtually every study. In this paper, Meehl and his colleagues cited a presentation by Grove which found that clinical prediction surpassed statistical prediction in only 6 of 117 comparative studies in medicine and the social sciences. However, according to Dawes et al., the studies that found a superiority for clinical prediction occurred primarily in medical and not psychological research and generally indicated only a slight advantage for clinical prediction. Thus, Dawes et al. did not think that these studies were sufficient to overturn the conclusion that statistical prediction always equals or surpasses clinical prediction.

Responses to Meehl

Following the publication of Meehl's (1954) book, there was a large and vigorous response from clinical psychologists. Many of these were supportive, recognizing along with Meehl the flaws in the early empirical comparisons of clinical and statistical prediction, but also recognizing the value of having an empirical foundation for the tasks performed by the clinical psychologist (Gough, 1962; Kogan, 1955; Mann, 1956). Others sought to clarify the assumptions underlying and the procedures followed in both statistical and clinical prediction, so as to clarify the similarities and dissimilarities between them (e.g., McArthur, 1956a; Tiedeman, 1956). Other responses were more critical, detailing additional flaws in the comparative studies reviewed by Meehl or arguing for some other method of determining the relative accuracies of the two procedures for making predictions.

Zubin (1956) termed the issue of the relative accuracies of clinical and statistical prediction a "pseudo-problem." In actual decision making, the two processes are used to supplement one another. In addition, just as Sarbin and Lundberg had regarded clinical prediction as a form of statistical prediction, Zubin now suggested that statistical prediction could be interpreted as a form of clinical prediction. After all, once a statistical prediction has been reached, a clinician makes a subjective decision whether or not to use the statistical prediction. This subjective decision is a form of clinical judgment and adds the clinical element to all statistical predictions.

Like Zubin, Hutt (1956) argued that the question of the relative accuracies of clinical and statistical prediction is meaningless. The answer will depend upon the specific context: What is being predicted? What variables are being used to make the prediction? Rather than attempt to answer such a broad question, Hutt (1956) suggested that it would be more useful to study the clinical process itself—to examine the influences on the accuracy of clinical prediction rather than to consider simply the global accuracy of clinical prediction.

Similarly, Holzberg (1957) detailed the steps in clinical prediction and suggested that they be examined in a scientific way. He argued that the studies reviewed by Meehl were flawed, and called for research that was better designed and more representative of actual clinical prediction than the initial empirical comparisons.

McArthur (1956b) and de Groot (1961) suggested alternative designs which they considered to be more appropriate for comparing the relative accuracies of clinical and statistical prediction. McArthur argued that a fair test of the relative accuracies of the clinician and the actuary would give both their choice of data, method of analysis, and type of prediction. McArthur stated that the data typically used by clinicians in actual decision making are plentiful, overlapping, open-ended, and fully recorded. Such "data" include verbatim transcripts and behavioral observations, in contrast with the summary scores from psychological tests used in statistical prediction. Similarly, McArthur stated that the predictions typically made by clinicians are contingent upon situational circumstances, rather than simple "yes-no" or multiple-choice responses, and are limited to the topic of the clinician's choice, rather than to the choice of the experimenter. Thus, the studies cited by Meehl, which did not permit clinicians their choice of data, method of analysis, and type of prediction, were not considered by McArthur to be fair tests of the relative accuracies of clinical and actuarial prediction.

It should be noted that Meehl (1954) addressed the criteria which he believed must be met for an adequate comparison of the accuracies of clinical and statistical prediction, including the criterion that the two methods should be given comparable or identical sets of information. Thus, what Meehl (1954) regarded as an adequate test of the relative accuracies of the two methods was regarded as "unfair" by McArthur.

Meehl and McArthur were asking different questions. It is certainly "fair" to provide an actuary and a clinician with identical sets of information if one asks, as did Meehl, about their relative accuracies of prediction given identical sets of information. What McArthur should question is not the "fairness" of the studies reviewed by Meehl (1954) but the external validity or the generalizability of the studies. If one is concerned with the relative accuracies of clinical and statistical prediction as these predictions are made in actual practice, then one should provide both the actuary and the clinician with the type and amount of information available for making predictions in actual practice. McArthur's criticism concerns the generalizability of these studies to actual practice and not the "fairness" of the comparison.

De Groot (1961) also suggested an alternative method for examining the relative accuracies of clinical and statistical prediction. Rather than pit the clinician against the actuary in a competitive design, de Groot wondered whether the clinician could improve upon the actuary's prediction in an incremental validity design. He suggested that a more appropriate test of the two methods would involve presenting the clinician with the prediction generated by the statistical formula and then determining whether the clinician could improve upon it, for example, by using clinical judgment to decide whether to discard the statistical prediction altogether or to modify in some way the statistical weights of the predictor variables included in the prediction equation. In other words, de Groot was describing a research design that would determine whether the clinician's judgment added incremental accuracy to the predictions made by a statistical formula. Like McArthur (1956b), de Groot also suggested that the clinician should have as much information available as possible, including information not included in the statistical formula. This would enhance the generalizability of the research comparisons to actual clinical predictions and would also be a more realistic test of the question of the clinician's incremental validity.

As an aside to the above argument, de Groot (1961) noted that he had conducted two small studies using this design. Although he did not present details concerning the procedures of the studies, he reported that one study found a small nonsignificant superiority of the clinician while the other found a significant superiority for the actuary. Indeed, in the second study, clinicians significantly reduced the accuracy of statistical predictions.

Of all the respondents to Meehl's (1954) book on the issue of clinical and statistical prediction, by far the most prominent and vocal has been Robert Holt. Holt published a series of articles (1958, 1961, 1970) in which he detailed the methodological flaws in the studies reviewed by Meehl and others, argued that statistical prediction is often a form of clinical prediction, and presented an alternative research design which he believed to be more appropriate for the scientific comparison of the accuracies of clinical and statistical prediction.

Like Zubin (1956), Holt (1958) suggested that statistical prediction involves clinical judgment and so can be regarded as a form of clinical prediction. Whereas Zubin (1956) only considered the clinical decision to accept, modify, or reject the statistical prediction, Holt (1958) detailed five different stages where clinical or subjective judgment enters into statistical decision making. These are the decisions involved in the selection of the (a) criterion variable to be predicted, (b) predictor variables to use in making the prediction, (c) assessment devices used to measure the criterion and predictors, (d) data-gathering methods, and (e) data-combination methods. (In 1970, Holt added a sixth step, suggesting that clinical judgment was involved in the design and implementation of empirical trials to evaluate the appropriateness of the first three decisions. Thus, a stage of preliminary pilot research was inserted prior to the actual data-gathering.)

These decisions are not automatic ones that can be made by an actuary or computer. They require familiarity with the practical problem to be predicted, theoretical formulations concerning the variable to be predicted, research concerning the utility of various measures, and knowledge of design and statistical considerations. Holt suggested that such decisions are clearly clinical, and so make much of what has been called statistical prediction actually a form of clinical prediction.

In order to question the appropriateness of the studies reviewed by Meehl which compared statistical and clinical prediction, Holt (1958) detailed the clinical decisions involved in statistical prediction. He suggested that these studies defined prediction methods as "clinical" or "statistical" only by what occurred in the final stage of the prediction process—how the data were combined. He argued that if the studies differed in any or all of the previous stages, then they are not fair comparisons of different methods of data combination.

For example, statistical prediction generally involves a preliminary study which is used to generate a prediction equation. Only after this study is completed is a regression equation used in the comparison of the relative accuracies of statistical and clinical prediction. Holt (1958) argued that clinicians should have the same opportunity as the statistician to conduct preliminary studies of the relationship between the criterion to be predicted and the predictor variables—that clinicians should not enter the experimental setting "cold" and be expected to be able to predict the criterion variable.

Holt (1958) distinguished among three approaches to making predictions: pure actuarial, naive clinical, and sophisticated clinical. The pure actuarial method involves objective or quantitative data which are combined statistically. The naive clinical method involves primarily qualitative data which are combined subjectively, without any opportunity for the clinician to conduct preliminary studies to determine the relationship between the criterion and likely predictor variables. Finally, the sophisticated clinical method involves both quantitative and qualitative data which are combined subjectively, after the clinician has had the opportunity for thorough study of the relationship between the criterion and predictor variables. (Holt [1961] argued that the clinical combination of quantitative data was not a form of clinical prediction. Rather, this was, as Sarbin and Lundberg maintained, a form of unsystematic statistical prediction, and so it is not surprising to learn that clinicians are outperformed by computers at this task.)

Holt (1958) considered the studies reviewed by Meehl (1954) to be mostly comparisons between the pure actuarial and naive clinical methods of making predictions. Hence, he was not surprised to learn that in these studies statistical prediction always equalled or surpassed clinical prediction. However, he thought that a fairer test of clinical prediction would be obtained by comparing the pure actuarial and sophisticated clinical methods. This would also be an evaluation of clinical prediction as done in actual practice and so would be a more externally valid or generalizable evaluation of clinical prediction. Holt (1958) briefly summarized the results of one such study which he conducted, which found that the sophisticated clinical method was more accurate than the other two methods of making predictions.

Sawyer's Review

In 1966, Jack Sawyer published an important review of the empirical comparisons of the accuracy of clinical and statistical prediction. Whereas Meehl's (1954) review of the research considered only how data were combined in order to generate predictions, Sawyer classified predictions according to both how the data were gathered and how they were combined.

For example, one can use clinical methods to combine either clinically collected data (the "pure clinical" method) or mechanically collected data (as in the case of profile interpretation). Similarly, one can use mechanical (statistical) methods to combine either mechanically collected data (the "pure statistical" method) or clinically collected data (as is the case in trait ratings). In addition, one can combine both types of data clinically (the "clinical composite") or mechanically (the "mechanical composite"). Finally, one can use both types of data along with the mechanical composite and combine this information clinically (the "clinical synthesis") or can use both types of information along with the clinical composite and combine this information mechanically (the "mechanical synthesis").

Sawyer reviewed 45 studies which yielded 75 empirical comparisons of the accuracies of two of these methods of generating predictions. Because the original authors of the studies did not classify the comparisons in the same way that Sawyer did, the number of times that two methods were compared to one another varied across pairs of methods. Sawyer tabulated the number of times that one method was found to be significantly more accurate than any other method. (In the case of nonsignificant differences, Sawyer "split the difference," counting each of the two methods as superior half of the time.) He then determined the percentage of times a particular method of generating predictions was found to be more accurate than any of the other methods to which it had been compared. This provided at least a rough estimate of the relative accuracies of the various methods.

On the basis of this analysis, Sawyer reached the following conclusions:

1. Within each mode of data collection, the mechanical method of data combination was superior to the clinical method. For example, pure clinical prediction was the more accurate method in 20 percent of its comparisons, whereas trait rating was the more accurate method in 43 percent of its comparisons. Profile interpretation was more accurate in 38 percent of its comparisons, whereas pure statistical prediction was more accurate in 63 percent of its comparisons. The mechanical composite outperformed the clinical composite by 75 percent to 26 percent, and the mechanical synthesis outperformed the clinical synthesis by 75 percent to 50 percent.

2. Within each mode of data combination, the clinical method of data collection was inferior to the mechanical method. As noted above, trait ratings were outperformed by pure statistical predictions, and pure clinical predictions were outperformed by profile interpretations.

3. With one exception, the difference between methods of data combination depended very little upon the methods of data collection, and vice versa.

4. The exception to the above statement concerned the clinical composite. When the method of data combination was mechanical, it was better to have both clinically and mechanically collected data. However, when the method of data combination was clinical, it was better to have only mechanically collected data. (That is, profile interpretations outperformed clinical composites.)
5. Predictions based on either clinical or mechanical syntheses did not appear promising. The mechanical synthesis did not surpass the mechanical composite in accuracy. Even though the clinical synthesis outperformed the clinical composite, the clinical synthesis was still outperformed by the mechanical composite.

Sawyer's review was an important one. It distinguished between statistical and clinical methods not only in data combination but also in data collection. Although Meehl (1954) and others had discussed the distinction between clinical and statistical methods of collecting data, Sawyer's paper was the first to systematically investigate the relative accuracies of predictions classified according to clinical and statistical methods of both data collection and combination.

Sawyer's review agreed with Meehl's (1954, 1957) conclusion. Regardless of how the data were collected, the statistical method of data combination outperforms the clinical method. However, by considering a factor not included in Meehl's reviews, Sawyer was able to extend Meehl's conclusions, showing how the clinician helps to improve the accuracy of prediction. Sawyer found that the most accurate methods of generating predictions included data collected both clinically and mechanically. "This suggests that the clinician may be able to contribute most not by direct prediction, but rather by providing, in objective form, judgments to be combined mechanically" (Sawyer, 1966, p. 193).

Although Sawyer's review reestablished a role for the clinician in prediction by showing that clinically collected data improved the accuracy of prediction, opponents of statistical prediction soon attacked his review. Holt (1970) published what is perhaps the most systematic critique of Sawyer's project. Holt detailed six major criticisms of Sawyer's review, many of which had previously been directed at the reviews of Meehl.

1. *Lack of cross-validation.* Holt noted that 15 of the 45 studies reviewed by Sawyer did not include cross-validations of the statistical prediction equations. Hence, these studies were biased in the favor of statistical methods of data combination.
2. *Inadequate prediction criteria.* Holt reported that only 12 studies employed criteria of the kind that clinicians actually deal with and that five of the studies included criterion measures that were completely inadequate (for example, one study employed a criterion

that was nonbehavioral—the number of live births—while another used a criterion that was unreliable and remote from the behavior of any one individual—winning a football game).

3. *Variability in the training and experience of clinicians.* Of the 45 studies reviewed by Sawyer, 23 employed judges who were not trained clinicians (psychologists or psychiatrists). Instead, they used untrained or less well-trained individuals (graduate students, military personnel, sportswriters) to make clinical-like judgments. The conclusions from such studies may well not generalize to clinical predictions made by trained clinicians.

4. *Small sample sizes.* Holt noted that several studies had small sample sizes, and so had limited statistical power to detect actual differences that may have existed between the modes of prediction. Two studies had sample sizes less than ten, while another six studies had samples with fewer than 50 subjects.

5. *Inadequate distinction between clinical and statistical prediction.* Holt repeated his argument that quantitative data combined clinically is not a form of clinical prediction. Rather, he considered such exercises (as clinical interpretation of MMPI profiles) not as a type of clinical judgment, but as a kind of informal actuarial prediction. Thus, he regarded many of the studies reviewed by Sawyer as inadequate evaluations of the accuracy of clinical prediction.

6. *Reviewer bias.* Holt suggested that Sawyer demonstrated a systematic bias in favor of statistical prediction and opposed to clinical prediction. Holt indicated three ways in which Sawyer demonstrated such a bias:

   a. Sawyer treated differently the best clinicians and the best statistical prediction methods. Holt argued that it was unfair of Sawyer to compare the average clinician (rather than the best clinician) to the best statistical formula (rather than the average formula).

   b. Sawyer employed inconsistent standards in determining whether there was a difference between the accuracies of two methods. For example, Sawyer's third conclusion appears to be inconsistent with his first two conclusions. He first observed that: (a) within each mode of data collection, the statistical mode of data combination was superior to the clinical mode; and (b) within each mode of data combination, the statistical method of data collection was superior to the clinical method. However, he then concluded that, with but one exception, the difference between methods of data combination depended very little upon the methods of data collection, and that the methods of data collection depended little upon the methods of data combination.

   c. Sawyer's review was based on a nonrepresentative collection of the available research. Holt cited a review by Korman (1968), based on over 40 studies of the relative abilities of clinical and statistical methods to predict managerial performance, which concluded that "there is no basis for assuming any superiority of the 'actuarial' over the 'clinical' method at this time. In fact, the evidence is to the contrary" (p. 316). Although Korman's review was published later than Sawyer's, and so included 10 papers that had not been available to Sawyer, none of the other papers in Korman's review was reviewed by Sawyer. In addition, Holt criticized Sawyer for failing to include in his review a book by Holt and Luborsky (1958) that presented data from a study comparing actuarial and sophisticated clinical prediction.

Overview of the Clinical-Statistical Prediction Issue

A Symposium on Clinical versus Statistical Prediction was presented at the 1984 meeting of the American Psychological Association. Three of the presenters at this symposium, Sarbin, Meehl, and Holt, had been leading contributors to the clinical-statistical prediction debate. Their remarks provide interesting overviews of the issue.

Sarbin (1986) was no longer concerned with the relative accuracies of clinical and statistical prediction, because he no longer regarded the clinician as merely an informal or unsystematic scientist. Sarbin cited the influence of Reichenbach's distinction between the contexts of discovery and justification (which had been highlighted by Meehl in 1954). He also cited the influence of recent works (e.g., Spence, 1982) that have argued that clinicians are not engaged in a scientific exercise, seeking historical truth judged on the basis of correspondence to actual events. Rather, clinicians are engaged in hermeneutic analysis, seeking a narrative truth which should be judged on the basis of its coherence and the degree to which it satisfies the client.

Although Sarbin (1986) indicated that he is no longer interested in the original question of the relative accuracies of clinical and statistical prediction and so has withdrawn from the original debate, he restated the question and so redefined the debate. He now considered the important question to be the relative utilities of the standards of historical truth (correspondence judged objectively) and narrative truth (coherence judged subjectively). The issue of the place of hermeneutic analysis in psychology has begun to be discussed in the professional journals (e.g., Packer, 1985) and is certain to receive more attention in the years to come.

Meehl (1986) stated that the empirical research from the last two decades would lead him to retract very little of his 1954 book. Although Meehl intended his 1954 book to be an impartial review of the arguments and empirical evidence on both sides of the debate, what Meehl would now retract would place his work more on the side of statistical prediction.

Meehl (1986) stated that he would retract his defense of clinical prediction on the grounds that it is configural or nonlinear (that is, it considers interactions among two or more variables) and so can make more accurate predictions than those generated by linear nonconfigural statistical methods. Two decades of research have shown that clinical prediction does *not* tend to be nonlinear or configural and that, when such nonlinearity is present, it is rare, unstable, difficult to detect, and low in incremental validity.

A second defense of clinical prediction which Meehl (1986) now retracted concerned the validity of complicated psychodynamic inferences. Meehl stated that the research of the previous two decades has questioned the reliability of psychoanalytic interpretations and the efficacy of psychoanalytic treatment, and so "psychoanalytic therapy is far less important quantitatively than it was 30 years ago" (p. 372).

Meehl (1986) noted that there were almost 90 studies which compared the accuracy of clinical and statistical prediction, with no more than 6 suggesting even a weak superiority of the clinician. Still, Meehl (1986) believed that this research has had very little impact on the way in which clinicians make predictions in actual practice. He identified several reasons, ranging from ignorance of the research through theoretical bias to fear of unemployment, for the reluctance of clinicians to incorporate empirically based statistical predictions in their practice. Since 1974, when Tversky and Kahneman showed that people in general make biased judgments when under conditions of uncertainty, many studies have demonstrated that clinicians are subject to these same biases. (The issue of the accuracy of clinical judgment in general is addressed in Chapter Seven.) Meehl (1986) suggested that such biases have led clinicians to continue to make less accurate clinical judgments than they could make. "I really didn't expect people to be able to think rationally about it. . . . I do not view human irrationality as confined to mentally ill patients or even to the milder maladjustments we see in outpatient psychotherapy, but rather as par for the course, as fairly standard for the human condition" (Meehl, 1986, p. 375).

A very different overview of the influence of the clinical-statistical prediction debate was presented by Holt (1986). Holt (1986) saw the clinical-statistical prediction issue as declining in importance. Thus, like Meehl (1986), Holt did not think that the issue would have much impact in the future.

Unlike Meehl, however, Holt believed that the issue has had a significant effect on clinical psychology over the previous two decades. Holt (1970) had earlier noted a decline of personality assessment in general and of diagnostic testing in particular and attributed this to the "rout of clinicians by exponents of statistical and actuarial prediction" (Holt, 1970, p.

337). One can argue that the decline in traditional assessment was due to factors other than the clinical-statistical prediction issue (for example, the increasing number of empirical studies of the reliability and validity of projective instruments, which are discussed in Chapter Four, and the increasing availability of alternative methods such as behavioral assessment). However, these alternative explanations are conceptually related to the clinical-statistical prediction issue in that they ultimately rest on the empirical evidence for the accuracy of clinical assessment.

Although Holt (1986) indicated that he thought that assessment was not emphasized as much today as it had been several decades ago (he perceived the field as having gone in the direction of therapy rather than assessment), he was no longer as pessimistic about the future of assessment as he had been in 1970. He cited recent studies that indicated that diagnostic testing was still "going strong."

Like Sarbin (1986), Holt (1986) suggested that science was not limited to only a single method of inquiry. Whereas Sarbin (1986) had recognized the hermeneutic method of interpretative analysis as appropriate in clinical psychology, Holt (1986) suggested that there was a place in science for subjective observation and verification. Although these issues cannot be examined in depth in this work, Sarbin's and Holt's arguments illustrate that there is at least a minority opinion within psychology that the methods of science are not as rigidly objective or empirical as traditionally held. These are certainly matters for scientists and philosophers of science to examine at greater length.

Because Holt (1986) accepted alternatives to what he regarded as the rigidly empirical or mechanical methods of traditional science, the relative accuracies of clinical and statistical prediction were no longer of major concern to him. Regardless of the outcomes of the almost 90 studies referred to by Meehl (1986), there are other means—personal, subjective, clinical—for verifying the accuracy and, ultimately, the usefulness of clinical prediction.

A final paper presented in the symposium along with those of Sarbin, Holt, and Meehl was that of Einhorn (1986). Einhorn (1986) suggested that the clinical approach to prediction is based on a deterministic, causal view that attempts to achieve perfect accuracy because of the important practical decisions, such as diagnosis and treatment, that follow prediction. On the other hand, Einhorn (1986) stated that statistical decision is based on a probabilistic model that accepts error as inevitable and that attempts to achieve, not perfect accuracy, but optimal accuracy. In other words, the statistical approach to prediction "accepts error to make less error."

Einhorn illustrated this distinction with the well-known example of probability matching. Suppose that a subject sits in front of a panel on which there are two lights and that the subject's task over a long series of trials is to predict which of the two lights will be turned on. Suppose further that the lights are programmed to follow a binomial distribution with a 60–40 ratio. That is, although the process is random, one light will be turned on 60 percent of the time while the other light will appear 40 percent of the time. Many studies have demonstrated that human subjects ultimately respond in a fashion that has been called "probability matching." That is, they predict the more frequent light on 60 percent of the trials and the less frequent light the other 40 percent.

The interesting point about these studies is that the subject, by attempting to predict every trial correctly, has engaged in a pattern that yields a less-than-optimal success rate! By predicting the more frequent light on 60 percent of the trials, the subject is correct on 36 percent (.60 x .60), of the trials. By predicting the less frequent light on 40 percent of the trials, the subject is correct on 16 percent (.40 x .40) of the trials. Thus, the overall success rate is 52 percent (.36 + .16).

On the other hand, if the subject had simply predicted the more frequent light every time, the accuracy rate would be optimized at 60 percent! Instead of trying to be correct on every trial, the subject could have been more successful by operating in a fashion that optimizes the overall success rate but also guarantees many failures.

Einhorn (1986) argued that this situation is at the heart of the clinical-statistical prediction issue. The clinician wishes to be correct on every occasion, because the cost of incorrect predictions with regard to practical outcomes such as treatment is so high. Thus, the clinician attempts to be right every time, adopting a "high-risk" strategy (Einhorn, 1988), with the result that the overall success rate is frequently lower than would occur by adopting a probabilistic approach, which guarantees many failures but also results in optimizing the overall success rate. Einhorn (1986) concluded that "the acceptance of error to make less error is likely to be a safer and more accurate strategy over a wide range of practical situations. Thus, the statistical approach leads to better performance on the average" (p. 394).

Summary and Conclusions

Following the publication of Meehl's (1954) book, the issue of the relative accuracies of clinical and statistical prediction became the focus of many empirical studies and theoretical discussions. The following conclusions can be drawn from an examination of this literature.

1. Statistical prediction almost always equals or surpasses clinical prediction. As Meehl (1986) indicated, there are now almost 90 empirical comparisons in the social sciences of the relative accuracies of predictions made by the two methods, with no more than half a dozen studies showing

a weak superiority of the clinician. All of the other studies suggest that statistical prediction is equal to or superior to clinical prediction. Meehl suggested that no single controversy in the social sciences had such "a large body of qualitatively diverse studies coming out so uniformly in the same direction as this one" (1986, pp. 373–374).

One may argue, in line with Holt, that these investigations have primarily examined "naive" and not "sophisticated" clinical prediction, from which one might conclude that statistical prediction almost always equals or surpasses naive clinical prediction. A problem with this tempering of the original conclusion is that it does not provide a substitute for empirical evidence for the superiority of sophisticated clinical prediction. Rather than simply dismiss almost 100 studies on methodological or conceptual grounds, proponents of the traditional position that clinical prediction is the superior method need to present research evidence for their position.

2. Despite the flurry of empirical studies comparing the two methods, and despite the near unanimity of the results of these studies, articles discussing the clinical-statistical prediction issue have declined since the 1960s in both number and emotional intensity. In contrast, the issue of the effectiveness of psychotherapy has experienced an ever-accelerating rate of outcome studies since Eysenck's (1952) review, with a heated debate continuing today over the efficacy of therapy in general and the relative efficacies of different therapies.

One reason for the relative decline in comparative studies of the accuracies of clinical and statistical prediction is that research has moved away from attempting to answer the broad question: Is clinical prediction superior to statistical prediction? As Hutt pointed out in 1956, such a broad question is unanswerable. The answer to the question will depend on the context in which it is asked: What criterion is being predicted? What information is being used to make the prediction?

Much research in the last several decades has been directed at specific types of clinical predictions. The issue is not whether clinical prediction is better than statistical prediction, but how to make the best prediction in each specific situation. For example, since the 1970s, clinical psychologists have directed an increased amount of empirical attention toward the topics of clinical diagnosis, the validity of psychodiagnostic assessment, and response to psychotherapy. These topics all concern the accuracy of predictions, and could well fit under the general heading of the accuracy of clinical and statistical prediction. These topics are discussed in other chapters of this book.

A second reason for the decline in comparative studies of the relative accuracies of clinical and statistical prediction is that clinical research has moved away from a focus on the overall accuracy of predictions toward a focus on the influences on the accuracy of predictions. As Hutt recommended in 1956, the focus has shifted from outcome to process. How are clinical decisions made? What factors decrease the accuracy of clinical judgments? How can such factors be countered?

These questions were first addressed by cognitive psychologists who examined influences on decision making in general, and then by clinical researchers who examined the operation of such influences on clinical decisions. For example, Tversky and Kahneman (1974) showed that, when subjects are under conditions of uncertainty, they tend to make judgments which are biased in systematic ways. Arkes (1981) discussed how such biases hinder the accuracy of clinical judgments and suggested ways that the clinician could attempt to overcome these biases. Wiggins (1981) expressed optimism that this focus on the process of clinical prediction will ultimately lead to the improvement of clinical practice. The accuracy of and influences on clinical judgments are the topic of Chapter Seven.

3. Another consequence of the clinical-statistical prediction debate has been that clinical psychologists now attend more closely to the criterion variables they attempt to predict. As Holt (1958, 1970) argued, clinical psychologists should study the outcome variables they intend to predict before they attempt to develop methods to predict them. If the outcome variable selected is itself unreliable, then no amount of clinical or statistical prediction methods will be able to accurately predict it. If the outcome variable is trivial or unrelated to the kinds of outcomes that clinicians must actually predict, then methods shown to be accurate in the laboratory may not generalize to clinical practice. Wiggins (1981) examined responses to the clinical-statistical prediction issue and concluded that clinical psychology has moved in the direction of developing more meaningful criterion measures.

For example, the school of behaviorism has insisted that psychologists assess psychological variables, such as response to psychotherapy, in terms of observable behaviors. Such outcome measures tend to be more objective, and so more reliable, than measures assessing internal constructs. Use of more reliable outcome measures will lead to the development of more accurate methods of predicting outcome.

Use of a behavioral outcome measure does not ensure that the measure is more meaningful than another kind of outcome measure. Indeed, early behavior therapists were criticized for addressing behaviors that were not meaningfully related to the clinical problems treated by clinicians in their daily practice (Goldfried & Davison, 1976). In response to this criticism, one movement within behavior therapy since the early 1970s has been to focus on behavioral outcomes that are clinically relevant (Bellack & Hersen, 1985). Thus, the rise and evolution of behavior therapy over recent decades provides one example of how clinical psychology has improved prediction by selecting reliable and meaningful criterion variables.

References

Allport, G. W. (1937). *Personality: A psychological interpretation.* New York: Holt.

Allport, G. W. (1942). *The use of personal documents in psychological science.* New York: Social Science Research Council.

Arkes, H. R. (1981). Impediments to accurate clinical judgment and possible ways to minimize their impact. *Journal of Consulting and Clinical Psychology, 49,* 323–330.

Bellack, A. S., & Hersen, M. (1985). General considerations. In M. Hersen & A. S. Bellack (Eds.), *Handbook of clinical behavior therapy with adults* (pp. 1–19). New York: Plenum.

Dawes, R. M., Faust, D., & Meehl, P. E. (1989). Clinical versus actuarial judgment. *Science, 243,* 1668–1674.

De Groot, A. D. (1961). Via clinical to statistical prediction. *Acta Psychologica, 18,* 274–284.

Einhorn, H. J. (1986). Accepting error to make less error. *Journal of Personality Assessment, 50,* 387–395.

Einhorn, H. J. (1988). Diagnosis and causality in clinical and statistical prediction. In D. C. Turk & P. Salovey (Eds.), *Reasoning, inference, and judgment in clinical psychology* (pp. 51–70). New York: Free Press.

Eysenck, H. J. (1952). The effects of psychotherapy: An evaluation. *Journal of Consulting Psychology, 16,* 319–324.

Freyd, M. (1925). The statistical viewpoint in vocational selection. *Journal of Applied Psychology, 9,* 349–356.

Goldfried, M. R., & Davison, G. C. (1976). *Clinical behavior therapy.* New York: Holt, Rinehart, and Winston.

Gough, H. G. (1962). Clinical versus statistical prediction in psychology. In L. Postman (Ed.), *Psychology in the making* (pp. 526–584). New York: Knopf.

Holt, R. R. (1958). Clinical and statistical prediction: A reformulation and some new data. *Journal of Abnormal and Social Psychology, 56,* 1–12.

Holt, R. R. (1961). Clinical judgment as a disciplined inquiry. *Journal of Nervous and Mental Disease, 133,* 369–382.

Holt, R. R. (1970). Yet another look at clinical and statistical prediction: Or, is clinical psychology worthwhile? *American Psychologist, 25,* 337–349.

Holt, R. R. (1986). Clinical and statistical prediction: A retrospective and would-be integrative perspective. *Journal of Personality Assessment, 50,* 376–386.

Holt, R. R., & Luborsky, L. (1958). *Personality patterns of psychiatrists* (Vol. 2). Topeka, KS: The Menninger Foundation.

Holzberg, J. D. (1957). The clinical and scientific methods: Synthesis or antithesis? *Journal of Projective Techniques, 21,* 227–242.

Hutt, M. L. (1956). Actuarial and clinical approaches to psychodiagnosis. *Psychological Reports, 2,* 413–419.

Kogan, L. S. (1955). Book review of Meehl, Paul E. *Clinical versus statistical prediction. Psychological Bulletin, 52,* 539–540.

Korman, A. K. (1968). The prediction of managerial performance: A review. *Personnel Psychology, 21,* 295–322.

Lundberg, G. A. (1941). Case studies vs. statistical methods—An issue based on misunderstanding. *Sociometry, 4*, 379–383.

Mann, R. D. (1956). A critique of P. E. Meehl's *Clinical versus statistical prediction. Behavioral Science, 1*, 224–230.

McArthur, C. (1956a). The dynamic model. *Journal of Counseling Psychology, 3*, 168–171.

McArthur, C. C. (1956b). Clinical versus actuarial prediction. In *Proceedings, 1955 invitational conference on testing problems* (pp. 99–106). Princeton, NJ: Educational Testing Service.

Meehl, P. E. (1954). *Clinical versus statistical prediction.* Minneapolis, MN: University of Minnesota Press.

Meehl, P. E. (1957). When shall we use our heads instead of the formula? *Journal of Counseling Psychology, 4*, 268–273.

Meehl, P. E. (1965). Seer over sign: The first good example. *Journal of Experimental Research in Personality, 1*, 27–32.

Meehl, P. E. (1986). Causes and effects of my disturbing little book. *Journal of Personality Assessment, 50*, 370–375.

Packer, M. J. (1985). Hermeneutic inquiry in the study of human conduct. *American Psychologist, 40*, 1081–1093.

Reichenbach, H. (1938). *Experience and prediction.* Chicago: University of Chicago Press.

Sarbin, T. R. (1941). Clinical psychology—Art or science? *Psychometrika, 6*, 391–400.

Sarbin, T. R. (1942). A contribution to the study of actuarial and individual methods of prediction. *American Journal of Sociology, 48*, 593-602.

Sarbin, T. R. (1944). The logic of prediction in psychology. *Psychological Review, 51*, 210–228.

Sarbin, T. R. (1986). Prediction and clinical inference: Forty years later. *Journal of Personality Assessment, 50*, 362–369.

Sawyer, J. (1966). Measurement and prediction, clinical and statistical. *Psychological Bulletin, 66*, 178–200.

Spence, D. P. (1982). *Narrative truth and historical truth: Meaning and interpretation in psychoanalysis.* New York: Norton.

Tiedeman, D. (1956). The trait model. *Journal of Counseling Psychology, 3*, 164–168.

Tversky, A., & Kahneman, D. (1974). Judgment under uncertainty: Heuristics and biases. *Science, 185*, 1124–1131.

Viteles, M. S. (1925). The clinical viewpoint in vocational psychology. *Journal of Applied Psychology, 9*, 131–138.

Wiggins, J. S. (1981). Clinical and statistical prediction: Where are we and where do we go from here? *Clinical Psychology Review, 1*, 3–18.

Zubin, J. (1956). Clinical versus actuarial prediction: A pseudo-problem. In *Proceedings, 1955 invitational conference on testing problems* (pp. 107–128). Princeton, NJ: Educational Testing Service.

CHAPTER SEVEN

The Validity of Clinical Judgment

Introduction

The previous chapter addressed the relative accuracies of clinical and statistical prediction. This chapter will discuss the topic of clinical judgment in general, apart from the issue of the comparison of clinical and statistical prediction.

Clinical judgment refers to the decisions concerning a client made subjectively by a clinician. For example, Wiggins (1973) wrote that "clinical" judgments occur when "human judgment enters into the combination of input data" (p. 142) when making decisions concerning a client's behavior. Similarly, Thorne (1961) stated that the "classical viewpoint, largely held among physicians, was that clinical judgment involves an intuitive Art which develops only after long experience" (p. 1).

Clinical judgments are made routinely with regard to fundamental matters such as personality dynamics, diagnosis, prognosis, and selection of treatment. Clinical judgments are also made frequently throughout a course of therapy; for example, the interpretations made during therapy are another kind of clinical judgment.

The information available to the clinician for such judgments includes data from psychological assessments (structured and projective personality tests, intelligence tests, and neuropsychological tests), behavioral observations, biographical and demographic information, and interview information.

Prior to the 1950s, the accuracy of clinical judgment was not often questioned by clinical psychologists. Since the time of Freud, clinicians assumed that their judgments were both accurate and useful, indeed a tool necessary to their trade.

Freud himself contributed to this belief in the accuracy of and the reliance on clinical judgment. For example, Freud hailed clinical observations over experimental investigation. According to Shakow and Rapaport (1964), when Rosenzweig wrote to Freud, describing the results of several empirical studies that supported psychoanalytic tenets, Freud responded that he saw little value in experimental tests of psychoanalysis, "because the wealth of dependable observations" on which psychoanalytic propositions rest "make them independent of experimental verification" (p. 129).

Similarly, Freud held a firm belief in the accuracy of his clinical interpretations. In an excellent biography of Freud, Gay (1988) noted that Freud's early writings led critics to perceive psychoanalytic interpretations in a "Heads I win; tails you lose" fashion. Gay wrote that Freud's "largely implicit claim to virtual omniscience invited criticism; it suggested that all psychoanalytic interpretations are automatically correct, whether the analysand accepts them or disdains them" (p. 250). According to Gay, Freud was aware of this criticism and regarded it as inaccurate. Gay indicated that, rather than accept a client's agreement with a psychoanalytic interpretation and perceive as resistance a rejection of the interpretation, Freud viewed both a client's agreement and disagreement with an interpretation skeptically.

Many traditionally trained psychologists shared Freud's assumption that clinical judgment is an intuitive or artistic enterprise, which cannot and should not be evaluated using empirical standards. Thorne (1961) wrote, "One of the most disturbing aspects of contemporary clinical practice has been the lack of criticality among clinicians in accepting and applying theories of unproven validity at a time when both clinical experience and accumulating research evidence indicated the actual invalidity of what was being done" (p. ix). Similarly, Wiggins (1973) suggested that clinicians contributed to a delay in the empirical evaluation of the accuracy of clinical judgments by maintaining that clinical judgments are "intuitive" and that, because they could not verbalize the processes that entered clinical judgment, clinical judgment was outside the scope of scientific investigation. Indeed, from early in the century there has been an ongoing debate within clinical psychology concerning its status as an art or a science (Bakan, 1956; Berenda, 1957; Chein, 1945; Hunt, 1951; Krech, 1946; Rogers, 1955; Rychlak, 1959; Skaggs, 1934).

According to one argument about clinical judgment, since people are unique individuals, judgments cannot be made using nomothetic (universal) laws, but instead must stem from an understanding of the individual. This position also holds that the process of clinical judgment is an intuitive one—clinicians themselves cannot articulate how and why they make their decisions—and so it is not possible to subject the clinical decision-making process to empirical examination.

The opposing position holds that clinical judgment, like any other judgment, is fallible. It is possible that clinical judgments are inaccurate. Indeed, the judgment that clinical judgments are accurate is in itself a clinical judgment and so may be erroneous. For this reason, empirical evaluations of clinical judgments are important to determine whether clinicians are as accurate as they hope and believe they are. If this research determines that clinical judgments are less accurate than commonly believed, then such results can be used in efforts to improve the clinical decision-making process.

From the 1950s on, clinical psychologists have directed an increasing amount of attention toward the accuracy of clinical judgment. This interest was sparked by several factors.

First, during this period, clinical psychologists began to question the empirical validity of many of their traditional assumptions and practices. As is shown throughout this book, the mid-1900s was a time when clinical psychology reevaluated many of its basic assumptions and methods. For example, the effectiveness of psychotherapy, the reliability and validity of projective tests, and the reliability of psychiatric diagnosis came into question. As empirical studies did not lend unequivocal support for these traditional practices, clinical psychologists became increasingly self-critical about other assumptions and practices. It was natural that, during such a period of self-appraisal, the accuracy of clinical judgment in general would be evaluated.

Second, psychologists in areas other than clinical psychology demonstrated that people in general tend to form inaccurate judgments when evaluating information or other people. For example, cognitive psychologists examined the systematic biases demonstrated when people process information in uncertain situations. Similarly, social psychologists examined the biases exhibited when people form impressions of others or try to determine the causes of the behavior of others. Because people in general demonstrate systematic errors when forming judgments in such situations, it seemed likely that clinicians might be susceptible to the same errors.

Thorne (1961) attributed the rise in empirical attention to the validity of clinical judgment to Meehl's (1954) review of the research on the relative accuracies of clinical and statistical prediction and the ensuing research that was conducted to contest Meehl's conclusion that statistical prediction almost always equalled or surpassed clinical prediction.

In addition to these factors, Kleinmuntz (1984) suggested several other influences on the rise of interest in the scientific investigation of clinical judgment: (a) the increased emphasis among cognitive psychologists on the information-processing model as a means of attempting to understand psychological processes, (b) the rise of behavioral decision theory as a means for understanding human decision making, (c) an increased emphasis among physicians and medical researchers on the scientific investigation of medical reasoning, and (d) the rise of the computer, especially in areas such as artificial intelligence where computer scientists and psychologists have made great strides in modeling problem-solving processes and other complex psychological functions.

Unlike the issues of the effectiveness of psychotherapy and the relative accuracies of clinical and statistical prediction, no single work sparked a controversy concerning and initiated the empirical investigation of the accuracy of clinical judgment. One of the first clinical psychologists to make a serious effort to examine empirically the accuracy of clinical judgment was Paul Meehl. In his 1954 book on clinical versus statistical prediction he wrote, "We of all people, ought to be highly suspicious of ourselves . . . [and] have no right to assume that entering the clinic has resulted in some miraculous mutations and made us singularly free from the ordinary human errors which characterized our psychological ancestors" (pp. 27–28).

Meehl (1960) followed this remark with an article in which he reported the results of several empirical studies of the "cognitive activity of the clinician." These studies addressed several traditional assumptions made by clinicians concerning the clinical decision-making process: (a) that their conceptualizations of clients consistently change and become increasingly complex as they acquire more information about the client; (b) that clinical judgment is configural (it considers interactions among two or more client variables) and so cannot be modeled adequately by and must be more accurate than linear statistical formulas; and (c) that their theoretical formulations of clients are complex, relying upon numerous theoretical constructs, all of which must be considered simultaneously when understanding and making predictions about a client.

Meehl (1960) reported evidence that questioned each of these assumptions. He described research results which found that clinicians' impressions of clients are formed early and remain relatively unchanging despite additional information, that nonlinear configural equations are not substantially superior to linear additive equations for modeling clinical judgments, and that a small number of theoretical constructs is about as able as a set of constructs ten times as large to capture the detailed characterizations made by clinicians of a set of clients.

Meehl (1960) concluded on an ambivalent note. Although he was encouraged by more and more sensible empirical examinations of clinical judgment being conducted, he was discouraged by the "cultural lag between what the published research shows and what clinicians persist in claiming to do" (p. 26).

In 1973, Meehl published an interesting paper in which he identified several dozen logical, statistical, and conceptual errors that commonly occur in clinical "reasoning" and that should be familiar to anyone who has attended case conferences or read case descriptions. The many threats to the validity of clinical reasoning described by Meehl include forgetting Bayes' Theorem (which requires the application of prior probabilities or base rates when making probabilistic judgments), the Barnum Effect (which refers to making statements about clients that are trivial and likely true of most people, and so are useless as a description of an individual), and the failure to distinguish between valid and invalid predictors when attempting to predict some behavioral criterion.

Although the many errors identified by Meehl overlap and are not clearly distinct from one another and although Meehl presented this material in a nontraditional manner that some may find caustic and confrontational, I have found this paper very valuable in the training of graduate student therapists. By identifying these errors, demonstrating why they are errors, and presenting more effective alternative ways of evaluating case material, Meehl sought to improve the quality of case conferences in particular and the quality of clinical judgment in general.

By the 1960s, other clinical psychologists were, like Meehl, aware of the importance of the empirical validation of clinical judgment and had begun to conduct such investigations. In 1959, for example, Hunt and Jones summarized a series of studies on clinical judgment. Hunt and Jones applied the methodology of psychophysics, which examines the accuracy of judgment of physical stimuli, to the area of clinical judgment. They found not only that this methodology was useful in the study of clinical judgment, but also that several of the features of psychophysical judgment (e.g., assimilation, contrast) characterize clinical judgment as well.

The remainder of this chapter will discuss the topic of the accuracy of clinical judgment. Several specific types of clinical judgment (for example, psychiatric diagnosis, interpretation of projective tests) or issues related to clinical judgment (for example, the relative accuracies of clinical and statistical prediction) have been addressed in previous chapters.

The organization of the material in this chapter will follow a structure employed by Hollon and Kriss (1984). They discussed the importance of cognitive factors in clinical practice. Although they were primarily interested in the cognitive operations of clients, they also addressed briefly the cognitive operations of clinicians. In their discussion of cognitive influences in clinical practice, Hollon and Kriss found it useful to categorize cognitive factors as Structures, Processes, or Products.

Cognitive structures, sometimes called "schemata," are "organizational entities that contain all of an individual's knowledge at any given moment about himself/herself and the world" (Hollon & Kriss, 1984, p. 36). Cognitive psychologists have shown that schemata are useful constructs for helping to understand how an individual organizes experiences (e.g., Neisser, 1976). As one engages in some experience, preexisting cognitive structures help to organize the information so that it is more readily understood. Schemata help to label and explain incoming information and to direct the search for additional information which may be required to label ambiguous material.

Cognitive processes refer to the ways in which incoming information is combined with existing knowledge structures to form judgments. Hollon and Kriss (1984) likened cognitive processes to computer software, noting that "these processes determine how incoming information is perceived, encoded, stored, combined, and altered with respect to information and structures already in the system, and how that existing information is retrieved and those existing structures are engaged, disengaged, or altered" (p. 40).

Cognitive products are the results of information processing, the outcomes generated by the individual as a consequence of the cognitive processes described above. Like cognitive structures, cognitive products have informational content. However, unlike cognitive structures (whose content may have to be inferred), cognitive products are directly accessible to the individual.

The distinction drawn by Hollon and Kriss (1984) among cognitive structures, processes, and products is somewhat arbitrary. If one operates on the basis of a biased cognitive structure, then one is likely to engage in an ineffective cognitive process and ultimately produce an inaccurate cognitive product. Thus, these concepts are interrelated. It could prove difficult to determine which cognitive factor was the single major influence in an example of a faulty clinical judgment. Still, despite their interrelatedness, they do provide a useful way of classifying the kinds of influences that can affect the accuracy of clinical judgment.

Cognitive Structures

It is clear that the accuracy of clinical judgment will be related to the cognitive structures of the clinician. If the clinician's cognitive structures are biased or inaccurate, then incoming information will be processed in a biased or distorted manner. This section of the chapter will examine studies of how cognitive characteristics of the clinician are related to the accuracy of the clinician's judgments. This discussion will include two issues: the problem of clinical bias and the role of individual characteristics of the clinician.

Clinical Bias

It is not possible to review here all of the possible biases that may decrease the accuracy of clinical judgment. However, three specific kinds of bias have received extensive attention in the research literature and so warrant inclusion in this summary of clinical bias. Clinicians may exhibit bias against their clients on the basis of the variables of patient status, minority status, and sex.

Patient Status

Several major studies have demonstrated the bias of clinicians toward individuals with patient status. Perhaps the most dramatic of these studies was that of Rosenhan (1973). In this study, eight normal individuals presented themselves at 12 mental hospitals, complaining of hearing voices which said "thud," "hollow," and "empty." Rosenhan reported that the pseudopatients were admitted to the hospital with the diagnosis of schizophrenia (the one exception received the diagnosis of manic-depression). Even though they acted normally while in the hospital, the pseudopatients were released with a discharge diagnosis of schizophrenia in remission after an average hospital stay of 19 days.

Although Rosenhan's study is usually cited as evidence for the invalidity of traditional psychiatric diagnosis, it also demonstrated the influence of bias on clinical judgment. Rosenhan recounted several incidents where the "patient" label led hospital staff to misinterpret normal behavior as abnormal. For example, the pseudopatients kept logs of their experiences in the hospital. In three cases, nursing notes indicated that this note-taking behavior was seen as evidence of psychopathology.

Another well-known study of the effect which the "patient" label has on clinical judgment is that of Temerlin (1968). Temerlin played an audiotaped interview to mental health professionals. In one condition, subjects were told that the target "looks neurotic, but actually is quite psychotic." In another condition, this suggestion was reversed. Subjects then monitored the tape and assigned a diagnosis to the target.

Temerlin found that expectation had a significant effect on clinicians' observations. Clinicians who believed that the target was psychotic assigned a greater frequency of severe diagnoses than did clinicians who believed that the target was neurotic.

Langer and Abelson (1974) conducted a similar study. They filmed an interview with a young man who had recently applied for a new job. He was asked a series of questions concerning his feelings and experience regarding his past work. Langer and Abelson described the man as "intense, but uncertain, so that he could easily be seen either as sincere and struggling or as confused and troubled" (p. 6). They then presented the film to psychologists from two theoretical schools: behavioral and psychodynamic. They also manipulated the psychologists' expectations regarding the target. Subjects were instructed that this was an interview with either a patient or a job applicant. Subjects then viewed the film and answered a series of questions concerning the adjustment of the target.

Langer and Abelson found, like Temerlin, that clinicians' expectations significantly affected their judgments of the target. Clinicians who expected the individual to be a patient perceived him to be more severely disturbed than clinicians who expected him to be a job applicant. However, Langer and Abelson also found that theoretical orientation was related to the degree to which clinicians demonstrated the labeling bias. Behaviorally oriented clinicians (who are trained to observe behaviors rather than to attempt to infer underlying constructs from observed behaviors) showed significantly less labeling bias than psychodynamically oriented clinicians.

These studies and others have demonstrated that the "patient" label may lead mental health professionals to misperceive and misinterpret an individual's behavior, thereby decreasing the accuracy of clinical judgment. Those interested in more detailed discussions of the effects of the patient label should consult the works of Braginsky, Braginsky, and Ring (1969), Goffman (1961), and Scheff (1966).

Minority Status

A second factor which may bias clinicians' judgments is minority (or counternormative) status. Abramowitz and Dokecki (1977) reviewed the empirical studies of the relationship between clinical judgment and the client's social class, race, values, and sex. Both analogue and correlational studies indicated that social class was significantly related to negative evaluations by clinicians. Patient value system was the second strongest elicitor of negative clinical judgments, although the results for this variable were mixed. Patient race was not found to be related to negative evaluations by clinicians in analogue studies. Similarly, Abramowitz and Murray (1983) reviewed the evidence concerning the effect of client's race on clinical judgments and concluded that there was little evidence of racial bias.

Lopez (1989) reviewed the research on the effect of such patient variables on clinical judgments, using a broadened definition of bias. Earlier attention to the issue of possible bias in clinical judgment defined bias in a unidirectional manner: clinicians were said to be biased when they evaluated members of a minority group more negatively than others. Lopez extended the definition of bias to include ratings of minorities which differ from those of others in either a positive or a negative direction. That is, according to Lopez, clinical judgment is biased when clinicians rate members of a minority group as either more or less severely disturbed than others.

Lopez tabulated the results of studies of clinical bias using both the traditional and his expanded definition of bias. Whereas the traditional definition led to findings of bias in 24 percent of studies using severity ratings and 22 percent of studies involving diagnostic judgments, the broadened definition led to findings of bias in, respectively, 44 and 60 percent of these studies. Lopez concluded that there are "nearly twice as many findings of bias with the new definition as with the old definition" and that "there is about equal evidence of bias as there is evidence of no bias" (p. 192).

In addition, Lopez found consistent evidence of bias against the mentally retarded and members of lower socioeconomic groups, some consistent evidence of racial bias in studies involving diagnostic decision making, but little evidence for gender bias.

Sex

A third factor that may bias clinicians' judgments is the client's sex. Since the demonstration by Broverman, Broverman, Clarkson, Rosenkrantz, and Vogel (1970) that mental health professionals share the sex-role stereotypes of their society and that these stereotypes are incorporated into the clinicians' definition of mental health, numerous studies have been conducted to examine the extent to which such sex-role stereotypes affect clinical judgments.

Studies of the influence of sex on the judgments of clinicians have been reviewed by Abramowitz and Dokecki (1977), Zeldow (1978), Whitley (1979), and Davidson and Abramowitz (1980). These reviews agreed that:

1. Mental health professionals share the sex-role stereotypes of their nonprofessional contemporaries, and that these stereotypes are related to the professionals' definition of mental health. In general, traits associated with the stereotypical female are judged as less healthy or desirable than traits associated with the stereotypical male.

2. The judgments of mental health professionals regarding severity of psychopathology, diagnosis, and prognosis are relatively uninfluenced by violations of their sex-role expectations. Analogue studies in which experimenters presented clinicians with case material while manipulating the sex of the patient generally found that there was little or no effect of patient sex.

However, these reviews also noted the limitations of analogue studies. Because what clinicians say they do in analogue studies may not accurately reflect their behavior in actual practice, it is possible that analogue research is not an adequate methodology for detecting sex bias in clinical judgments. For example, Abramowitz and Dokecki (1977) noted that correlational studies based on archival records consistently reported results at odds with those of analogue studies and which support the claim of an anti-female bias among clinicians.

At best, the evidence concerning sex-related bias in clinical judgments is inconclusive. Although it is clear that clinicians share the sex-role stereotypes of their society, it is unclear to what extent, if any, these stereotypes affect actual clinical judgments.

Other Factors

Other biases may affect clinical judgments. Biases related to religious, ethnic, regional, or other prejudices may all affect the observations of clinicians. Although there are relatively few empirical examinations of how these factors affect clinical judgments (Lopez, 1989), it is well known that members of the general population have such prejudices. It is likely that individual clinicians or subgroups of clinicians may share these prejudices. For example, Jones, Hansson, and Phillips (1978) demonstrated that students' ratings of the psychological disturbance of patients were significantly affected by the physical attractiveness of the patients (even when subjects were instructed that attractiveness is not important in the evaluation of patients). Judgments based on such biased perceptions must be less accurate than those based on nonbiased and more accurate observations. For example, Snyder and Thomsen (1988) cited numerous studies that have demonstrated how therapists' stereotypes concerning clients' sex, race, appearance, and class affect their judgments about clients. Hence, the accuracy of clinical judgments, like that of judgments made by nonclinicians, will be related to the degree to which observations are influenced by preexisting biases.

Characteristics of the Clinician

In addition to the problem of bias, many individual characteristics of clinicians have been examined which may be related to clinicians' cognitive structures and so may influence their judgmental accuracy. Of these, the training and experience of the clinician have received the most attention.

Clinical Training and Experience

Taft (1955) reviewed the research to date concerning individual characteristics that were related to the "ability to judge people." Several of the factors that were positively correlated with the ability to judge others supported traditional assumptions concerning the accuracy of clinical judgment. For example, intelligence, social skill, good emotional adjustment, and insight into one's own emotional states and psychological traits, all of which have traditionally been viewed as important characteristics of clinicians, were positively correlated with the ability to judge others. However, the research to date also found that training in psychology was unrelated to the ability to judge others and that the relationship between being a clinical psychologist and the ability to judge others was uncertain. Thus, the empirical evidence did not unequivocably support the assumption of the accuracy of clinical judgment.

Taft's review did not provide conclusive results regarding the accuracy of clinical judgment. Although it supported several traditional assumptions concerning the characteristics of a good clinician, it failed to show that training in psychology or in general or clinical psychology in particular was related to increased accuracy of judgment. Clinicians were not compelled by this review to alter their views on clinical judgment. Much of the research reviewed by Taft consisted of analogue studies, wherein judgments were made by subjects who were not trained clinicians under conditions that were not representative of the ways in which clinicians make judgments in actual practice. Hence, the conclusions had only limited generalizability to actual clinical judgments.

Since Taft's review, there have been many efforts to determine the degree to which clinical training and experience are related to judgmental accuracy. Unfortunately, many of these studies have failed to show that training or experience improve the accuracy of clinical judgments.

One of the most commonly cited studies of this issue is that of Goldberg (1959). Goldberg compared the abilities of staff psychologists, psychological trainees, and untrained secretaries to use the Bender-Gestalt Test to diagnose brain damage. He found that these groups did not differ in accuracy.

Another classic study was conducted by Oskamp (1962). Oskamp had undergraduate students, psychological trainees, and clinical psychologists attempt to classify patients as either medical or psychiatric on the basis of the patients' MMPI profiles. Oskamp reported that initial judgmental accuracy was moderately related to experience; however, a brief training period was sufficient to raise the accuracy of undergraduates to the level of experienced clinicians.

In another study, Oskamp (1965) had undergraduates, psychology graduate students, and psychologists make a series of ratings of a case study, which had been divided into segments presented sequentially. Oskamp found that the three groups did not differ in the accuracy of their judgments of the case. In addition, he reported that increasing the amount of information did not necessarily increase the accuracy of judgments. In fact, the addition of childhood information to the case material caused a decrease in the accuracy of judgments.

Since these early studies, many reviewers of the literature have concluded that there is little empirical support for the claim that clinical training or experience enhances clinical judgment. For example, Wiggins (1973) concluded that "there is little empirical evidence that justifies the granting of 'expert' status to the clinician on the basis of his training, experience, or information-processing ability" (p. 131). Similarly, Watts (1980) wrote that "there are many studies . . . suggesting that the clinical judgement of psychologists is no better than that of, say, physical scientists; and that psychologists with a clinical training have no better judgement than those without" (p. 95). A task force of the American Psychological Association (1982) found no evidence that either professional training or experience is related to professional competence.

More recently, evaluations of the research by Faust (1986; Faust & Ziskin, 1988) have not revised these earlier conclusions. Faust and Ziskin, for example, concluded that "there is almost no evidence that a select group of professionals with extensive experience or special qualifications performs better than other professionals" (p. 32) and that "Virtually every available study shows that amount of clinical training and experience are unrelated to judgmental accuracy" (p. 32).

Rock, Bransford, Maisto, and Morey (1987) examined the issue of the validity of clinical judgment. They selectively reviewed the literature and found that much of the evidence fails to support the validity of clinical judgments. However, they also criticized this research on methodological grounds and suggested that researchers in this area should adopt a four-factor model when investigating the clinical decision-making process. This model includes: (a) the characteristics of the clinician, (b) the information-processing strategies available to the clinician, (c) criterial tasks that specify the major focus of the judgments, and (d) the nature of the information made available to the clinician. When Rock et al. applied this model to two classic studies of clinical judgment (Goldberg, 1959; Oskamp, 1962), they interpreted selected results from these studies in ways much more favorable to the validity of clinical judgment than had the original authors.

Perhaps the most vocal proponent of the validity of clinical judgment in recent years has been Garb (1988, 1989). Garb (1988) took Rock et al. (1987) to task for what Garb believed was an overly negative interpretation of the research on clinical judgment. Garb noted that Rock et al. only cited studies of negative findings and failed to cite studies in which clinicians performed well.

Garb (1989) reviewed research on the relationships between the validity of clinical judgment and the factors of clinical training and experience. Even though he is a strong proponent of the validity of clinical judgment, Garb concluded that the "results on experience and validity were disappointing" (p. 391). In the studies he reviewed, Garb found that experience was not related to the validity of either personality or neuropsychological assessments (except when "expert" neuropsychologists were compared to other clinicians).

Garb (1989) also reported that the "results for training and validity were more positive. Training was positively related to validity for some assessment instruments and some tasks" (p. 391). For example, although clinicians were not found to be superior to graduate students in their judgments based on biographical data from nonpatients, projective tests, or neuropsychological tests, clinicians did outperform nonprofessionals when judgments were based on patients' biographical data, the WAIS, and the MMPI.

In summary, despite traditional beliefs that the accuracy of clinical judgment is related to the clinician's training and experience, there is relatively little empirical evidence to support this. One of the recommendations made by the APA (1982) Task Force on Education was that researchers should obtain "persuasive evidence" demonstrating that training and experience are related to professional competence.

Other Characteristics

Besides training and experience, other personal characteristics may also affect the accuracy of the clinician's perceptions and subsequent judgments. For example, Raines and Rohrer (1955) examined the interrater reliability of psychiatrists' evaluations of military candidates' likelihood of success in an officer training program. They found relatively low agreement between the psychiatrists' ratings and reported that one of the reasons for the unreliability was that the psychiatrists' own personalities seemed to influence their assessments. In other words, Raines and Rohrer likened the psychiatric evaluation to a projective test where the final evaluation reflected the personality of the examiner as well as of the examinee.

Raines and Rohrer (1960) examined this suggestion more closely. They randomly assigned 116 military personnel to 4 psychiatrists who interviewed and evaluated them on 41 symptom dimensions. Raines and Rohrer also obtained personality descriptions of the 4 psychiatrists from a senior psychiatrist. When they analyzed the 116 evaluations, Raines and Rohrer found that the psychiatrists differed significantly in their use of the

11 dimensions that had been used frequently enough to be subject to statistical analysis. In addition, they found that each psychiatrist exhibited a unique pattern of use of the symptoms and that these patterns were related to their own personalities as described by the senior psychiatrist. Raines and Rohrer concluded that their projection hypothesis was supported— that the evaluations of professional clinicians are in fact related to their own personalities—and that the influence of clinicians' personalities on other clinical judgments needed to be investigated.

Clinicians' theoretical orientations may also affect their perceptions of clients. For example, Snyder (1977) reanalyzed the data from the Langer and Abelson (1974) study on the susceptibility to suggestion bias of therapists from different theoretical schools. Snyder found that a major difference between the perceptions of psychodynamic and behavioral clinicians was an attributional one. Psychodynamic therapists perceived the cause of the client's condition to be more within the client himself, whereas behavioral clinicians perceived the cause of the client's condition to be more situational.

Similarly, Houts (1984) played a videotaped interview of an actress portraying a fear of elevators to clinicians with three theoretical orientations—psychodynamic, behavioral, and cognitive—who then rated the client's responsiveness to therapy. Houts found that psychodynamic clinicians expressed significantly more negative judgments concerning the client's prognosis than did clinicians with the other two orientations.

In summary, then, research has shown that factors related to the cognitive structures of the clinician are associated with the validity of clinical judgments. Clinicians' biases and other individual characteristics may decrease the accuracy of clinical judgments. However, despite the general belief in their value, the clinician's training and experience have not been consistently found to be related to clinical accuracy.

In other words, clinical judgment resembles judgment in general: factors which distort incoming information or which lead to the information's being processed in an ineffective fashion lead to decreased accuracy in judgments.

Cognitive Processes

The characteristics of the clinician discussed in the previous section of the chapter affect not only the accuracy of the clinician's observations, but they also influence the cognitive processes employed to gather and process information. For example, a clinician's bias against a certain group of people will affect both the perceptions of a client who belongs to this group and the cognitive processes used to gather and evaluate additional information about the client. Thus, the clinician is likely to engage in a series of ineffective cognitive processes that will ultimately reduce the accuracy of his or her clinical judgments.

For example, suppose a clinician's cognitive structure contains the assumption that "All neuroses are caused by childhood experiences during the first five years of life." As the clinician gathers information about the client, it is processed—organized, labeled, understood—in a manner consistent with this assumption. Regardless of the actual age at which the disorder was caused, the clinician will develop a conceptualization of the problem consistent with the model of childhood causation. The clinician need only gather information in a biased fashion, seeking to learn about traumatic events, actual or fantasized, during early childhood. By entertaining only the hypothesis of early childhood causation of pathology, it is a simple matter to probe until some childhood stressful event is revealed and then conclude that this is causally related to the present disorder.

This example illustrates a faulty cognitive process that has been labeled the *confirmatory bias*. The purpose of this section of the chapter is to discuss research on this and other faulty or ineffective cognitive processes which may affect the validity of clinical judgments.

Confirmatory Bias

Wason (Wason, 1960; Wason & Johnson-Laird, 1972) investigated people's hypothesis-testing strategies in the following way. He presented a sequence of numbers (e.g., 2 4 6) and informed subjects that the sequence followed some mathematical rule. The task was to identify the underlying rule through experimentation. Subjects would present their own sequence of numbers and receive feedback as to whether or not this sequence followed the rule.

Wason reported that subjects had difficulty identifying the rule, even though it was very basic (e.g., $x < y < z$). In general, subjects tended to use confirmatory rather than disconfirmatory strategies. That is, when subjects formed hypotheses about the rule, they presented sequences that conformed to rather than deviated from the hypothesis. If the hypothesis also followed the underlying rule (e.g., $x, x + 2, x + 4$), it was possible for subjects to obtain multiple confirmations of their hypothesis, even though they made no progress toward identifying the underlying rule.

Since Wason's study, cognitive psychologists have demonstrated the confirmatory bias many times. People in general tend to look for evidence to confirm their hypotheses and tend to ignore or to undervalue disconfirming evidence.

This bias has also been shown to occur in clinical-like judgments made by nonprofessional subjects. For example, Snyder (1981; Snyder & Swann, 1978; Snyder, Tanke, & Berscheid, 1977) has shown that subjects who are asked to seek evidence concerning a hypothesis (e.g., that an individual is an introvert) most often ask confirmatory questions.

It should be noted that, since the work of Karl Popper (1959, 1963), science itself has been associated with a disconfirmatory strategy. Popper argued that science was best distinguished from nonscience in that scientific theories were falsifiable. Science made progress through the refutation of inadequate theories and their replacement with more accurate ones. The scientist, according to Popper, has been trained to employ a disconfirmatory strategy because it is the most effective means of determining the "truth-value" of a claim and is bound to lead to the overturning of incorrect hypotheses or theories in favor of better ones.

Given that clinical psychologists are generally trained in a scientist-practitioner model (Barlow, Hayes, & Nelson, 1984), one might expect that clinical judgments are less likely than judgments by the general public to demonstrate the confirmatory bias. Unfortunately, however, studies have shown that the confirmation bias occurs in the judgments of clinicians as well as nonclinicians—in the judgments of scientists as well as nonscientists.

For example, Mahoney (1976) presented Wason's task to 15 psychologists, 15 physical scientists, and 15 Protestant ministers. Mahoney found that neither scientists nor nonscientists used the scientific method of disconfirmation to a significant degree—85 percent of the experiments were confirmatory. In fact, on several measures of reasoning ability, the ministers actually outperformed the scientists.

Other studies have also demonstrated that professional training does not shield one from the confirmatory bias. Mahoney (1976) described a second study in which 77 natural and social scientists completed a survey and a test of logical reasoning skills. Mahoney reported that fewer than 8 percent of the scientists correctly identified two of four irrelevant tests of an experimental hypothesis (with psychologists somewhat more successful than biologists, physicists, and sociologists), and that over half of the scientists failed to recognize modus tollens (disconfirmation) as a valid logical form.

In a similar study by Einhorn and Hogarth (1978), with statisticians or graduate students in statistics as subjects, only 5 of 23 subjects correctly identified the two of four logical possibilities that were the minimum number required to test a hypothesis. More than half of the subjects failed to indicate that disconfirmatory tests were required.

Elstein, Shulman, and Sprafka (1978) studied diagnostic decision-making processes of physicians. They reported that the less accurate physicians tended to discount evidence that was inconsistent with their initial hypothesis. That is, a nonscientific approach to diagnostic decision making was less accurate than an approach which included the consideration of disconfirming evidence.

Hindsight Bias

Another general reasoning error, related to confirmatory bias, has been shown to occur in the judgments of both professional and nonprofessional subjects. Several studies of judgment have found what has been termed hindsight bias. *Hindsight bias* is "the tendency to believe, once the outcome of an event is known, that the outcome could have been predicted more easily than is actually the case" (Wedding & Faust, 1989, p. 237). For example, Fischhoff (1975) had one group of subjects read psychotherapy case studies and judge the likelihoods of four possible outcomes. Other subjects were given the case studies along with their outcomes and were asked to judge the likelihoods of the known outcomes. Fischhoff reported that subjects with hindsight knowledge judged the known outcomes as highly likely and as significantly more likely than subjects without such foreknowledge.

Arkes, Wortmann, Saville, and Harkness (1981) demonstrated the same effect in physicians. A case history was presented to four groups of physicians, each of which was informed that the case had been assigned a different diagnosis. When physicians rated the likelihoods of the four diagnoses given the presenting symptoms, each group assigned the highest probability to the diagnosis which it believed had been assigned.

Arkes, Faust, Guilmette, and Hart (1988) repeated this finding with neuropsychologists as subjects. In hindsight, subjects rated as most probable the diagnosis which they had been informed was ultimately assigned to the case. An interesting aspect of this report is that Arkes et al. demonstrated a method of reducing hindsight bias. Hindsight bias was eliminated when subjects were asked to list the supportive evidence for all possible diagnoses before they rated the probabilities of the conditions.

Thus, hindsight bias, or the tendency to think that "I knew it all along," may affect the judgments of clinicians in several ways. First, hindsight bias may contribute to anchoring errors. When a clinician weighs new evidence, hindsight is likely to bias such considerations so as to support the initial judgment.

Second, hindsight bias may contribute to labeling bias. When a clinician is presented a case with a diagnostic label, hindsight bias is likely to lead the clinician to interpret the case in a way consistent with the label. Finally, the hindsight bias may contribute to overconfidence in the accuracy of a clinician's judgments. Because reviews of the evidence which led to a judgment are interpreted in a biased fashion so as to support the initial judgment, clinicians who review their decisions in this way are likely to develop an inflated view of their accuracy, and so make future judgments with an unrealistically high degree of confidence.

It should also be clear that hindsight bias and the confirmatory bias are related to one another. Confirmatory bias may lead a clinician to seek out and weigh most heavily information that is consistent with the initial hypothesis. Similarly, hindsight bias may lead a clinician, when reviewing the evidence of a case, to weigh most heavily the evidence consistent with the final hypothesis.

Anchoring and Adjustment Heuristic

Tversky and Kahneman (1974) described a general reasoning error that closely resembles the confirmation bias. Tversky and Kahneman investigated how people make judgments when under conditions of uncertainty. They found that people use several heuristics or "short-cuts" to reduce complex judgmental tasks to simpler ones. Although such heuristics are useful when processing large amounts of information, they may also yield inaccurate conclusions. Thus, Tversky and Kahneman (1974) found that, under conditions of uncertainty, people tend to make errors in systematic ways.

Tversky and Kahneman (1974) described three heuristics which people commonly use to simplify complex decisions. The first of these is the *anchoring and adjustment heuristic*, which occurs in situations where people are presented with information in a sequential fashion. Tversky and Kahneman found that people tend to form their initial judgments on the basis of some salient dimension and then make insufficient adjustments away from the initial estimate as additional information is obtained. That is, anchoring errors occur when final estimates are biased in the direction of initial estimates.

The anchoring error is related to the confirmatory bias: in both cases, one's initial judgment leads to an inadequate consideration of later, possibly disconfirming information.

Tversky and Kahneman (1974) demonstrated that anchoring errors occur in a variety of contexts. For example, in one study, subjects estimated unknown quantities and were assigned arbitary initial starting points. Tversky and Kahneman found that subjects' median estimates were biased in the direction of the initial value.

Several studies have examined anchoring in clinical judgment. For example, Dailey (1952) presented case material sequentially to students and found that subjects who made initial judgments based on limited information were less accurate in their later judgments than those who had not made initial judgments. The initial judgments apparently biased subjects' processing of later information. Similarly, Richards and Wierzbicki (1990) presented case material sequentially to undergraduate subjects. They found that initial judgments, which contained no information indicative of the severity of the case, were significantly related to later judgments about severity and prognosis.

Other studies have examined the diagnostic practices of clinicians. These studies have reported that initial judgments of clients are formed rapidly and then maintained over time by professional clinicians, including psychologists (Meehl, 1960), psychiatrists (Gauron & Dickinson, 1966; Sandifer, Hordern, & Green, 1970), and physicians (Elstein et al., 1978). Although these studies do not demonstrate that anchoring errors have occurred (since it is possible that the initial impressions of clinicians are accurate), they are consistent with the prediction that the anchoring heuristic may adversely affect the judgment of clinicians.

Other studies have examined the anchoring effect in judgments by clinicians. For example, Oskamp (1965) presented case material sequentially to both students and professional clinicians. After each segment, subjects rated the case along several dimensions. Oskamp reported that predictive accuracy peaked early in the information-gathering process; beyond this peak, additional information failed to increase the accuracy of subjects' ratings. Similarly, Perez (1976) presented increasing amounts of information to graduate students and interns who attempted to classify cases into two groups. Perez found that subjects performed at about the chance level, and that increasing the amount of available information about cases did not increase the accuracy of judgments.

Clavelle and Turner (1980) reported that both professional clinicians and paraprofessionals reach their final decision concerning a case early in the decision-making process. They found that 66 percent of all subjects and 80 percent of professionals reached their final decision after receiving only 10 of 30 categories of information about a case.

Friedlander and Stockman (1983) found that anchoring occurred in the judgments of professional clinicians for one of two cases examined. However, Friedlander and Phillips (1984) were unable to demonstrate anchoring in the judgments of students using this same case material. They also reported that professional clinicians made their judgments with greater confidence than students, and so they suggested that high confidence may predispose individuals for making anchoring and other decision-making errors.

These studies demonstrate that anchoring errors decrease the accuracy of clinical (and clinical-like) judgments just as they affect judgments in general.

Representativeness Heuristic

The second heuristic used to simplify complex judgments is what Tversky and Kahneman (1974) termed the *representativeness heuristic*. When people are asked to judge the likelihood that an individual has some characteristic, they tend to judge this likelihood according to the degree to which the individual *is representative of* the class of individuals with the characteristic. Judgments are influenced by the degree to which the individual *resembles* the prototypical member of the class.

This heuristic will increase judgmental accuracy when the target individual's resemblance to the class is evaluated along a valid indicator of class membership. However, such judgments are often made on the basis of invalid predictors, such as the biases or stereotypes discussed earlier in this chapter, and so use of the representativeness heuristic in these cases will decrease judgmental accuracy.

Tversky and Kahneman (1974) described the results of several studies which demonstrated that the representativeness heuristic led to decreased judgmental accuracy when this heuristic was used when other, more valid information concerning the judgment was ignored. They showed that representativeness influenced subjects' judgments when subjects should have taken into consideration statistical information such as: (a) prior probabilities (base rates), (b) sample size, (c) the nature of random fluctuation (especially within small samples), (d) the reliability of predictors, (e) the validity of predictors, and (f) the occurrence of regression to the mean.

Several investigators have demonstrated or discussed the fact that clinicians, like other people, fail to consider sufficiently the statistical limits of judgmental accuracy listed above.

Prior Probabilities

A classic paper by Meehl and Rosen (1955) alerted clinical psychologists to the need to incorporate base rates in their judgments. Meehl (1973) again identified the problem of forgetting Bayes' Theorem as a common error in the clinical judgments exhibited in case conferences.

It is easy to demonstrate that prior probabilities have a profound impact on judgments. Suppose that a disorder has a prevalence of 1/10,000. Suppose further that a test has been developed which correctly identifies 90 percent of the afflicted individuals and only mistakenly identifies 10 percent of nonaffected individuals as having the disorder. Now, suppose that the test is used on a widespread basis, testing a population of 100,000.

How should a clinician interpret a positive test result? What is the probability that an individual who tests positive for the disorder actually has the disorder?

In the population tested, there are 10 patients with the disorder, of whom 9 test positive. There are another 99,990 individuals who do not have the disorder, of whom 9,999 test positive. Thus, the likelihood that an individual who tests positive for the disorder actually has the disorder is 9/9,999, or somewhat higher than one chance in a thousand.

Although the best decision about an individual who tests positive should include the likelihood as calculated above, many clinical judgments will be formed on the basis of the representativeness heuristic—by the degree to which the individual resembles patients with the condition— rather than on the basis of both the test result and the prior probabilities.

Schwartz, Gorry, Kassirer, and Essig (1973) demonstrated that this is exactly what medical students and physicians do when presented with examples similar to the one above. They overestimate the likelihood that a test result is a true rather than a false positive.

Tversky and Kahneman have also demonstrated that subjects employ the representativeness heuristic and consider prior probabilities insufficiently in clinical and clinical-like decision making. For example, Tversky and Kahneman (1974) presented a personality sketch to two groups of subjects and asked them to judge whether the person was a lawyer or an engineer. The personality sketch contained no information relevant to the target's occupation, but instead contained descriptors stereotypically associated with the two professions. Subjects were told that the person had been selected randomly from a population. The two subject groups differed in that they were presented with dramatically different base rates for the two professions. Tversky and Kahneman found that subjects made the mistake of judging the target's profession on the basis of their resemblance to population stereotypes and failed to consider sufficiently the information concerning the occupations' prior probabilities.

Kahneman and Tversky (1973) described a similar study where subjects were graduate students in psychology. Results were the same: subjects judged the likelihood that a target would have one of nine educational specialties on the basis of the target's similarity to population stereotypes rather than the specialties' base rates.

Sample Size

Another factor identified by Tversky and Kahneman as underutilized by subjects when forming judgments is sample size. Tversky and Kahneman (1971) reported several studies which found that psychologists tend to believe in the "law of small numbers." In these studies, psychologists were shown to: (a) overestimate the power of their experimental tests, "gambling" research hypotheses on samples that are too small; (b) overestimate the significance of their results, placing undue weight on early trends in their observations; (c) underestimate the breadth of confidence intervals, by overestimating the likelihood that a research result will be replicated; and (d) underestimate the role of sampling variation, attributing deviations from expectations to post hoc hypotheses rather than to sampling variability. These results suggest that psychologists may be too quick to develop causal hypotheses. This can lead to erroneous clinical judgments, expecially when judgments are based on a small number of observations or when initial observations do not conform to the clinician's expectations. Judgments based on such small sample sizes have more sampling error and lower reliability than judgments based on larger numbers of observations.

Tversky and Kahneman (1971) concluded that "acquaintance with formal logic and with probability theory does not extinguish erroneous intuitions" (p. 109). Although they observed these errors in the judgments of psychologists on statistically oriented problems, it is likely that clinical psychologists will also exhibit these errors in their clinical judgments.

Reliability and Validity of Predictors

Other factors clinicians fail to consider sufficiently when forming judgments are the reliability and validity of predictors. Tversky and Kahneman (1974) discussed how these factors may contribute to the invalidity of clinical judgments. They also noted how these factors may produce the paradoxical result that confidence in a clinical judgment may be inversely related to its accuracy!

As discussed later in this chapter, confidence in clinical judgment increases with the amount of information the clinician receives about the target (Oskamp, 1965). Kahneman and Tversky (1973) demonstrated that confidence increases with the consistency of the information received. Thus, when clinicians obtain consistent information, they make judgments with increased confidence.

However, when the validity of a prediction equation is determined, information obtained from highly correlated (statistically dependent) sources is given less weight than would be the case for noncorrelated (statistically independent) sources. Or, as Kahneman and Tversky point out, a multiple correlation with a criterion variable is inversely related to the intercorrelations among the predictors.

Thus, if the consistent information presented to a clinician comes from highly correlated sources, then the accuracy of judgments based on this information will be little higher than would be the case if only a single piece of information was obtained. However, the clinician's confidence in the judgment is likely to be higher than is warranted by the validity of the predictors.

Regression to the Mean

Kahneman and Tversky (1973) also described how statistical regression to the mean may contribute to the invalidity of clinical judgment and to an inverse relationship between confidence and accuracy of clinical judgments. They noted that confidence in judgments increases when judgments are based on observations of extreme deviations from normative behavior. For example, Tversky and Kahneman reported that confidence in judgments is higher when predicting very high achievement or utter failure than when predicting mediocre performance. However, statistical regression to the mean indicates that observations of extreme predictor variables are likely to be followed by somewhat less extreme observations. Thus, predictions based on extreme observations ought to be less extreme than the observations themselves.

Kahneman and Tversky observed that people's intuitive predictions are insufficiently regressive and so predictions of extreme performance are somewhat less accurate than predictions of average performance. In other words, clinical judgments regarding pathology—based on observations of extreme levels of functioning—may have high confidence but low accuracy. Again, there is an inverse relationship between the confidence in and accuracy of clinical judgments. This tendency for individuals to have high confidence when making fallible judgments was termed by Kahneman and Tversky (1973) the "illusion of validity."

Conjunctive versus Disjunctive Events

The representativeness heuristic may decrease the accuracy of clinical judgments in another way. Tversky and Kahneman (1983) have investigated the way in which people make judgments about the probability of conjunctive events versus disjunctive events. Basic probability theory states that the probability of a conjunction (A *and* B) cannot exceed the probability of either of its components (A, B) in isolation. Yet Tversky and Kahneman have found that people's intuitive judgments of probability often violate this principle.

For example, Tversky and Kahneman (1983) had physicians judge the representativeness of symptoms for each of five medical conditions. They then presented case studies to another sample of physicians and asked them to rank the probabilities that each of six symptoms or symptom combinations would be experienced by the case. Symptom lists included one symptom (B) that was not representative of the case and one conjunction of B with a symptom (A) that was highly representative of the case. Tversky and Kahneman found that, for all five case studies, the conjunction of symptoms A and B was judged as more probable than symptom B alone—a fundamental violation of the laws of probability. In other words, trained clinicians attended to the likelihood of the highly representative symptom alone rather than to the conjunction of both symptoms, thus ignoring basic logic and probability theory.

Availability Heuristic

The third heuristic described by Tversky and Kahneman (1974) is the *availability heuristic.* According to this heuristic, people tend to make judgments concerning the likelihood of an event according to the ease with which instances of the event can be brought to mind. People tend to overestimate the frequency of highly salient events that can be recalled easily.

Tversky and Kahneman reported research results which showed that the availability heuristic limited the accuracy of judgments across a variety of contexts. For example, when subjects estimated the number of words which either began with the letter *r* or which had *r* in the third position, they incorrectly judged the former to be more numerous. Tversky and Kahneman explained this result in terms of the effectiveness of the search strategies used by subjects in the two conditions. Because it is easier to recall words which begin with a letter than to recall those which have a letter in the third position, people tend to judge the more easily recalled class as more numerous.

The availability heuristic can also affect clinical judgments. For example, Lichtenstein, Slovic, Fischhoff, Layman, and Coombs (1978) showed that people tend to overestimate the frequency of lethal events (illnesses, accidents) which are highly publicized and to underestimate the frequency of lethal events which are less highly publicized. When a clinician judges the likelihood of possible diagnostic labels for a patient, it is possible that this judgment will similarly be influenced by the salience of or publicity surrounding the labels.

Clinical psychology has witnessed several examples where a diagnostic label becomes "fashionable," receives a great amount of attention in the popular and professional literatures, and then experiences a marked increase in its frequency of diagnosis (anorexia nervosa and multiple personality disorder are two such conditions). These examples may have resulted, at least in part, from clinicians' reliance on the availability heuristic.

The availability heuristic can also affect the judgments of clinicians in other ways. Personal testimony (Borgida & Nisbett, 1977) and vivid case material (Hamill, Wilson, & Nisbett, 1980) have been found to be more powerful than statistical information in influencing judgments. It is possible that clinicians, like other people, can be so persuaded by the personal accounts of their clients that they weigh this information more heavily than is warranted by the statistical value of the information. This may be one reason why clinicians and others underutilize prior probabilities and other statistical information when forming judgments.

Another way in which the availability heuristic may influence clinical judgments is through illusory correlations (which will be discussed in more detail in the next section of the chapter). Chapman (1967; Chapman & Chapman, 1967, 1969) reported that subjects tended to misperceive the relationship between a patient's symptoms and projective test signs, especially when there was a strong associative connection between these factors. The availability heuristic easily explains the occurrence of illusory correlations. A clinical psychologist may recall a vivid example of a patient who exhibited a "textbook" psychodiagnostic sign (e.g., a paranoid patient who drew a figure with large eyes). In judgments of the general association between the symptom and the sign (when determining whether to use the association when interpreting the test results of another case), the clinician may readily recall the case where the two factors occurred, ignore other cases where the two did not co-occur, and so overestimate the association between the variables.

Avoidance of Risk

Another cognitive process which may decrease the validity of clinical judgment is the tendency for people to act in ways in order to minimize potential risk. Tversky and Kahneman (1981) demonstrated that when problems are reframed so as to emphasize either the gain or risk involved (although the problems remain essentially the same), people act to avoid salient risk.

Elstein (1988) discussed several studies which suggested that clinicians act according to the "minimax" principle—that is, they act in order to minimize the maximum loss. For example, Feinstein (1985) observed that physicians' decisions are influenced by their wish to minimize the maximum possible "regret." Feinstein labeled this the "chagrin factor" and suggested that it was a significant influence on medical decision making.

Cognitive Products

The third cognitive factor identified by Hollon and Kriss (1984) as important in clinical practice was cognitive products. In the present context, cognitive products represent the actual judgments made by clinicians. Clearly, there are many kinds of clinical judgments which can be evaluated on their accuracy.

Other chapters of this book discuss specific kinds of clinical judgments which have been found to have limited validity (or at least to have lower validity than clinicians traditionally believed). The clinical judgments which warrant entire chapters and which are addressed in other chapters of this book are those concerning the effectiveness of psychotherapy, the relative accuracies of clinical versus statistical prediction, the stability of traditional personality traits, the reliability and validity of projective personality tests, and the reliability of psychiatric diagnoses. Other kinds of clinical judgments have also been evaluated for their accuracy. This section of the chapter will discuss the validity of several other kinds of clinical judgments.

Throughout this discussion, it should be noted that the distinction drawn here between cognitive processes and cognitive products is somewhat arbitrary. When a cognitive product is invalid, it is possible that some ineffective or inaccurate cognitive process was employed to derive that product. Thus, erroneous clinical judgments of the kind presented here may well have resulted from the biases or heuristics discussed previously.

Misperception of Configural Process

One clinical judgment whose validity has been questioned concerns the very manner in which clinicians form their judgments! Traditionally, clinicians have reported that their judgments are based on complex interpretations of many client variables. Clinical judgments have been characterized as configural or patterned, indicating that they are not based on simple linear combinations but rather on more complex methods of combining variables, including their interactions (configurations, patterns).

Indeed, this is one of the major criticisms that was raised against Meehl's (1954) conclusion that statistical methods of data combination always equalled or surpassed clinical methods. Meehl (1954) himself suggested that an exception to the general finding of the inferiority of clinical prediction was when clinical predictions were based on such configural methods of data combination.

Despite the traditional claim that clinical prediction is based on complex configural methods of data combination, there is little research evidence to support this. Ever since an early study by Hoffman (1960) which compared linear and configural models of clinical judgment, empirical investigations (e.g., Anderson, 1972; Dawes & Corrigan, 1974; Fisch, Hammond, & Joyce, 1982; Goldberg, 1968, 1970; Wiggins & Hoffman, 1968) have consistently reported that clinical judgments can be adequately modeled and often surpassed by linear models of data combination. Meehl's (1986) overview of the clinical-statistical prediction literature led him to retract his 1954 defense of the configural nature of clinical judgment. In his opinion, two decades of research have consistently found that clinical judgment is not configural. Thus, the clinical judgment that clinical judgment itself is based on configural or patterned interpretations of data is of dubious validity.

Misperception of Association

Another product of human judgment which has been found to have limited validity is the perception of the association (covariation) between variables. Jenkins and Ward (1965) had subjects attempt to determine the contingency between one of two responses and one of two outcomes. Some subjects made the response themselves while other subjects simply observed the trials. Jenkins and Ward found that subjects did not accurately judge the relationship between a response and an outcome. In general, subjects' perception of association was a function of the number of instances in which a response co-occurred with an outcome. In other words, subjects attended to positive pairings of the variables, but ignored the occasions where one variable was paired with the absence of the other. Jenkins and Ward also found that pretraining did not remove this bias.

Ward and Jenkins (1965) conducted a similar study, varying the format in which information trials were presented to subjects. One group of subjects received a serial presentation of the trials, a second group received only a tabular summary of the results, while a third group received the results in both formats. Ward and Jenkins found that a majority of subjects accurately perceived the association between variables only in the group which received the tabular summary of results. That is, subjects who viewed the trials in a serial fashion tended to judge the association in terms of the number of instances in which the two variables co-occurred.

This finding has been demonstrated in other contexts and may well affect the judgments of clinicians. For example, Smedslund (1963) investigated the ability of nurses to determine the association between a symptom and a disease from a serial presentation of 100 cases. Smedslund found that most of the nurses misperceived the association, basing their judgments on the number of co-occurrences of the symptom with the disease.

Similarly, clinical judgments of the association between a client's symptoms and psychodiagnostic test behaviors have been shown to have limited accuracy. Chapman (1967) presented word-pairs to subjects, ensuring that all words from one list were paired equally frequently with all words from another list. Chapman found that subjects mistakenly perceived an association between word-pairs which had an associative (i.e., meaningful) connection. Because these word-pairs did not have a statistical association but were mistakenly perceived to be associated, Chapman labeled this phenomenon the *illusory correlation*. Chapman suggested that such illusory correlations might adversely influence the judgments of clinicians. For example, they might account for the "reported observations of disconfirmed correlations between patients' symptoms and performance on diagnostic tests" (p. 155).

Chapman and Chapman (1967) conducted a series of studies to investigate this possibility. They presented to undergraduate students a series of Draw-A-Person drawings along with the symptoms of the patients who apparently produced the drawings. Chapman and Chapman found that subjects mistakenly perceived associations between characteristics of the drawing and the patient, that these associations were similar to the traditional projective interpretations of psychologists, and that these illusory correlations were closely related to the associative strength between symptoms and features of the drawings.

Chapman and Chapman (1969) conducted a related study with professional psychologists as subjects. They surveyed practicing psychodiagnosticians concerning the kinds of Rorschach signs that they have seen associated with homosexuality in males. Chapman and Chapman then compared these responses to Rorschach signs which empirical research had shown to be valid or invalid indicators of homosexuality. They found that most of the respondents reported that one or more of five invalidated signs were associated with homosexuality. They also found that these invalid signs of homosexuality had a stronger "verbal associative connection" to homosexuality than any of the valid Rorschach signs. Interestingly, a series of studies with undergraduate students mirrored the clinicians' reports. Students mistakenly perceived the invalid Rorschach signs to be associated with homosexuality and failed to perceive the valid signs.

Since this initial work by Chapman and Chapman, clinical psychologists have demonstrated that illusory correlations occur across a variety of contexts. For example, Starr and Katkin (1969) demonstrated the occurrence of illusory correlations in graduate students in clinical psychology who were interpreting an incomplete sentences test.

In addition, psychologists have investigated several factors which influence the occurrence of illusory correlations. Kurtz and Garfield (1978) found that pretraining designed expressly to reduce the occurrence of illusory correlations was ineffective with undergraduate subjects. Lueger and Petzel (1979) reported that the occurrence of illusory correlations varied with the amount of information to be processed—as the judgment became more complex because more information had to be processed, the likelihood of illusory correlations increased.

Misperception of Causation

Another of the clinician's cognitive products which may have limited accuracy is the perception of the degree to which the clinician has control over or has effected some improvement in the client.

Langer and Roth (1975) demonstrated that subjects in a purely chance task misperceived the degree of control they exerted in the situation—what Langer (1975) labelled the *illusion of control*. Langer and Roth found that the illusion of control was enhanced by subjects' involvement in the task (performing responses themselves rather than simply observing the trials). Subjects justified their perceived control through use of the availability heuristic; that is, they remembered successes and so tended to overestimate their degree of control as well as their future performance.

Social psychologists have since demonstrated that several factors influence the illusion of control. For example, across a variety of chance tasks, the illusion of control has been found to be related to control over one's responses and selection of the desired outcome (Wortman, 1975), belief in one's ability to control the outcome (Ayeroff & Abelson, 1976; Benassi, Sweeney, & Drevno, 1979), and experience with (number of practice trials) and selection of task materials (Benassi et al., 1979). In addition, an internal locus of control has also been found to be related to the illusion of control (Benassi et al., 1979; Wolfgang, Zenker, & Viscusi, 1984).

Clinicians in actual practice are not engaged in chance tasks such as those employed in the above studies, and so these factors may not generalize to clinical judgments. However, it is possible that the illusion of control may contribute to misperceptions of the degree to which one exercises control in nonchance tasks—the illusion of control may lead clinicians to overestimate their control. Also, some clinical situations may be so difficult (e.g., there may not be an effective treatment for some clients; there may not be a validated method of recognizing a disorder from the symptoms presented) that clinical judgment becomes essentially a chance task. Thus, it is possible that the illusion of control, and the factors cited above, may influence clinical judgments.

Overconfidence

Related to this issue is a large body of research on the degree to which a clinician's confidence in his or her judgments is related to the accuracy of the judgments. Goldberg (1959) found that clinicians were not more accurate than nonprofessionals in diagnosing organic brain damage from the results of the Bender Gestalt test. However, he also found that clinicians made their judgments with a much higher degree of confidence than other subjects. Thus, confidence was unrelated to the accuracy of clinical judgments.

Similarly, Oskamp found that confidence was not a good index of the validity of clinical judgments. For example, Oskamp (1962) found that confidence was not related to the accuracy of clinical-like judgments in either experienced or inexperienced subjects. Similarly, Oskamp (1965) found that additional case material led to increases in the confidence, but not in the accuracy, of clinical judgments.

In a series of studies, Friedlander (Friedlander & Phillips, 1984; Friedlander & Stockman, 1983) found that professional clinicians make more anchoring errors than student subjects and that clinicians make these judgments with more confidence than students. Again, this suggests that the confidence of clinical judgments is not a useful index of their accuracy.

Reviewers of the relationship between confidence and accuracy of judgments in general have typically concluded that there is little positive relationship (and may even be a negative relationship) between them. For example, Kahneman and Tversky (1973) wrote that "factors which enhance confidence, for example, consistency and extremity, are often negatively correlated with predictive accuracy. Thus, people are prone to experience much confidence in highly fallible judgments" (p. 249). Similarly, Einhorn and Hogarth (1978) indicated that neither "experimental evidence" nor "casual empiricism" have supported the view that judgmental confidence is related to accuracy.

Reviewers of the relationship between confidence and accuracy of clinical judgments have typically reached similar conclusions. For example, Goldberg (1968), Mischel (1968), and Rock et al. (1987) all questioned whether confidence was related to the accuracy of clinicians' judgments.

Garb (1986), on the other hand, reviewed this literature and came to a more positive conclusion concerning clinical judgment. He criticized previous reviewers for overlooking positive findings in the literature and for relying upon studies of clinical-like judgments which are not representative of the judgments made by clinicians in actual practice. Garb limited his review to studies with mental health professionals as subjects who were engaged in judgment tasks related to clinical psychology.

Garb's review supported the appropriateness of clinicians' confidence ratings. He found that experienced clinicians tended to make more appropriate confidence ratings than inexperienced clinicians and that confidence ratings were more likely to be related to judgmental accuracy when the information on which judgments were based had higher validity. For example, in three studies of clinical judgments based on projective test data, accuracy of judgments was not found to be related to confidence ratings. However, accuracy of neuropsychological judgments was related to confidence when judgments were made using the Halstead-Reitan neuropsychological test and the Wechsler-Bellevue intelligence test.

Thus, there is evidence that clinicians succumb to the illusion of control, making clinical judgments with more confidence than is warranted by their accuracy. However, as Garb (1986) demonstrated, confidence in clinical judgments is not without merit. For example, confidence becomes an index of clinical accuracy when judgments are based on validated procedures.

Another body of research speaks to the issue of the illusion of control in clinical judgment. Numerous studies have attempted to determine the accuracy of clinicians' judgments concerning their effectiveness. Although this literature is too large to review comprehensively in this chapter, evidence suggests that clinicians tend to overestimate their effectiveness. For example, Feifel and Eells (1963) showed that clinicians overestimate their clients' improvement. In a similar vein, Pekarik and Finney-Owen (1987) found that clinicians underestimate their own clients' dropout rates and overestimate the average duration of their clients' therapy.

These results are consistent with the hypothesis that the illusion of control influences clinicians' judgments. Clinicians perceive themselves as more effective therapists and as more accurate diagnosticians than they actually are. Thus, the confidence with which they make clinical judgments does not always reflect the accuracy of their judgments.

Misperception of Validity

Another of the clinician's cognitive products which may have limited accuracy is the perception of the validity of some psychodiagnostic technique. Although this is related to both illusory correlations and illusion of control, the fallacy of subjective validation of psychological tests has received sufficient research attention to warrant its own discussion.

Forer (1949) had college student subjects complete a personality questionnaire. One week later, they received what they believed to be a personalized interpretation of their test results and rated the accuracy of individual interpretations, the entire personality description, and the validity of the test. What subjects did not realize was that all of them had been given the same personality description, which consisted of a series of vague or ambiguous descriptions which are true of most people. For example, these statements included the following: "You have a tendency to be critical of yourself." "At times you are extroverted, affable, and sociable, while at other times you are introverted, wary, and reserved." Forer found that students rated the personality descriptions as very accurate and judged the personality test as having good validity.

Since this initial report by Forer, vague or general statements which can be interpreted as true of almost everyone have been termed "Barnum statements" (Paterson, cited by Meehl, 1956), and the fact that people tend to accept such statements as accurate descriptions of themselves and to accept as valid the instruments generating the statements has been called the *Barnum effect* (named after P. T. Barnum, the noted nineteenth-century showman to whom has been attributed the cynical observation, "There's a sucker born every minute" [Beck, 1980]).

Following Forer's demonstration of the fallibility of subjective validation, psychologists have replicated the result on many occasions. Snyder, Shenkel, and Lowery (1977) summarized the results of over 25 studies of the Barnum effect. They concluded that Barnum statements are more likely to be accepted as accurate when: the statements are high in globality and ambiguity; the examinee believes that the description was prepared specifically for him; the personality description is favorable (or at least contains more favorable than unfavorable statements); the description is generated by a brief assessment or by a projective technique (which may add to the client's perception of the ambiguity of the situation); and the examiner has high status.

In addition, Snyder et al. identified several reasons why the Barnum effect is especially likely to occur in clinical contexts. Personality descriptions are generated by high-status clinicians for specific clients using instruments which may appear mysterious to and are not clearly understood by the clients. In addition, clients are commonly characterized by stress and low self-esteem, which have been identified by social psychologists as factors which increase an individual's persuasibility.

For these reasons, clinicians must be aware that a client's endorsement of a clinical judgment (personality description, therapeutic interpretation, theoretical conceptualization) is a fallible index of the accuracy of the judgment. To rely exclusively on the client's (or one's own) subjective validation of clinical judgments is a risky and error-prone enterprise. The clinician should rely on independent and more objective sources than the client's personal endorsement to validate clinical judgments.

Summary and Recommendations

This chapter examined the influences on and the accuracy of clinical judgment. The following conclusions can be drawn from this review.

1. Cognitive structures, such as biases and expectations, influence clinicians' perceptions and so may detract from the accuracy of clinical judgments based on these perceptions.

2. Personal characteristics of clinicians, such as personality traits and theoretical orientation, may also detract from the accuracy of clinical judgments. Interestingly, despite traditional belief, there is relatively little empirical evidence to support claims that clinical training and experience are positively related to the accuracy of clinical judgments.

3. Many cognitive processes have been identified which decrease the accuracy of judgment in general and which may also decrease the accuracy of clinical judgment. These include confirmatory bias, hindsight bias, and Tversky and Kahneman's anchoring, representativeness, and availability heuristics.

4. Several specific types of judgment, related to the judgments made routinely by clinicians, have been found to have limited validity. These include judgments of the very process used to generate clinical judgments, the associations between variables, the degree of control exerted by the clinician in clinical situations, the accuracy of the clinician's judgments, and the validity of the methods used to generate clinical judgments.

Whereas early research (1950s–1960s) addressed the accuracy of clinical judgment, more recent research has examined the processes of clinical judgment, including the heuristics and biases that detract from the accuracy of such judgments (Elstein, 1988). Research has shown that clinical judgments are subject to the same kinds of influences that limit the accuracy of nonclinical judgments. Clinical judgment can thus be interpreted as a subtype of the more general heading of human judgment. Viewed in this way, it is not surprising that clinical judgments are affected by the same biases and cognitive distortions which affect the accuracy of judgments in general. After all, clinicians are people, too!

After recognizing that clinical judgments are fallible and that they are subject to the same limitations as other judgments, the next question to consider is how to improve clinical judgment. Several recent works (Arkes, 1981; Dumont & Lecomte, 1987; Gambrill, 1990; Lourens, 1979; Turk & Salovey, 1985, 1988; Wedding & Faust, 1989) have examined the limitations of clinical judgment and have suggested methods for improving its accuracy. In general, these authors have suggested that clinicians (and clinicians in training) should:

1. Recognize personal biases. It is clear that clinicians' expectations will influence the accuracy of their clinical judgments. If expectations regarding certain clients are invalid, then judgments concerning these clients will have limited accuracy. Clinicians should be aware that they may share community stereotypes concerning the age, race, gender, and social class of their clients. Similarly, clinicians should be aware that their theoretical orientations and value systems carry expectational sets that may limit the accuracy of clinical judgments.

Although there may be no way to eliminate altogether this threat to the accuracy of clinical judgment, a first step to controlling this threat is to encourage clinicians to become aware of their personal biases. Traditional approaches to the training of psychotherapists recommended that a clinician undergo personal therapy, a part of which would be directed toward an examination of the clinician's biases. Less traditional approaches to the training of therapists, which do not require that clinicians receive personal therapy, should encourage trainees to self-examine their biases, and should address such biases in therapy supervision when they are manifested in interactions with clients.

2. Recognize the threats to the accuracy of judgment in general. Clinicians should recognize that clinical judgment is a special case of the more general area of judgment under uncertainty. The same threats or limits to the accuracy of judgment in general also influence clinical judgments. The clinician's training, experience, and confidence do not ensure that clinical judgments are error-free. Thus, relying on clinical "intuition" to support a judgment on the basis of evidence with questionable validity is a dubious practice. The training of clinicians should include presentations on the threats to the accuracy of judgment under uncertainty and on how such threats operate in actual clinical judgments.

3. Receive training in decision-making processes that counter the threats to the validity of judgment. Several studies have shown that simply making subjects aware of the threats to the accuracy of judgment and instructing them not to be influenced by the threats is not sufficient to overcome them (e.g., Kurtz & Garfield, 1978). What is needed is explicit training in decision-making procedures which overcome the threats to the validity of judgment.

One method of reducing the threats to the validity of clinical judgment is to engage in a disconfirmatory process of data gathering and hypothesis testing. Rather than simply looking for evidence to support one's initial hypothesis (and so risk anchoring errors and overconfidence), the clinician should be trained to consider alternative hypotheses and seek information regarding the validity (or invalidity) of each.

Interestingly, this method has been formalized in DSM-III-R (American Psychiatric Association, 1987), the current diagnostic system. Many of the disorders listed in DSM-III-R require that exclusion criteria be met before a diagnosis is assigned. That is, the clinician must consider and rule out alternative diagnoses before assigning a diagnostic label.

This method of considering alternative hypotheses and then seeking information that will disconfirm them is fundamental to the scientific method. Clinicians who are trained as scientist-practitioners should be exposed to this scientific approach to problem solving. After mastering this method in the laboratory, it can easily be generalized to the clinic.

Arkes (1981) listed three techniques which have been shown to reduce the degree to which judgmental errors occur. The first of these is to consider alternative hypotheses. For example, Slovic and Fischhoff (1977) found that having subjects explicitly consider how initial events could have led to both of the possible outcomes significantly reduced the impact of hindsight bias. Similarly, Koriat, Lichtenstein, and Fischhoff (1980) reported that having subjects list arguments for and against each of two options before choosing one significantly reduced the problem of overconfidence in the judgments.

The second technique identified by Arkes is to think Bayesian. Arkes reported a study which demonstrated that graduate students in psychology could be trained to utilize prior probabilities and so make more accurate estimates regarding the likelihood of low-probability events.

The third technique identified by Arkes is to decrease reliance on memory. Ward and Jenkins (1965) found that subjects accurately judged the association between two variables when they evaluated a tabular summary of the data, but not when they received a serial (case-by-case) presentation of the data. In other words, subjects who relied on their own memories of the outcomes of individual trials were much less accurate than subjects who viewed a statistical summary of the data.

4. Make judgments on the basis of the most valid methods available. Clearly, clinical judgments will be most accurate when based on the most valid indicators. Clinical practice will be improved if it is based on more accurate judgments. Although this recommendation seems self-evident, the research on clinical judgment demonstrates that it is not always followed.

Wedding and Faust (1989) made several recommendations for improving clinical judgment which concern the validity of the methods employed by the clinician. They suggested that clinicians should: (a) avoid the premature abandonment of useful decision rules, (b) start with the most valid information, (c) avoid overreliance on highly intercorrelated measures, (d) regress extreme estimates and confidence in one's judgments to the level of uncertainty in the data, and (e) obtain feedback following the judgments.

Many of these recommendations were anticipated by Meehl (1973) in his discussion of the errors in clinical reasoning which he observed in case conferences. He suggested that case conferences be run in such a way that initial information is presented to clinicians who then have to seek out the information necessary to establish the appropriate diagnosis and treatment.

Clinicians would have to use the most valid information and tests to formulate their initial hypotheses, consider alternative hypotheses and the information necessary to confirm or disconfirm each, select the most valid methods of obtaining this information, and then reconsider the hypotheses in the light of the new information. In this way, clinicians would be using essentially a scientific procedure to arrive at the clinical "truth" of a case. I have made Meehl's (1973) paper required reading in my graduate courses in psychotherapy and have recommended that my students read this paper annually after obtaining jobs in clinical settings.

These recommendations are consistent with the "scientist-practitioner" model of clinical training which will be discussed in the final chapter of this book. They are also consistent with the argument presented throughout this book that objective or empirical approaches to clinical psychology are superior to subjective approaches in resolving issues concerning traditional assumptions and practices of clinical psychology.

References

Abramowitz, C. V., & Dokecki, P. R. (1977). The politics of clinical judgment: Early empirical returns. *Psychological Bulletin, 84*, 460–476.

Abramowitz, C. V., & Murray, J. (1983). Race effects in psychotherapy. In J. Murray & P. R. Abramson (Eds.), *Bias in psychotherapy* (pp. 215–255). New York: Academic Press.

American Psychological Association. (1982). *Report of the task force on the evaluation of education, training, and service in psychology.* Washington, DC: American Psychological Association.

Anderson, N. H. (1972). Looking for configurality in clinical judgment. *Psychological Bulletin, 78*, 93–102.

Arkes, H. R. (1981). Impediments to accurate clinical judgment and possible ways to minimize their impact. *Journal of Consulting and Clinical Psychology, 49*, 323–330.

Arkes, H. R., Faust, D., Guilmette, T. J., & Hart, K. (1988). Eliminating the hindsight bias. *Journal of Applied Psychology, 73*, 305–307.

Arkes, H. R., Wortmann, R. L., Saville, P., & Harkness, A. R. (1981). The hindsight bias among physicians weighing the likelihood of diagnosis. *Journal of Applied Psychology, 66*, 252–254.

Ayeroff, F., & Abelson, R. P. (1976). ESP and ESB: Belief in personal success at mental telepathy. *Journal of Personality and Social Psychology, 34*, 240–247.

Bakan, D. (1956). Classical psychology and logic. *American Psychologist, 11*, 655–662.

Barlow, D. H., Hayes, S. C., & Nelson, R. O. (1984). *The scientist-practitioner: Research and accountability in clinical and educational settings.* New York: Pergamon.

Beck, E. M. (1980). (Ed.). *Bartlett's familiar quotations* (15th ed.). Boston: Little, Brown.

Benassi, V. A., Sweeney, P. D., & Drevno, G. E. (1979). Mind over matter: Perceived success at psychokinesis. *Journal of Personality and Social Psychology, 37*, 1377–1386.

Berenda, C. W. (1957). Is clinical psychology a science? *American Psychologist, 12*, 725–729.

Borgida, E., & Nisbett, R. E. (1977). The differential impact of abstract vs. concrete information on decisions. *Journal of Applied Social Psychology, 7*, 258–271.

Braginsky, B. M., Braginsky, D. D., & Ring, K. (1969). *Methods of madness: The mental hospital as a last resort.* New York: Holt, Rinehart, and Winston.

Broverman, I. K., Broverman, D. M., Clarkson, F. E., Rosenkrantz, P. S., & Vogel, S. R. (1970). Sex-role stereotypes and clinical judgments of mental health. *Journal of Consulting and Clinical Psychology, 34*, 1–7.

Chapman, L. J. (1967). Illusory correlation in observational report. *Journal of Verbal Learning and Verbal Behavior, 6*, 151–155.

Chapman, L. J., & Chapman, J. P. (1967). Genesis of popular but erroneous psychodiagnostic observations. *Journal of Abnormal Psychology, 72*, 193–204.

Chapman, L. J., & Chapman, J. P. (1969). Illusory correlation as an obstacle to the use of valid psychodiagnostic signs. *Journal of Abnormal Psychology, 74*, 271–280.

Chein, I. (1945). The logic of prediction: Some observations on the Sarbin exposition. *Psychological Review, 52*, 175–179.

Clavelle, P. R., & Turner, A. D. (1980). Clinical decision-making among professionals and paraprofessionals. *Journal of Clinical Psychology, 36*, 833–838.

Dailey, C. A. (1952). The effects of premature conclusion upon the acquisition of understanding of a person. *Journal of Psychology, 33*, 133–152.

Davidson, C. V., & Abramowitz, S. I. (1980). Sex bias in clinical judgment: Later empirical returns. *Psychology of Women Quarterly, 4*, 377-395.

Dawes, R. M., & Corrigan, B. (1974). Linear models in decision making. *Psychological Bulletin, 81*, 95–106.

Dumont, F., & Lecomte, C. (1987). Inferential processes in clinical work: Inquiry into logical errors that affect diagnostic judgments. *Professional Psychology: Research and Practice, 18*, 433–438.

Einhorn, H. J., & Hogarth, R. M. (1978). Confidence in judgment: Persistence of the illusion of validity. *Psychological Review, 85*, 395–416.

Elstein, A. S. (1988). Cognitive processes in clinical inference and decision making. In D. C. Turk & P. Salovey (Eds.), *Reasoning, inference and judgment in clinical psychology* (pp. 17–50). New York: Free Press.

Elstein, A. S., Shulman, L. S., & Sprafka, S. A. (1978). *Medical problem solving: An analysis of clinical reasoning.* Cambridge, MA: Harvard University Press.

Faust, D. (1986). Research on human judgment and its application to clinical practice. *Professional Psychology: Research and Practice, 17*, 420–430.

Faust, D., & Ziskin, J. (1988). The expert witness in psychology and psychiatry. *Science, 241*, 31–35.

Feifel, H., & Eells, J. (1963). Patients and therapists assess the same psychotherapy. *Journal of Consulting Psychology, 27*, 310–318.

Feinstein, A. R. (1985). The "chagrin factor" and qualitative decision analysis. *Archives of Internal Medicine, 145*, 1257–1259.

Fisch, H. U., Hammond, K. R., & Joyce, C. R. B. (1982). On evaluating the severity of depression: An experimental study of psychiatrists. *British Journal of Psychiatry, 140*, 378–383.

Fischhoff, B. (1975). Hindsight ≠ foresight: The effect of outcome knowledge on judgment under uncertainty. *Journal of Experimental Psychology: Human Perception and Performance, 1*, 288–299.

Forer, B. R. (1949). The fallacy of personal validation: A classroom demonstration of gullibility. *Journal of Abnormal and Social Psychology, 44*, 118–123.

Friedlander, M. L., & Phillips, S. D. (1984). Preventing anchoring errors in clinical judgment. *Journal of Consulting and Clinical Psychology, 52*, 366–371.

Friedlander, M. L., & Stockman, S. J. (1983). Anchoring and publicity effects in clinical judgment. *Journal of Clinical Psychology, 39,* 637–643.

Gambrill, E. (1990). *Critical thinking in clinical practice: Improving the accuracy of judgments and decisions about clients.* San Francisco: Jossey-Bass.

Garb, H. N. (1986). The appropriateness of confidence ratings in clinical judgment. *Journal of Clinical Psychology, 42,* 190–197.

Garb, H. N. (1988). Comment on "The study of clinical judgment: An ecological approach." *Clinical Psychology Review, 8,* 441–444.

Garb, H. N. (1989). Clinical judgment, clinical training, and professional experience. *Psychological Bulletin, 105,* 387–396.

Gauron, E. G., & Dickinson, J. K. (1966). Diagnostic decision-making in psychiatry: 2. Diagnostic styles. *Archives of General Psychiatry, 14,* 233–237.

Gay, P. (1988). *Freud: A life for our time.* New York: Norton.

Goffman, E. (1961). *Asylums.* Garden City, NY: Doubleday.

Goldberg, L. R. (1959). The effectiveness of clinicians' judgments: The diagnosis of organic brain damage from the Bender-Gestalt Test. *Journal of Consulting Psychology, 23,* 25–33.

Goldberg, L. R. (1968). Simple models or simple processes? Some research on clinical judgments. *American Psychologist, 23,* 483–496.

Goldberg, L. R. (1970). Man versus model of man: A rationale plus some evidence for a method of improving on clinical inferences. *Psychological Bulletin, 73,* 422–432.

Hamill, R., Wilson, T. D., & Nisbett, R. E. (1980). Insensitivity to sample bias: Generalizing from atypical cases. *Journal of Personality and Social Psychology, 39,* 578–589.

Hoffman, P. J. (1960). The panamorphic representation of clinical judgment. *Psychological Bulletin, 57,* 116–131.

Hollon, S. D., & Kriss, M. R. (1984). Cognitive factors in clinical research and practice. *Clinical Psychology Review, 4,* 35–76.

Houts, A. C. (1984). Effects of clinician theoretical orientation and patient explanatory bias on initial clinical judgments. *Professional Psychology: Research and Practice, 15,* 284–293.

Hunt, W. A. (1951). Clinical psychology—Science or superstition. *American Psychologist, 6,* 683–687.

Hunt, W. A., & Jones, N. F. (1959). The experimental investigation of clinical judgment. In A. J. Bachrach (Ed.), *Experimental foundations of clinical psychology* (pp. 26–51). New York: Basic Books.

Jenkins, H. M., & Ward, W. C. (1965). Judgment of contingency between responses and outcomes. *Psychological Monographs: General and Applied, 79* (Whole No. 594), 1–17.

Jones, W. H., Hansson, R. O., & Phillips, A. L. (1978). Physical attractiveness and judgments of psychopathology. *Journal of Social Psychology, 105,* 79–84.

Kahneman, D., & Tversky, A. (1973). On the psychology of prediction. *Psychological Review, 80,* 237–251.

Kleinmuntz, B. (1984). The scientific study of clinical judgment in psychology and medicine. *Clinical Psychology Review, 4,* 111–126.

Koriat, A., Lichtenstein, S., & Fischhoff, B. (1980). Reasons for confidence. *Journal of Experimental Psychology: Human Learning and Memory, 6,* 107–118.

Krech, D. (1946). A note on fission. *American Psychologist, 1,* 402–404.

Kurtz, R. M., & Garfield, S. L. (1978). Illusory correlation: A further exploration of Chapman's paradigm. *Journal of Consulting and Clinical Psychology, 46,* 1009–1015.

Langer, E. (1975). The illusion of control. *Journal of Personality and Social Psychology, 32,* 311–328.

Langer, E. J., & Abelson, R. P. (1974). A patient by any other name . . . : Clinical group differences in labeling bias. *Journal of Consulting and Clinical Psychology, 42,* 4–9.

Langer, E. J., & Roth, J. (1975). Heads I win, tails it's chance: The illusion of control as a function of the sequence of outcomes in a purely chance task. *Journal of Personality and Social Psychology, 32,* 951–955.

Lichtenstein, S., Slovic, P., Fischhoff, B., Layman, M., & Coombs, C. (1978). Judged frequency of lethal events. *Journal of Experimental Psychology: Human Learning and Memory, 4,* 551–578.

Lopez, S. R. (1989). Patient variable biases in clinical judgment: Conceptual overview and methodological considerations. *Psychological Bulletin, 106,* 184–203.

Lourens, P. J. D. (1979). All too human: Some limitations of professional judgment. *Psychologia Africana, 18,* 65–80.

Lueger, R. J., & Petzel, T. P. (1979). Illusory correlation in clinical judgment: Effects of amount of information to be processed. *Journal of Consulting and Clinical Psychology, 47,* 1120–1121.

Mahoney, M. J. (1976). *Scientist as subject: The psychological imperative.* Cambridge, MA: Ballinger.

Meehl, P. E. (1954). *Clinical versus statistical prediction.* Minneapolis, MN: University of Minnesota Press.

Meehl, P. E. (1956). Wanted—A good cookbook. *American Psychologist, 11,* 263–272.

Meehl, P. E. (1960). The cognitive activity of the clinician. *American Psychologist, 15,* 19–27.

Meehl, P. E. (1973). Why I do not attend case conferences. In P. E. Meehl, *Psychodiagnosis: Selected papers* (pp. 225–302). Minneapolis, MN: University of Minnesota Press.

Meehl, P. E. (1986). Causes and effects of my disturbing little book. *Journal of Personality Assessment, 50,* 370–375.

Meehl, P. E., & Rosen, A. (1955). Antecedent probability and the efficiency of psychometric signs, patterns, or cutting scores. *Psychological Bulletin, 52,* 194–216.

Mischel, W. (1968). *Personality and assessment.* New York: Wiley.

Neisser, U. (1976). *Cognition and reality: Principles and implications of cognitive psychology.* San Francisco: Freeman.

Oskamp, S. (1962). The relationship of clinical experience and training methods to several criteria of clinical prediction. *Psychological Monographs: General and Applied, 76* (No. 547), 1–28.

Oskamp, S. (1965). Overconfidence in case-study judgments. *Journal of Consulting Psychology, 29,* 261–265.

Pekarik, G., & Finney-Owen, K. (1987). Outpatient clinic therapist attitudes and beliefs relevant to client dropout. *Community Mental Health Journal, 23,* 120–130.

Perez, F. I. (1976). Behavioral analysis of clinical judgment. *Perceptual and Motor Skills, 43,* 711–718.

Popper, K. R. (1959). *The logic of scientific discovery.* London: Hutchinson.

Popper, K. R. (1963). *Conjectures and refutations.* New York: Harper & Row.

Raines, G. N., & Rohrer, J. H. (1955). The operational matrix of psychiatric practice. I. Consistency and variability in interview impressions of different psychiatrists. *American Journal of Psychiatry, 111,* 721–733.

Raines, G. N., & Rohrer, J. H. (1960). The operational matrix of psychiatric practice. II. Variability in psychiatric impressions and the projection hypothesis. *American Journal of Psychiatry, 117,* 133–139.

Richards, M. S., & Wierzbicki, M. (1990). Anchoring errors in clinical-like judgments. *Journal of Clinical Psychology, 46,* 358–365.

Rock, D. L., Bransford, J. D., Maisto, S. A., & Morey, L. (1987). The study of clinical judgment: An ecological approach. *Clinical Psychology Review, 7,* 645–661.

Rogers, C. R. (1955). Persons or science? A philosophical question. *American Psychologist, 10,* 267–278.

Rosenhan, D. L. (1973). On being sane in insane places. *Science, 179,* 250–258.

Rychlak, J. F. (1959). Clinical psychology and the nature of evidence. *American Psychologist, 14,* 642–648.

Sandifer, M. G., Hordern, A., & Green, L. M. (1970). The psychiatric interview: The impact of the first three minutes. *American Journal of Psychiatry, 126,* 968–973.

Scheff, T. J. (1966). *Being mentally ill: A sociological theory.* Chicago: Aldine.

Schwartz, W. B., Gorry, G. A., Kassirer, J. P., & Essig, A. (1973). Decision analysis and clinical judgment. *American Journal of Medicine, 55,* 459–472.

Shakow, D., & Rapaport, D. (1964). *The influence of Freud on American psychology.* New York: International Universities Press.

Skaggs, E. B. (1934). The limitations of scientific psychology as an applied or practical science. *Psychological Review, 41,* 572–576.

Slovic, P., & Fischhoff, B. (1977). On the psychology of experimental surprises. *Journal of Experimental Psychology: Human Perception and Performance, 3,* 544–551.

Smedslund, J. (1963). The concept of correlation in adults. *Scandinavian Journal of Psychology, 4,* 165–173.

Snyder, C. R. (1977). "A patient by any other name" revisited: Maladjustment or attributional locus of problem? *Journal of Consulting and Clinical Psychology, 45,* 101–103.

Snyder, C. R., Shenkel, R. J., & Lowery, C. R. (1977). Acceptance of personality interpretations: The "Barnum effect" and beyond. *Journal of Consulting and Clinical Psychology, 45,* 104–114.

Snyder, M. (1981). "Seek and ye shall find. . . ." In E. T. Higgins, C. P. Herman, & M. P. Zanna (Eds.), *Social cognition: The Ontario symposium on personality and social psychology* (pp. 277–303). Hillsdale, NJ: Erlbaum.

Snyder, M., & Swann, W. B. (1978). Hypothesis-testing processes in social interaction. *Journal of Personality and Social Psychology, 36,* 1202–1212.

Snyder, M., Tanke, E. D., & Berscheid, E. (1977). Social perception and interpersonal behavior: On the self-fulfilling nature of social stereotypes. *Journal of Personality and Social Psychology, 35,* 656–666.

Snyder, M., & Thomsen, C. J. (1988). Interactions between therapists and clients: Hypothesis testing and behavioral confirmation. In D. C. Turk & P. Salovey (Eds.), *Reasoning, inference and judgment in clinical psychology* (pp. 124–152). New York: Free Press.

Starr, B. J., & Katkin, E. S. (1969). The clinician as an aberrant actuary: Illusory correlation and the incomplete sentences blank. *Journal of Abnormal Psychology, 74,* 670–675.

Taft, R. (1955). The ability to judge people. *Psychological Bulletin, 52,* 1-23.

Temerlin, M. K. (1968). Suggestion effects in psychiatric diagnosis. *Journal of Nervous and Mental Disease, 147,* 349–353.

Thorne, F. C. (1961). *Clinical judgment: A study of clinical errors.* Brandon, VT: Journal of Clinical Psychology.

Turk, D. C., & Salovey, P. (1985). Cognitive structures, cognitive processes, and cognitive-behavior modification: II. Judgments and inferences of the clinician. *Cognitive Therapy and Research, 9,* 19–33.

Turk, D. C., & Salovey, P. (Eds.). (1988). *Reasoning, inference and judgment in clinical psychology.* New York: Free Press.

Tversky, A., & Kahneman, D. (1971). Belief in the law of small numbers. *Psychological Bulletin, 76,* 105–110.

Tversky, A., & Kahneman, D. (1973). On the psychology of prediction. *Psychological Review, 80,* 237–251.

Tversky, A., & Kahneman, D. (1974). Judgment under uncertainty: Heuristics and biases. *Science, 185,* 1124–1131.

Tversky, A., & Kahneman, D. (1981). The framing of decisions and the psychology of choice. *Science, 211,* 453–458.

Tversky, A., & Kahneman, D. (1983). Extensional versus intuituve reasoning: The conjunction fallacy in probability judgment. *Psychological Review, 90,* 293–315.

Ward, W. C., & Jenkins, H. M. (1965). The display of information and the judgment of contingency. *Canadian Journal of Psychology, 19,* 231–241.

Wason, P. C. (1960). On the failure to discriminate hypotheses in a conceptual task. *Quarterly Journal of Experimental Psychology, 12,* 129–140.

Wason, P. C., & Johnson-Laird, P. N. (1972). *Psychology of reasoning.* Cambridge, MA: Harvard University Press.

Watts, F. N. (1980). Clinical judgement and clinical training. *British Journal of Medical Psychology, 53,* 95–108.

Wedding, D., & Faust, D. (1989). Clinical judgment and decision making in neuropsychology. *Archives of Clinical Neuropsychology, 4,* 233-265.

Whitley, B. E. (1979). Sex roles and psychotherapy: A current appraisal. *Psychological Bulletin, 86,* 1309–1321.

Wiggins, J. S. (1973). *Personality and prediction: Principles of personality assessment.* Reading, MA: Addison-Wesley.

Wiggins, N., & Hoffman, P. J. (1968). Three models of clinical judgment. *Journal of Abnormal Psychology, 73,* 70–77.

Wolfgang, A. K., Zenker, S. I., & Viscusi, T. (1984). Control motivation and the illusion of control in betting on dice. *Journal of Psychology, 116,* 67–72.

Wortman, C. B. (1975). Some determinants of perceived control. *Journal of Personality and Social Psychology, 31,* 282–294.

Zeldow, P. B. (1978). Sex differences in psychiatric evaluation and treatment: An empirical review. *Archives of General Psychiatry, 35,* 89–93.

CHAPTER EIGHT

Overview

Introduction

This book has discussed six issues which have been debated by clinical psychologists since the 1950s. Each issue concerns the relative merits of traditional subjective versus objective approaches. For every issue, when the field subjected the traditional assumption or practice to empirical test, it found sufficient evidence to question the value of the traditional approach. For this reason, many clinical psychologists since the 1950s have emphasized objective or empirical approaches to clinical psychology over more traditional subjective approaches.

The purpose of this final chapter is to discuss briefly two other kinds of evidence which support the claim that clinical psychology has adopted an increasingly empirical or objective orientation: the development and affirmation of the scientist-practitioner model of training of clinical psychologists, and the development of the ethical standards of psychologists and the standards of practice of clinical psychologists.

The Scientist-Practitioner Model

Although the term *clinical psychology* was introduced by Lightner Witmer as early as the 1890s (Kendall & Norton-Ford, 1982), the role of the clinical psychologist remained uncertain throughout the first half of the twentieth century. The different interests and needs of academic experimental psychologists and applied clinical psychologists led to an uneasy relationship between them, characterized by a series of clear separations followed by cautious alliances (McNamara, Jones, & Barclay, 1982; Strickland, 1988).

Even among practitioners, the proper role of the clinical psychologist has been debated. For example, whereas the major role of clinical psychologists in the 1920s was psychological testing (Strickland, 1988), the need for increased numbers of providers of treatment services in World Wars I and II led many clinical psychologists by the 1940s to adopt the role of therapist (Strickland, 1988).

The increased demand for clinical services and the increasing numbers of psychologists seeking to provide clinical services following World War II led the APA to address formally the educational and training requirements of clinical psychologists. In 1944, the APA decided to train clinical psychologists in existing doctoral training programs in psychology (Reisman, 1981). An APA committee was established to examine and make recommendations concerning the educational requirements of clinical psychology training programs. The committee report (Shakow, Hilgard, Kelly, Luckey, Sanford, & Shaffer, 1947) set forth the basics for what has become known as the *Scientist-Practitioner model* of training in clinical psychology.

As elaborated by Thorne (1947), the scientist-practitioner adopts a scientific or experimental approach to the treatment of individual cases. Each case is treated as an N-of-one study in which a scientific (i.e., critical, empirical) approach is taken to the assessment, conceptualization, treatment selection, and follow-up evaluation of the client. In addition, each case is viewed as a part of a larger sample of cases, so that information gathered sequentially concerning individual clients can eventually be integrated into a systematic group analysis. Thus, the clinical psychologist serves a scientific role even in the context of applied clinical practice.

A two-week conference was held in 1949 in Boulder, Colorado, to discuss this and other possible models of clinical training. The result of this conference was a unanimous endorsement of the scientist-practitioner model (Barlow, Hayes, & Nelson, 1984), henceforth also referred to as the *Boulder model*. According to the report of this conference (Raimy, 1950), the reasons for the approval of the Boulder model included the fundamental lack of knowledge in the field which mandated the conduct of clinical research, and the need to train psychologists in applied techniques to enable researchers to develop a better understanding of and increased interest in important clinical research issues.

Following this official endorsement by the APA of the scientist-practitioner model of clinical training, the empirical examination of traditional clinical assumptions and practices began. The issues discussed throughout this book—the effectiveness of psychotherapy, the relative accuracies of clinical and statistical prediction, the reliability of diagnosis, the reliability and validity of projective psychological tests, the stability of personality traits, and the validity of clinical judgment—all became the focus of empirical investigation.

Since 1949, several major conferences have been convened to address the issue of the graduate training of clinical psychologists. These have included conferences in Miami in 1958 (Roe, Gustad, Moore, Ross, & Skodak, 1959), Chicago in 1965 (Clark, 1965), Vail in 1973 (Korman, 1974), and Salt Lake City in 1987 (Bickman, 1987). Although the Vail and Salt Lake City conferences endorsed a professional model of training of clinical psychologists as an alternative to the scientist-practitioner model, all the conferences recognized the importance of training in research and scientific principles for clinical psychologists.

It should be stressed that clinical psychologists have not unanimously endorsed the scientist-practitioner model. Frank (1984, 1986a, 1986b, 1987) has been particularly vocal in his criticism of the Boulder model. According to Frank (1984), APA committees on graduate training in clinical psychology prior to the Boulder conference had recommended that "clinical training should be grounded *in* and *on* research in psychology," and that Shakow et al. (1947) changed this emphasis by recommending that clinical psychologists "should be trained to *do* research" (Frank, 1984, p. 425).

Frank (1984) also identified two major criticisms that have been directed against the scientist-practitioner model: that there is little evidence to support the assumption of the importance of scientific training for clinical psychologists and that interest in and the skills necessary to succeed as a researcher are incompatible with those required for applied clinical work.

Much evidence has been presented to support these arguments. For example, a classic and often-cited report by Levy (1962) followed almost 800 clinical psychologists who earned their degrees from 1948 to 1953 and found that the modal number of publications for this group was zero! The mean number of publications was 3.7, with a median of 1.6. In general, the distribution of the number of publications was highly skewed, with 10 percent of the group accounting for 45 percent of the total publications. Thus, even though clinical psychologists had been trained in the scientist-practitioner model, relatively few of them engaged in scientific research (and publication of this research) following the completion of their degree programs.

Another often-cited report is the survey of clinical psychologists conducted by Garfield and Kurtz (1976). They found that a majority of clinical psychologists would have preferred a decreased emphasis on research training during their graduate educations.

Such results are not uncommon (Frank, 1984). Many clinical psychologists have exclusively applied rather than research interests and so view their scientific training as unrelated to their professional activities or even as a detriment to their clinical training.

In addition, from the 1940s through the present, there has been an increased demand for clinical services (Reisman, 1981). The numbers of clinical specialties, settings in which clinical psychologists are employed, and positions for clinical psychologists have all increased. Reisman (1981), Canter and Canter (1982), and Pryzwansky and Wendt (1987) have documented both the increase in the number of clinical psychologists and the shift among psychologists toward applied rather than academic careers. With the increased demand for and interest in applied clinical positions, there has been an increased demand for programs that emphasize the practitioner over the scientific component of clinical training.

For these reasons, the Vail Conference of 1973 endorsed the practitioner model of clinical training as an alternative to the Boulder model. This model emphasizes professional training over scientific training. However, this model continues to recognize that clinical practice should be founded on scientifically demonstrated principles and techniques, and so has been referred to occasionally as the "practitioner-scientist" model.

This practitioner model forms the basis of Psy.D. programs, which were introduced in 1968 at the University of Illinois (Peterson, 1968). By the 1980s, this model of clinical training had become well established (Peterson, 1985). By 1987, 45 professional schools of psychology had been established, with 22 of them APA-approved (Strickland, 1988). The Salt Lake City conference of 1987 reaffirmed this practitioner model as an alternative to the Boulder model of clinical training and recognized the Psy.D. as a "distinct and legitimate" degree (Strickland, 1988).

However, the scientist-practitioner model has lost neither its following nor its influence. Thelen and Ewing (1970) surveyed clinical psychologists in academia and found that this group strongly supported the Boulder model of clinical training. Perry (1979) argued that the increase in APA-approved Ph.D. programs in clinical psychology from 67 in 1975 to 102 in 1977 demonstrated that the field had not rejected the Boulder model of clinical training. All the major conferences on graduate training—even those endorsing the practitioner model of training—affirmed the importance of the scientific foundations of clinical psychology (Kendall & Norton-Ford, 1982). For example, the participants of the Salt Lake City conference recommended that "research and scientific inquiry be an essential part of every psychologist's training . . . ." (Strickland, 1988, p. 107).

Thus, since the Boulder conference of 1949, the APA has formally recognized the importance of the scientific training of clinical psychologists. From 1949 to the present, the APA has endorsed the scientist-practitioner model of clinical training, with the practitioner-scientist model recognized as an alternative model from 1973 to the present. The APA has recognized that scientific principles (e.g., learning, motivation, cognition) underlie clinical practice and that scientific methods of evaluation are crucial for the evaluation and improvement of clinical techniques. This formal endorsement by the APA of the scientific training of clinical psychologists therefore supports the thesis of this book that clinical psychology has moved in a more empirical or scientific direction.

Standards of Psychologists

Another way of illustrating the movement of clinical psychology in a more empirical or objective direction is to examine the development of the ethical standards of psychologists.

The APA first established a committee to consider the adoption of a formal ethical code in 1938 and then created the Committee on Scientific and Professional Ethics in 1940 as a standing committee to consider ethical complaints against psychologists (Pryzwansky & Wendt, 1987).

In 1948, the APA asked its members to submit incident reports on ethical problems they had encountered. On the basis of over 1,000 reports, the APA developed an initial set of standards which was first published formally in 1953 (APA, 1953). Since then, the APA has revised the general ethical principles of psychologists on several occasions and has developed standards for psychologists engaged in specific professional activities. Schofield (1982) regarded the codification of these ethical principles as one of the major indices of the development of psychology as a true profession.

The most recent version of the ethical standards of psychologists appeared in 1990 (APA, 1990). This set of ethical standards contains ten principles: Responsibility, Competence, Moral and Legal Standards, Public Statements, Confidentiality, Welfare of the Consumer, Professional Relationships, Assessment Techniques, Research with Human Participants, and Care and Use of Animals. Each principle is presented briefly in paragraph form, followed by a series of elaborations concerning the application of the principle to specific situations.

Several of the ethical principles speak to the issue of the empirical or scientific foundation of clinical psychology. For example, the principle of Competence includes the statement that "[psychologists] maintain knowledge of current scientific and professional information related to the services they render" (APA, 1990, p. 391). Similarly, an elaboration of the principle of Competence indicates that "Psychologists responsible for decisions involving individuals or policies based on test results have an understanding of psychological or educational measurement, validation problems, and test research" (APA, 1990, p. 391).

The principle of Assessment Techniques also addresses the empirical foundations of clinical psychology. An elaboration of this principle indicates that psychologists who develop and standardize psychological tests must use "established scientific procedures" (APA, 1990, p. 394). Similarly, psychologists who use psychological tests must "indicate any reservations that exist regarding validity or reliability because of the circumstances of the assessment or the inappropriateness of the norms for the person tested" and must be "able to produce appropriate evidence for the validity of the programs and procedures used in arriving at interpretations" (APA, 1990, p. 394).

Thus, the ethical principles of psychologists require that clinical psychologists maintain current scientific knowledge concerning the services they provide and that they use psychological tests in ways that have been appropriately validated. In both of these respects, then, ethical clinical practice has empirical roots.

In addition to the ethical principles of psychologists in general, the APA has also developed sets of ethical standards to regulate the ethical behavior of psychologists engaged in specific professional activities. In 1954, the APA co-published a set of recommendations concerning the development and use of psychological and educational tests (APA & Educational Research Association and National Council on Measurement in Education, 1954). These standards were revised several times with the most recent version appearing in 1984 (APA, 1984). These recommendations spell out in detail the procedures to be followed by those who develop, standardize, and use psychological and educational tests.

In general, test developers should demonstrate empirically both the reliability and validity of their tests (including the various types of reliability and validity discussed in Chapter Four on projective tests) and should specify the populations in which test reliability and validity have been documented. Clinicians and other users of psychological and educational tests should be aware of the reliability and validity of the tests employed, know the psychometric properties of the assessment technique when used in the population being examined, and use the test for the purpose for which it was developed and validated. In other words, APA standards require that psychological testing—a major activity of clinical psychologists—be founded on empirical grounds.

The APA has also developed a set of ethical standards for psychologists who provide psychological services. These standards were initially adopted by the APA in 1974 and have been revised on several occasions, with the most recent version appearing in 1987 (APA, 1987). These standards are presented under four major headings: Providers, Programs, Accountability, and Environment. Each heading includes a set of related principles along with interpretations and discussions of the principles.

Several of the principles for psychologists who provide psychological services address the empirical foundations of clinical psychology. For example, under the heading of Accountability, providers of psychological services are instructed, "There are periodic, systematic, and effective evaluations of psychological services" (APA, 1987, p. 8).

Similarly, under another guideline, providers "are encouraged to develop and/or apply and evaluate innovative theories and procedures, to provide appropriate theoretical or empirical support for their innovations, and to disseminate their results to others" (p. 4). To illustrate this last statement, psychotherapists are further informed that their profession is "rooted in a science" (p. 4) and, as such, they should continually explore, study, and evaluate their procedures. Thus, providers of psychological services are expected to conduct ongoing evaluations of their treatments and to be able to provide theoretical and empirical support for their treatments.

The ethical standards of psychologists in general, of psychologists who develop and use psychological tests, and of psychologists who provide psychological services all demonstrate that the profession expects clinical psychologists to operate under empirical scientific guidelines. Even those clinical psychologists whose primary role is that of practitioner rather than scientist must still have empirical evidence to support their assessment and treatment techniques and should be engaged in ongoing empirical evaluations of their activities. Thus, this brief overview of the ethical standards of psychologists supports the thesis of this book that clinical psychology has moved in an empirical or scientific direction.

This review of the ethical standards of psychologists focused exclusively on standards related to the issue of the empirical foundations of clinical psychology. Certainly, many of the ethical standards are not related to this issue. Readers should consult other works for more extensive discussions of the history of the development of psychology's ethical standards (Mills, 1982; Pryzwansky & Wendt, 1987) and for discussions of ethical issues in clinical research and practice (Hedberg, 1981).

Summary

This book discussed six issues that have been debated by clinical psychologists from the 1950s to the present and which concern the relative merits of subjective versus objective approaches to the field. These issues examined traditional assumptions (e.g., the stability of personality traits, the superiority of clinical over statistical prediction, the validity of clinical judgment) and practices (e.g., psychotherapy, psychiatric diagnosis, projective psychological tests) of clinical psychology. When clinical psychology examined these issues empirically, it found sufficient evidence to question both the validity of the assumptions and the utility of the practices.

The development and affirmation by the APA of the scientist-practitioner model of clinical training, the increase in cognitive, behavioral, and physiological theories of psychopathology and treatments for clinical disorders, the increase in use of behavioral and structured personality assessments, and the development of the operational diagnostic system DSM-III (and DSM-III-R) illustrate the increased emphasis of clinical psychology on an objective or empirical orientation.

Please note that it is not my intention to claim that each of these issues was decided conclusively in favor of the objective position. Throughout this book, I have presented the major criticisms of the research and the major arguments raised in favor of the traditional assumptions and practices. Still, even if readers are advocates of the subjective approach to clinical psychology, they should be aware that a substantial number of clinical psychologists were convinced by the findings and arguments described in this book and so adopted a more objective or scientific approach to the field than was common in the first half of the 1900s.

Proponents of the traditional subjective approaches to clinical psychology should also be aware that this scientific orientation has influenced their own camp. Not all of the research on these issues since the 1950s has been conducted by critics of the traditional approaches. Much of it has been conducted by proponents of traditional assumptions and practices who wish to provide empirical evidence of the validity of their positions. For example, Holt's efforts to demonstrate the accuracy of clinical prediction (Holt, 1958; Holt & Luborsky, 1958), Truax's research on the relationship to therapeutic outcome of Rogerian therapist characteristics (Truax, Wargo, Frank, Imber, Battle, Hoehn-Saric, Nash, & Stone, 1966a, 1966b), and research on the effectiveness of psychodynamic therapy (Sifneos, 1972, 1979; Sloane, Staples, Cristol, Yorkston, & Whipple, 1975) illustrate efforts from this period to generate empirical evidence to support traditional clinical practices.

References

American Psychological Association. (1953). *Ethical standards of psychologists.* Washington, DC: American Psychological Association.

American Psychological Association. (1977). *Standards for providers of psychological services.* Washington, DC: American Psychological Association.

American Psychological Association. (1984). *Joint standards for educational and psychological measurement*. Washington, DC: American Psychological Association.

American Psychological Association. (1987). *General guidelines for providers of psychological services*. Washington, DC: American Psychological Association.

American Psychological Association. (1990). Ethical principles of psychologists. *American Psychologist, 45,* 390–395.

American Psychological Association, & Educational Research Association and National Council on Measurement in Education. (1954). Technical recommendations for psychological tests and diagnostic techniques. *Psychological Bulletin, 51,* 201–238.

Barlow, D. H., Hayes, S. C., & Nelson, R. O. (1984). *The scientist practitioner: Research and accountability in clinical and educational settings*. New York: Pergamon.

Bickman, L. (1987). Proceedings of the National Conference on Graduate Education in Psychology, University of Utah, Salt Lake City, June 13–19, 1987 [Special issue]. *American Psychologist, 42* (12).

Canter, S., & Canter, D. (1982). Professional psychology. In S. Canter & D. Canter (Eds.), *Psychology in practice: Perspectives on professional psychology* (pp. 1–22). New York: Wiley.

Clark, K. E. (1965). Committee on the scientific and professional aims of psychology: Preliminary report. *American Psychologist, 20,* 95–100.

Frank, G. (1984). The Boulder model: History, rationale, and critique. *Professional Psychology: Research and Practice, 15,* 417–435.

Frank, G. (1986a). The Boulder model revisited: The training of the clinical psychologist for research. *Psychological Reports, 58,* 579–585.

Frank, G. (1986b). The Boulder model revisited. *Psychological Reports, 59,* 407–413.

Frank, G. (1987). Clinical psychology in a new context. *Psychological Reports, 60,* 3–8.

Garfield, S. L., & Kurtz, R. M. (1976). Clinical psychologists in the 1970s. *American Psychologist, 31,* 1–9.

Hedberg, A. G. (1981). Professional and ethical issues in providing clinical services. In C. E. Walker (Ed.), *Clinical practice of psychology: A guide for mental health professionals* (pp. 367–396). New York: Pergamon.

Holt, R. R. (1958). Clinical *and* statistical prediction: A reformulation and some new data. *Journal of Abnormal and Social Psychology, 56,* 1–12.

Holt, R. R., & Luborsky, L. (1958). *Personality patterns of psychiatrists (Vol. 1). A study of methods for selecting residents*. New York: Basic Books.

Kendall, P. C., & Norton-Ford, J. D. (1982). *Clinical psychology: Scientific and professional dimensions*. New York: Wiley.

Korman, M. (1974). National conference on levels and patterns of professional training in psychology. *American Psychologist, 29,* 441–449.

Levy, L. (1962). The skew in clinical psychology. *American Psychologist, 17,* 244–249.

McNamara, J. R., Jones, N. F., & Barclay, A. G. (1982). Contemporary professional psychology. In J. R. McNamara & A. G. Barclay (Eds.), *Critical issues, developments, and trends in professional psychology* (pp. 1–28). New York: Praeger.

Mills, D. H. (1982). Ethical standards in professional psychology. In J. R. McNamara & A. G. Barlow (Eds.), *Critical issues, developments, and trends in professional psychology* (pp. 270–294). New York: Praeger.

Perry, N. W. (1979). Why clinical psychology does not need alternative training models. *American Psychologist, 34,* 602–611.

Peterson, D. R. (1968). The doctor of psychology program at the University of Illinois. *American Psychologist, 23,* 511–516.

Peterson, D. R. (1985). Twenty years of practitioner training in psychology. *American Psychologist, 40,* 441–451.

Pryzwansky, W. B., & Wendt, R. N. (1987). *Psychology as a profession: Foundations of practice.* New York: Pergamon.

Raimy, V. C. (1950). *Training in clinical psychology (Boulder Conference).* New York: Prentice-Hall.

Reisman, J. M. (1981). History and current trends in clinical psychology. In C. E. Walker (Ed.), *Clinical practice of psychology: A guide for mental health professionals* (pp. 1–32). New York: Pergamon.

Roe, A., Gustad, J. W., Moore, B. V., Ross, S., & Skodak, M. (1959). *Graduate education in psychology: Report of the Conference on Graduate Education in Psychology.* Washington, DC: American Psychological Association.

Schofield, W. (1982). Clinical psychology in transition: The evolution of a profession. In J. R. McNamara & A. G. Barlow (Eds.), *Critical issues, developments, and trends in professional psychology* (pp. 29–64). New York: Praeger.

Shakow, D., Hilgard, E. R., Kelly, E. L., Luckey, B., Sanford, R. N., & Shaffer, L. F. (1947). Recommended graduate training program in clinical psychology. *American Psychologist, 2,* 539–558.

Sifneos, P. E. (1972). *Short-term psychotherapy and emotional crisis.* Cambridge, MA: Harvard University Press.

Sifneos, P. E. (1979). *Short-term dynamic psychology therapy: Evaluation and technique.* New York: Plenum Press.

Sloane, R. B., Staples, F. R., Cristol, A. H., Yorkston, N. J., & Whipple, K. (1975). *Psychotherapy versus behavior therapy.* Cambridge, MA: Harvard University Press.

Strickland, B. R. (1988). Clinical psychology comes of age. *American Psychologist, 43,* 104–107.

Thelen, M. H., & Ewing, D. R. (1970). Roles, functions, and training of clinical psychology: A survey of academic clinicians. *American Psychologist, 25,* 550–554.

Thorne, F. C. (1947). The clinical method in science. *American Psychologist, 2,* 161–166.

Truax, C. B., Wargo, D. G., Frank, J. D., Imber, S. D., Battle, C. C., Hoehn-Saric, R., Nash, E. H., & Stone, A. R. (1966a). Therapist empathy, genuineness and warmth and patient therapeutic outcome. *Journal of Consulting Psychology, 30,* 395–401.

Truax, C. B., Wargo, D. G., Frank, J. D., Imber, S. D., Battle, C. C., Hoehn-Saric, R., Nash, E. H., & Stone, A. R. (1966b). Therapists' contribution to accurate empathy, nonpossessive warmth and genuineness in psychotherapy. *Journal of Clinical Psychology, 22,* 331–334.

Index